# BE BULLETPROOF

## How to achieve success in tough times at work

JAMES BROOKE & SIMON BROOKE

Vermilion
LONDON

1 3 5 7 9 10 8 6 4 2

Published in 2012 by Vermilion, an imprint of Ebury Publishing
Ebury Publishing is a Random House Group company

The Random House Group Limited Reg. No. 954009

Addresses for companies within the Random House Group can be found at
www.randomhouse.co.uk

A CIP catalogue record for this book is available from the British Library

Designed and set by seagulls.net

Printed and bound by CPI Group (UK) Ltd, Croydon, CR0 4YY

ISBN 9780091939816

Copies are available at special rates for bulk orders. Contact the sales
development team on 020 7840 8487 for more information.

To buy books by your favourite authors and register for offers, visit
www.randomhouse.co.uk

# CONTENTS

# INTRODUCTION

Getting really bad news or suffering a serious professional setback can sometimes feel like being hit by a bullet.

However, this does not need to be a downward spiral. How is it that, for some people, having these bullets fired at them seems to lead to greater opportunity? What can we learn from these people? What are the common beliefs and attitudes of resilient people?

Can we identify a pattern? Here is an interesting analogy:

As they thundered across the plains of Central Asia on horseback, the Mongols must have been a terrifying sight. Few warriors have ever matched their leader, Genghis Khan, for military prowess, ruthless determination and the ferocity of his attacks. Despite their fearsome reputation and unparalleled military successes, the Mongols were relatively lightly protected, unlike many of the soldiers that they defeated. Heavy metal armour would have slowed them down and a large part of the Mongols' success was due to the speed and agility of their horsemen.

In fact the most innovative and effective part of their armour was not made from iron or leather but from silk. The Mongols were great supporters of trade and, in particular, the Silk Road. As well as profiting from the trade in silk, the Mongols used it to create shirts, which they wore into battle.

What, you might wonder, do Mongol warriors' silk shirts have to do with you if you're struggling with an overbearing boss, being ostracised by your colleagues, or suffering rejection, setbacks or brutal criticism? Well, we can't avoid the slings and arrows of the modern workplace but we can learn to minimise the damages caused and recover rapidly. Let's look at how those silk shirts worked to protect their owners – and what we can learn from them.

Often, because of the shape of the barbs on an arrow, simply trying to pull it out would tear the flesh far more severely than when the arrow first hit. Although the Mongols' silk shirts wouldn't prevent an arrow from entering the body, when it did the arrow would not break the fine, yet robust, layer of fabric. So, it was relatively easy for the warrior to simply remove the arrow by gently pulling away the silk around the wound. He could then continue fighting.

Fast forward to the twenty-first century. Have you ever worn a bulletproof jacket? The most common variety is called a 'soft vest'. Soft vests are made of high-tech fibres, which are densely woven together for extra strength and then usually covered in resin and plastic. Bullets cause damage because they hit the body with a huge force focused in just one very small area. Most bulletproof vests work by diffusing this energy across a much wider surface, allowing that wearer to live and fight another day.

Imagine the challenges we face in the workplace as bullets: rejection; unfair bosses; negative feedback; uncooperative colleagues; and antagonistic, job-threatening meetings. *Be Bulletproof* provides a range of practical ways in which you can create your own version of the Mongols' silk shirts and the modern-day 'soft vest'. It's not about being the hardest, toughest warrior in the office; instead, it's about diffusing or absorbing the impact of attacks. After all, if you attempt to trudge around the office – and through your career – in your own thick, heavy and apparently impenetrable suit of armour, you're going to find life hostile and pretty lonely. It might be tempting to think like this when you're under attack but the problem is that if you do you won't learn anything, you won't interact with colleagues effectively and, worst still, you will waste energy that could be better used elsewhere.

There is a saying: *Yea, though I walk through the valley of the shadow of death I shall fear no evil … because I'm the biggest bastard there.* Well, maybe. But another way of looking at this is that such an attitude is probably going to make your life in an organisation nasty, brutish and short.

So, how do you create your own Mongol silk shirt or develop your own individual bulletproof vest? Over the last 20 years, we have been looking at the psychology of communication – more specifically how companies communicate with their staff and how those staff interact. At our training company, Threshold, we have helped literally tens of thousands of people in business across the world. What we have learnt from them has been as valuable as the lessons we have learnt from academics and other specialists.

Together we have looked at the wisdom of ancient thinkers and how that has been tested by modern psychology, and then developed. We've conducted interviews with other experts in our fields, such as psychologists, sports coaches and writers, for additional information and advice. We've also spoken to those who have suffered serious setbacks themselves – but recovered from them – in order to gain their insights and to learn from their personal experience.

The chapters of this book address the most common forms of attack that we face in the workplace and then introduce the tools and techniques you need to 'bulletproof' yourself.

**Think of this book as a way of constructing your own bulletproof jacket.**

We have identified three key themes:

- *'Mindfulness' and its modern scientific descendant: cognitive behavioural theory.* This is about being self-aware. Being conscious of your thoughts, why you're thinking something and how this can affect your emotions.
- *The new science of Positive Psychology.* This doesn't mean pretending that everything's great. Instead, it involves the use of a new strand of psychology to change the way you view events in order to increase your resilience.

- *Understanding your 'Story'.* Thinking of things in terms of your ongoing story will help you to reframe difficult incidents and put knock-backs into perspective so that you can learn from them and move on.

This book looks at the theories behind personal resilience, flowing on from these three main pillars, and offers practical tips and advice to help you become more resilient in a variety of different scenarios. We have organised the ideas in this book broadly, under the scenarios in which they might be most relevant, but they are certainly not limited to only these scenarios. Each is helpful in the light of the wide range of life's knocks and setbacks, so we strongly recommend that you familiarise yourself with them all.

So, what explains the difference in success between individuals? Intelligence? IQ is indeed important, but estimates suggest that it only explains between 4% and 25% of the difference in career success between individuals[1]. Even if we accept the upper parameter, that still leaves a lot to be explained.

Is the difference explained by motivation? Time to explode a myth about motivation: motivation is not an innate character trait. We all possess motivation, but for most of us it is largely situational; it varies according to the circumstance we are in. Any intelligent organism that lacked motivation would not survive long enough to pass its genes to the next generation. Indeed, studies show that the most motivated individuals can readily become the most demotivated when things go against them.[2]

While motivation per se is a human universal, sustained motivation in the face of setbacks certainly does vary between individuals. This important predictor of life and career success can be learnt.

And then there's the 'talent' myth: the corrosive idea that has so gripped the corporate world that some employees are differentiated from the rest by the fact that they are innately talented. We only need to look as far as research in the classroom to debunk this. Research among school children shows that those who have been labelled as 'clever' are the ones who crumble most when they fail at a task. Children who make the best progress are those who willingly persist at a task despite setbacks. In the words of psychologist Carol Dweck of Stanford: 'For the ones who simply figure that "these are just harder problems, I just need to figure out how to do them", their confidence remains high, their enjoyment of the task remains high and their performance gets better and better.'[3] Resilience makes the crucial difference when it comes to performance. It is worth reflecting on how today's corporate leaders would benefit from learning from the classroom.

The Enron débâcle was said to be exacerbated by the organisation's addiction to labelling certain employees as 'talent'. When these individuals experienced failures the organisation – convinced of the innate 'talent' of these people – would typically confabulate explanations which attributed the causes of failure to factors outside of their control (typically market conditions or having been let down by others). The result was that these individuals – who were happy to go along with the more comforting explanation – failed to learn from their mistakes and grow resilient in the way that more durable top performers do.[4]

Look at the biographical details of most high achievers. Far from leading consistently gilded lives, most of these people spent long periods in the wilderness. Many successful entrepreneurs, for instance, cite an enforced redundancy as an important springboard to their success. For many successful people, there is no epic incident. It is simply a case of turning life's day-to-day 'micro-aggression' into opportunities.

# CHAPTER 1
## HOW THE BULLETPROOF MIND WORKS

Much of what we feel, and the way we react to situations, is inherited from our evolutionary past. These instinctive reactions are strong, but can be counterproductive in our modern lives. Recognising this is key to developing the silk shirt that will make you bulletproof.

Why do incidents at work seem to be capable of wounding us so much? That voice in your head tells you to get over it. Your friends reassure you that it is no big deal. Common sense tells you that you are not physically injured. You are not in any physical danger. It is probably unlikely that your immediate livelihood is really in danger. Unless you happen to work in a very small number of professions – such as healthcare or the military – it is very unlikely that you or anybody else is likely to die. But we do know that toxic incidents at work – which may seem scarcely apparent to an onlooker – can and do have a disproportionate effect on our sense of well-being. This, in turn, can have an impact on our levels of stress, and on our relationships, cognitive functions and health.

We use the term 'toxic' as an incident, which, if left to go unchecked, will infect other aspects of life such as self-confidence, relationships, cognitive ability, stress and health – and, of course, future success and relationships. Toxic incidents include rejection, mistakes, redundancy, dysfunctional bosses, ostracism, antagonistic meetings and brutal feedback.

There is plenty of leadership advice on resilience and adversity of the 'blind-man-climbs-Everest' type, as we call it. The assumption here is that tales of heroic achievement in the light of great adversity (at least, far greater than what you are going through) will help you to put your own more mundane travails into perspective, and subsequently inspire you to heroic feats. There is certainly a place for this approach, but it can prove counterproductive. The problem with this sort of advice is that, if you are feeling low, it can often serve to emphasise the gulf that you are feeling between your own self-image and the noble or heroic, rather than inspire. We feel low following what should be viewed as a fairly trivial incident, and the critical parent in our minds tells us that we have no right to feel that way, and that we should get over it. Then we feel more critical of ourselves for allowing ourselves to be affected in this way. You are unlikely to go blind and we assume that you are unlikely to climb Everest. For reasons that you'll soon understand, how you deal with the mundane knocks and bruises is a key predictor of success in life.

## Introducing your inner cave dweller

An arrogant colleague, a bullying boss, unfair or aggressive criticism, repeated rejection and ostracism by the group can wear us down. The pain caused by these things is real. It is what Professor Kip Williams, University of Purdue, Indiana, refers to as 'Social Pain'. Social Pain serves the same purpose as any other form of pain. It is there to tell us that something is wrong, and that if the situation continues our well-being is in danger.

Ostracism by the group, an undermining of our status and the removal of our autonomy might be unpleasant for us now, but these things would have had very serious consequences for our ancestors. They posed direct threats to whether we got to eat, with whom we mated, and the extent to which we could rely on the collective protection of the group against external threats.[5]

How often have you reacted to a situation in a way that you know – as an intelligent modern human with the benefit of reflection – will be counterproductive? Sometimes it can almost seem that to be human is to know the right thing to do but to fail to do it. It's hardly surprising, then, that we often end up reacting to a situation in a way that the modern civilised part of our mind knows will be counter-productive.

Many psychological instincts that developed over time were excellent for our survival for 99.9% of human history, but in a sophisticated modern environment they let us down. We know that the foods that kept our ancestors alive – salty, fatty or sugary foods – are bad for us, but we still crave them. Similarly, when confronted with a setback or aggressive or negative behaviour from colleagues, we may know that anger, hostility, sulking, sabotage, self-justification or denial are not helpful responses, but we react in this way nonetheless.

The good news, however, is that we're not powerless to do something about these historic, cave-dweller emotions. On the contrary, once we understand where these emotional responses are coming from, we can take a step back and make the most productive choices. It sounds simple, but simple is not the same as easy. Being able to do this takes some practice but it can be done – and you can feel the benefits almost immediately.

Too frequently, leadership and management training focuses on *knowing* what's the right thing to do in a situation, but this is the smaller part of the equation. What matters is the ability to develop methods and strategies to make sure that you naturally, and automatically, *do* the right thing.

We use the term 'inner cave dweller' simply as shorthand to describe the impulsive, emotional responses that are driven by our ancestors' survival needs. Our inner cave dweller is far from stupid – after all, we wouldn't be here today had he not been so adept at staying alive. In a similar vein, we shouldn't make the mistake of viewing emotions as an inferior form of psychological processing. The evolutionary psychologist, Steven Pinker, argues that emotions are very effective shortcuts by which we prioritise high-order goals. Our instinctive responses are powerful. They evolved because they kept our ancestors alive – excellent back then, but not always so useful today.

The point is that we are at our most effective when we become aware of our inner cave dweller speaking. Being bulletproof means making the right choice when confronted with a situation – and making the right choice means calming and restraining our inner cave dweller.

As Steven Pinker puts it, our minds have evolved for *survival*, not for *truth*. In other words, seeing the truth of a situation may be helpful, but the main priority of our evolving minds is to view a situation in a way that has the greatest chance of keeping us alive. In times where communities and social structures were very much more straightforward, simply categorising people as 'good' or 'bad', 'safe' or 'dangerous' may not have been pleasant, but it was a simple and crude way of keeping us alive. So, our instinct to survive encourages us to go for the lowest risk approach – that means thinking the worst and asking questions later. The more we can be aware of these instincts, the better we can make choices to bulletproof ourselves in today's complex workplace.

## Summary

- ◯ The cave dweller reminds us that the legacy of our evolutionary past is always with us
- ◯ Our instinctive responses evolved because they kept our ancestors alive – excellent back then, but not always so useful today
- ◯ Bulletproof people know how to calm and quieten their inner cave dweller

## The guide and the cave dweller

### Case Study 1.1

Sean was under pressure. His department had to service another department down the corridor and they had not been delivering. But that was only part of the story – at least according to Sean. The other department had been unreasonable and incompetent, making requests for service that were late or incomplete. Sean had now been invited into a colleague's office for some feedback. It was going to be an uncomfortable dressing down. But

> Sean, the consummate professional, knew how to handle it: be professional; take the feedback; agree a constructive way forward. In reality he did nothing of the sort. Sean explained that he had delivered some home truths to his colleague and ... err ... may have gone a little too far. But nothing that the guy didn't deserve, you understand.

Metaphorically, Sean's cave dweller had sensed attack, moved Sean out of the way and struck back. Literally, while Sean's frontal cortex was thinking what to say, his limbic system and amygdala had sensed threat and struck.

The emotional and cognitive processing that we have inherited from our ancestors is not only ever-present, but also influences us more than we realise. That is why so often the reasoning parts of our mind can see the appropriate way to act in a certain situation but, nonetheless, almost before we realise it, we have done something quite different. But that is not all. The instinctive, emotional part of our minds is immensely powerful and the *reasoning* part of our minds is no match for it.

Imagine a football pitch. You get down on your knees and focus on two blades of grass. These two blades of grass represent the time in which humans have functioned in the modern commercial-industrial setting. Then you look back along the full length of the pitch, over yards and yards of grass. Imagine that all of these blades of grass represent the timeline stretching back to our earliest modern human ancestors. Now visualise almost 5,000 soccer pitches laid out beyond the end of this one. This is the length of time stretching right back to the earliest clump of neurons that functioned as a brain. Most of the instinctive, emotional processing part of our brain resides in the large, ancient limbic system. For humans, evolution added a frontal cortex, allowing us to reason, think rationally, make choices and participate in complex social interactions, alongside the limbic system and the amygdala, which process the more fundamental instinctive emotions that relate to survival.

To illustrate the constantly chafing, forever clashing relationship between these two parts of the mind, imagine that you are handcuffed to your inner cave dweller. You are your inner cave dweller's guide. In some respects, your inner cave dweller is a strong and powerful resource to you. The problem is that he comes with a mind of his own. The guide knows where he's supposed to be going and believes that he should be in charge. The cave dweller is big, strong and quick to react. The responsible, sensible guide is constantly trying to drag him back on track. The guide represents your ability to reason and make wise choices in social situations, typified by the frontal cortex, while the cave dweller represents the powerful, instinctive, emotional processing part of our mind.

This distinction matters, because to help us to become bulletproof it's not enough for us simply to give advice to the guide. The crucial thing is to help the guide to manage the cave dweller. The ability to step back from our instinctive or automatic responses and to make choices, both in the way we think about things and the way we behave, is central to becoming psychologically bulletproof.

## Summary

- O The cave dweller reminds us of the sheer power of our automatic responses to situations
- O The reasoning part of our mind is no match for our emotional mental processing
- O If we become more aware of our instinctive emotional processing, we can make more productive choices for today's complex organisations

## Our minds love to see patterns and stories in events

To look for meaning in events is human. If our ancestors saw an unexplained shape crouching behind a rock, it made sense to surmise pretty quickly that it could be a threatening animal and to take evasive action. Getting all of the facts before making a considered decision – or giving things the benefit of the doubt – was not a good survival strategy.

Take a look at the figure below. Most people see a white triangle overlaid on small black discs at each corner. Rotate one of the discs slightly and the triangle disappears. It was never there. Our minds instinctively piece together bigger meaning from smaller clues, seeking out consistent stories, patterns and themes from the things that we experience directly.

Let's take another example. The photograph below, showing a UFO hovering above the coast of Cornwall in England, generated a lot of interest when it was released to the media by a team of UFO investigators. There's no denying, even to us sceptics, that it's pretty clearly the way we expect a UFO to look. However, if you introduce the image as a seagull to even the greatest UFO enthusiast they will not understand what all the fuss was about. Our minds make up the picture, depending on what we expect to see.

© Apex news and pictures

When something undesirable happens at work – you make a mistake, a prospective customer slams the door on you, your boss rubbishes a piece of work, colleagues cut you out of a project – your mind seeks to explain it by looking for a pattern or a theme. It seeks to make the incident mean something either about you or about the world in general. This is one of the ways in which the toxic effects of incidents become amplified. That relatively small incident affects you more than you feel it should, because the unconscious processing part of your mind is looking to give it greater meaning. It is asking whether this is part of a consistent story or theme for which you should be wary.

For our ancestors who faced the threat from behind the rock, it made sense to assume there was a theme: *rocks similar to this one mean danger; when I see one, prepare for flight or fight mode.* This might make for a stressed, nervous, pessimistic ancestor but one who was more likely to stay alive.

To be human is to seek to make sense of the things we observe or experience. We are natural meaning-makers. We could not function without this instinct, but it is also means that our minds readily start to ascribe meaning to the things that we experience in a way that can be unhelpful. What can seem like a relatively small and survivable incident at work triggers our 'meaning-making' processes. Typical reactions are:

- This means that I am not up to the job
- This means that I have been 'found out'
- This means that things will keep on going wrong
- This means that people are generally mean and hostile towards me

These feelings start to contaminate other situations; the incident has become toxic.

When analysing the facts and the story, it is key to avoid distorting the reality of the situation. 'Distortion' is the term that psychologists use when they refer to people interpreting an incident in a way that makes it mean more than it does. For example, if somebody does something that we interpret as hostile, it proves that either:

- I deserve or attract people's hostility
- People are generally hostile
- I must have messed up again

On the other hand, it could simply be that the person is having a bad day, or tends to be that way with most people. The fact is that we simply don't know. Any analysis beyond that risks becoming a thinking distortion. And because our inner cave dweller evolved in a hostile and dangerous environment, it made sense to be pessimistic and more acutely aware of risk. For this reason, negative thinking distortions are more common than positive ones.

Bulletproof people, however, will ask, 'What am I making this mean?' They'll challenge their distortions and thinking errors by testing these against the real-world evidence. As we often put it, it is a case of separating out what actually happened in a situation (the facts) from what we make it mean (the story). This is the first step in decontaminating a toxic incident.

## Summary
- Our mind seeks out consistent themes and patterns because it tries to create meaning for us
- As natural 'meaning-makers', we frequently make things mean more than they do
- Being bulletproof means recognising your mind's tendency to make an incident mean more than it does, and decontaminating the incident to prevent it becoming toxic

# CHAPTER 2
## CHANGING YOUR MINDSET

Learning how to change your mindset and defuse distortions in your thinking is key in making yourself more bulletproof. The way we think about things affects the way we feel, which in turn affects what we do and the outcomes we achieve. This was the insight of the psychologist Aaron Beck, who recognised that many of the people he was treating for anxiety, stress and depression – the opposite of being bulletproof – seemed to be affected by distortions in their thinking. Beck felt that if he could encourage people to test out the validity of their thoughts – in much the same way that a scientist would interrogate the hard evidence – thinking distortions might be reduced and the disorders might improve. Beck's approach yielded remarkably beneficial results and this has been borne out by numerous trials under clinical conditions. This is the essence of cognitive behavioural therapy (CBT).

Dr Amy Silver is a clinical psychologist who, in addition to her work with individuals in a clinical setting, has been adapting the principles of CBT to help leaders and managers to become more bulletproof in the workplace. By following that belief that all of us, at some stage, risk getting caught in *distorted* thinking – and that that is when our interpretation of the situation and our reactions to it are unhelpful – Dr Silver helps people in business to recognise common ways in which their thinking can become unhelpful. She often comes across people in business who are simply not functioning as effectively as they could be, because they have allowed their thinking about an incident to become distorted and this affects other aspects of their game. This distortion comes from only selecting the negative aspects of a situation and ignoring the positive, or vice versa. These thought distortions can happen at any time for us and can be so automatic that we don't even have a chance to assess them for the truth. We find it intuitively hard to grasp that our thoughts might be wrong. But the truth is they can be – and a lot of the time. In varying degrees, this phenomenon affects everyone.

The principles of CBT are core to being bulletproof. If three-letter acronyms put you off, don't worry – it's the principles that matter, and the rudiments of these are easy to understand and master.

## Summary

○ How we think about things affects the way we feel
○ The way we feel drives what we do and affects the outcomes we achieve – but not always for the better
○ Bulletproof people develop the habit of choosing how to think about an incident or situation

# Putting it into practice

When something happens or somebody does something, we typically go on to assume that this incident or this person has made us feel a certain way:

● When he ignored me, it made me feel …
● When I made that mistake, it made me feel …

In reality an incident does not *make* us feel anything. The feeling that follows on from an incident is not inevitable. There needs to be a thought in between in order for the events that we experience to turn into feelings. And, as we've said, our thoughts are often distorted. We weave things into stories or we look for themes and consistencies that aren't really there. So, an **incident** or event triggers a **thought**, which triggers an **emotion**, which affects our **behaviour**.

## Case Study 2.1

Jane switched on her computer on Monday morning and discovered an email from a client rejecting her proposal [the incident]. Jane started to think, this just proves that I'm not good enough and I've been found out [the thought]. So she felt low and lacked confidence [the emotion]. In turn, this led to a certain type of behaviour. She was snappy and irritable with colleagues and family. As a result of how she processed the incident, she might end up being less inclined to approach her next proposal in a bold and creative way.

For a bulletproof version of Jane, the *incident* is identical but the *way* in which she thinks about it is not. Bulletproof Jane recognises the idea that 'this proves that I'm not good enough' is just that: it's an *idea*, and not a *fact*. When she has these thoughts, she recognises that there may be thinking distortions at play. She distinguishes between facts and assumptions. She considers other possible explanations for what has happened: perhaps the client's priorities changed; maybe it was all down to budget. She weighs the evidence for these alternative thoughts. The unhelpful effects of her emotions subside more quickly. She's able to think more clearly and take more constructive action.

You can try this for yourself the next time something similar happens to you, by following these steps:

1. Take a breath and relax. Imagine yourself literally taking a step back from the incident and viewing it on a screen
2. Then ask yourself what thoughts you had in relation to the incident. What did you make it mean? How true are these thoughts? How much do you know and how much are you just guessing? What other interpretations could exist?
3. Imagine you could choose which thought would work best for you; try out the new thought and become aware of how you feel
4. If your mind starts to spring back to the old unhelpful thoughts, remind yourself that you are just trying out the new thought. What could be the harm in that?

Ultimately there are five elements that impact on any scenario:

- What is going on in the surroundings
- What you feel physically
- What you think
- How you feel emotionally
- What you do – in other words, your behaviour

These five elements interact to determine your experience. The very same situation can trigger different aspects of these five elements for different people. In other words, each person will experience the same situation in different ways. But if you want your experience of a situation to be different, you have *learn to manage* it. You need to change one, or more, of these five elements.

For example, you could change something about what's going on around you – in other words, your *surroundings*. This might be something major, such as changing or moving to a different department, or it could be something as simple as changing your desk layout or your working routine.

You could change something *physically* by doing some simple breathing exercises – ensuring that you are breathing down to the lower part of the lungs and lowering your diaphragm – or going for a walk regularly. As we know, the physical and the psychological are closely related.

You could challenge the way you *think* about something by questioning your thoughts. This essentially means trying to look at the validity and/or the usefulness of your thoughts by standing back from them and examining them dispassionately. It's about trying to capture your thoughts and evaluate them. You can ask if they're actually true; for example, do you mean 'I can't cope,' or is the thought that most accurately describes the situation, 'This is a really tricky situation that I'm struggling with, but I will get through this as I have other tricky situations'?

You could change something *emotionally*, with the view to becoming almost dispassionate about your own emotions so that they alone don't decide what happens in your life. Rather than telling yourself 'I can't cope,' which makes you feel anxious, you could take more of a dispassionate view. You could say: 'Oh, look, there is that feeling of anxiety' or 'there goes that "I can't cope" thought. Isn't it interesting that it's come up again?' This is a much more practical and effective way to react than, 'Oh, no, I must do something about that thought. This feeling is unbearable and so I must push against it.' This process of stepping back from your emotions and becoming aware of them in a more dispassionate way fits with the Buddhist concept of 'mindfulness'.

You could also change your *behaviour*. Perhaps you could be more assertive or be less assertive.

When people push against their emotions, those emotions tend to get stronger. Rather than battling against your emotions, with CBT you distance yourself from them and become a sort of scientist, reviewing your thoughts and emotions objectively. Sometimes the very process of distancing yourself from your thoughts and emotions can have a dramatic effect in calming the mind and gaining control over challenging situations.

### Summary
○ Asking, 'What am I making this mean?' helps us to challenge our distortions and understand our thinking errors
○ Bulletproof people are able to reframe their thoughts and take out the inevitable distortions

## Positive self-talk

Telling ourselves that we can't cope decreases our ability to cope, and it is remarkable how readily we slip into this cycle. But we can do something about it.

## Case Study 2.2

Gemma was facing a tough board meeting at 8am in the morning. She fully expected a grilling over her department's sales figures during an unexpectedly tough trading period. She'd discovered that a colleague on whom she was relying had let her down, absenting himself at the last minute on a flimsy premise. Gemma would now also have to take care of his part of the presentation. She worked late. Her partner was away on business, and when she eventually got home her two young children had come down with a stomach bug that would keep them and her awake all night. She needed to be up at 6am. As she tended to sick children and changed bed linen throughout the night, what did she tell herself?

If she is similar to most of us, her self-talk will instinctively be of the 'I can't do this' variety. 'I can't' self-talk is very common. It goes hand in hand with a low-tolerance threshold. There are many variations on this theme:

- 'I can't possibly …'
- 'Nobody could be expected to …'
- 'This is intolerable …'

When a situation is far from ideal – when it is stressful, tiring or uncomfortable – another thinking error is at risk of taking over our thinking: we start to see the situation as intolerable, unbearable and insufferable.

The key is to recognise that difficult-to-cope is not the same as impossible-to-cope. Hard-to-tolerate is not the same as intolerable. Questioning the sort of language that we use about a situation is an important step in reframing our view of the situation in a way that is more helpful.

Sports psychologist Julie Douglas uses this technique with the young athletes with whom she works. She feels that self-talk is important and that it helps to take people through a process of developing more positive self-talk. The first step is to encourage them simply to become aware of self-talk, and then to take them through a method that she calls 'Thought Stopping'. When they notice unhelpful thoughts, she encourages them to stop those thoughts and come back with more positive ones.

Bulletproof Gemma understands that her situation is far from ideal, but that, at the same time, it is far from impossible. When she finds herself slipping into 'I can't' self-talk, she stops and replaces it with 'I can' self-talk. She recognises that, in reality, she can actually cope. As she changes one more sheet on the bed, she takes a breath and says to herself, 'I can do it. I'll be okay.'

Many self-help books will exhort you to love and relish whatever adversity will come your way. Some even ask people to love and welcome their malignant tumour as a friend. We feel this isn't helpful. To maintain pretence takes considerable energy. It wears you down until the reality seeps through. What Gemma is doing is something quite different. She doesn't make herself gush with enthusiasm about the hardship. She does not pretend that the situation is something that it isn't. It's far from ideal, but in spite of this she reminds herself that she can cope and that she can do it.

Become aware of your self-talk. Is it helping? Is it strengthening you or is it draining you? Simply saying to yourself 'I can' seems to work like magic in its ability to give you strength and increase your tolerance and ability to cope.

## Summary
- Accept that you're facing a challenge – don't deny it
- Become aware of draining, weakening self-talk ('I can't') – and drop it
- Find a phrase that is honest but positive, such as 'I can', and say it to yourself

# Acknowledging thoughts and letting go

Stepping back and understanding what you're feeling is one good way to get an insight into the thought that is governing those feelings.

The more aware you are of your thoughts and feelings, the more you can influence them. And when we say aware, we mean 'actively aware'. Most of us are driven by our thoughts and emotions, but we don't take the time to pause, take a look at them and reflect on them.

A useful technique for you to employ is to take a moment and try to step out of your thoughts, in order to gain an 'observer perspective' on your thinking. Then, in a more detached way, you can effectively examine the evidence for, and the evidence against, your thoughts.

The mind does not respond to the command: do not think about something. Most of us recognise those negative thoughts, memories or associations that get in the way of our performance. If you have ever tried to push these negative thoughts out of your mind, you will have noticed how they tend to keep springing back bigger and bolder than before. Jennifer Borton and Elizabeth Casey of Hamilton College in New York sought to test this idea with an experiment. People were asked about the most upsetting incident in their lives, and the group was then split in half, with half of the participants asked actively to push thoughts of this incident out of their minds. The remaining half were given no such brief and asked to carry on life as normal. At the end of each day, participants were required to assess their mood. At the end of the eleven-day period when the results were assessed, the difference between the two groups was clear. The group that had been briefed actively to suppress their negative thoughts were significantly more depressed and anxious than the other group.[6]

By using mindfulness and letting go, you observe this thought. It's about not telling yourself off. Not only does this give you a calm spot in your mind, the sense of calm allows you to make better choices rationally rather than irrationally, giving our guide more control over the cave dweller.

Stepping outside of yourself is an important part of becoming bulletproof. It creates an awareness that will allow you to manage your emotions calmly and effectively. Imagine a calm and clear-thinking friend alongside yourself: a 'meta-you'. This friend is supportive but is not afraid to challenge the clarity of your thinking and to ask you about the balance of evidence. For simplicity, let's refer to the meta-you as the 'wiser-you'.

This is a simple exercise you can do when an event that you experience troubles you, or you sense yourself feeling tense or not functioning well. Imagine the calmer and 'wiser-you' simply stepping to one side and describing what has happened and how you feel.

As we'll explore throughout this book, the ability to develop awareness in a calm and detached way is a life skill that you can learn, and once you learn it you will wonder how you ever functioned without it.

## Summary

- ○ Don't try to fight against negative or unhelpful thoughts; let them drift into your mind. Practise becoming aware of them in a more detached way
- ○ Stepping outside yourself is important in becoming bulletproof
- ○ Developing a calm self-awareness is an essential life skill for bullet-proof people
- ○ Imagine the 'wiser-you', standing alongside yourself and seeing your thoughts and feelings with a bit of objective distance

# Recognising negative thoughts – becoming 'mindful'

When we suffer stress at work, or feel that we're suffering because of the actions of others – perhaps because we believe people are being unfair to us or have rejected us – mindfulness can help. It offers a new way of being aware of our experience and a way of noticing our negative emotions coming and going, rather than maintaining them with justification, judgement or the desire to 'solve' them. This can help prevent them from overwhelming us as they can so very easily do – and usually without our realising.

Professor Mark Williams, of the Oxford Centre for Mindfulness, argues that our state of mind is closely connected to our memories. 'Whenever something goes wrong or we feel depressed, our minds naturally refer back to find times at which we've had similar experiences,' he says. 'For instance, if you feel rejected or ignored, your mind will start to bring up other instances when you felt like this so that it can find similarities and see how you handled the situation then.' It's a technique that has developed over millions of years of evolution. Our cave dweller is looking for patterns and meaning.

The same process can be triggered by almost any negative thought, including anxiety, fear and stress. The danger is that these thoughts, emotions and damning judgements snowball and make us feel unhappy, threatened and fearful.

Context and location have a powerful effect on memory. If you've ever gone back to your old school, or visited a town in which you used to live, you'll suddenly find all kinds of memories flooding unexpectedly into your mind – memories that you'd never have recalled otherwise.

Mood can act as a context in the same way as a particular location, says Mark Williams. A feeling of being threatened or of being rejected can stimulate memories. Soon you can be lost in gloomy thoughts and negative emotions, and often you don't know where they came from – they just suddenly arrived. Suddenly you're miserable and bad tempered and you don't even know why.

It's impossible to stop these memories but you can learn how to prevent such memories from spiralling out of control. You can learn to see them for what they are: propaganda. They're just one way of looking at the world; they're not you as a person. They're a point of view, not some objective truth. Once you've understood that, you can then observe them dispassionately and watch them float past you. Now, when people learn to do this, we find that they experience something else instead – and that's a profound sense of contentment. Recognise these thoughts as they float into your mind. Remind yourself that they are just propaganda, and not truth.

Much of the time we're thinking, planning and referring back to past experiences to find comparisons in an effort to find solutions for life's challenges. But we can also be aware of the fact that we are doing this; we can be aware of our mind and its habit of thinking, planning and judging. When you feel that spiral of negative feelings, remind yourself of your cave dweller seeking out pattern and meaning – and name that feeling for what it is: propaganda.

This is something that you can readily try out. Become more aware of your thoughts and feelings as they come into your mind. Feelings might be anxious or comforting, happy or melancholy, light or dark. The important point is not to judge them, fight them or suppress them. A useful technique is to view each thought as if it were a cloud drifting across the sky. Become aware of its size, colour and shape; appreciate the way it looks against the backcloth of the sky. Become aware of how it drifts and changes shape. The thought may drift away again, but the important point is that you do not need it to do so. You are now both detached from it and comfortable with its presence.

## Summary

○ Identify memories and thoughts as they enter your mind
○ See them for what they are: a point of view, and not some objective truth
○ Observe them dispassionately and watch them float past you

# Stop mind reading

Our minds have evolved to interpret things. If they didn't we couldn't function. Unfortunately our interpretations often go too far, make leaps of logic or become hard baked. There are common thinking distortions that weaken us and make us less effective. The more aware we are of these, the better equipped we are to avoid slipping into their trap, and the more bulletproof we can make ourselves.

One of the most common thinking traps is 'mind reading'. We once worked with a project team leader who was convinced that a team member did not respect his authority and was looking to usurp him. When we worked with him to examine the evidence, we discovered that this thought was triggered by an incident where the team member had arrived late at the first project meeting. Once mind reading started, based on this one small incident, the situation spiralled. We encouraged the team leader to keep separating the facts from his 'story' (his interpretation). We also encouraged him to try out the Buddhist practice of meeting his colleague 'anew' (meeting a familiar person as if we had never met them before, i.e. leaving the baggage at the door). Following this, the relationship thawed. We do not know what was really in the mind of his colleague. What we do know is that once the project leader stopped acting as if he knew, the situation improved.

An example that psychologists often use is this: a colleague walks past you in the corridor and does not greet you as you expect. If you are mind reading, you might feel that it is because the colleague is clearly harbouring feelings of resentment over some past incident and acting accordingly. It may simply be that the colleague was distracted. Mind reading makes you less effective. There is little benefit, and the risk is that you create problems by increasing your own stress.

Mind reading is not the same as putting yourself in other people's shoes or seeing things from their point of view. These exercises are useful, and bulletproof people make a point of doing them, but they remain aware that they never actually *know* what the other person is thinking. When we introduce you to Bob in chapter five you will see how his decision to stop mind reading helped with a severe dose of office politics.

Don't waste time and energy mind reading. If you do so, you are likely to exacerbate any potential problems. Remind yourself that you do not know what other people are thinking and you will be at your best when you keep an open mind.

## Summary

- ◯ One of the most common thinking traps is mind reading
- ◯ Even when we are convinced that we know what is in another's mind, we are often wrong
- ◯ Mind reading is not the same as putting yourself in other people's shoes
- ◯ Don't waste time and energy mind reading

# Banish self-scrutiny

If you've made a mistake and you think that everyone has noticed, the chances are that they probably haven't. If you have made a fool of yourself and think everyone is talking about it, they're probably not. If there is something that you are embarrassed or self-conscious about, the chances are that nobody pays it anything like the amount of attention that you pay to it.

### Case Study 2.3

Charles had to give a tough presentation about his divisional performance to the executive board of his company. Charles was very anxious that, as a relatively young senior officer, he should come across with a gravitas and confidence that would build confidence in his newly formed division. We coached Charles and he gave an excellent presentation.

Straight after he said to a colleague who had been in the meeting: 'I know what you were thinking: everyone was distracted by that tick in my left eye.'

'Sorry?' said his colleague.

'That twitch ... I couldn't stop the eye twitching ... it always does that at the most crucial moments.'

'Charles,' said his colleague, 'we couldn't see it. The board didn't notice. Nobody cares. Forget about it.'

Good advice.

Bulletproof people remind themselves that nobody is paying them nearly as much attention as they at first assume. 'Nobody is looking at me.' In fact, it is a very liberating thing to remember. We tend to over-estimate the extent to which people notice our blunders or shortcomings. Researchers at Cornell University designed an experiment to test this (also known as the 'spotlight effect'[7].) They gathered a sample of students in a room under the pretext of doing a written memory test. The experimenters created a ruse to cause one of the participants (known as the 'target participant') to be late. The target participant was informed that the rest of the group had already started. He was then asked to put on an article of clothing before entering the room to join the group.

Here's the rub. The article of clothing was a T-shirt emblazoned with a large picture of Barry Manilow (previous research indicated that Barry Manilow is considered about as embarrassing as it gets at Cornell University). The room was arranged so that all of the seats were facing the entrance. The target participant entered the room late and sporting the Barry Manilow T-shirt. After a couple of minutes, he was told that the other participants were already too far ahead and he was escorted out of the room. The target participant was then asked to estimate the proportion of participants in the room whom he believed noticed the Barry Manilow T-shirt. This was compared to the number of participants who *actually* noticed the T-shirt. Consistently the target participant overestimated the proportion of participants who noticed the T-shirt, generally estimating the figure at roughly a half, whereas in reality only about a *fifth* noticed the T-shirt. The exercise was repeated several times to ensure that there was a robust sample size of participants. There was no discernible difference in the finding between men and women.

If you find yourself worrying that people are noticing something embarrassing about you, perhaps a blush or a tic, or if you stumble, knock something over or have any other kind of mishap, here is a very useful tip: think Barry Manilow.

## Summary

○ Bulletproof people know that when they make a mistake, most people don't notice
○ Bulletproof people liberate themselves from potentially embarrassing situations: 'Hey! No one is looking at me'
○ Remember, even a Barry Manilow T-shirt flies under most people's radar

# Flexible is stronger than rigid

Another thinking trap is the *rigid rule*. We lose effectiveness in a situation when our attitude is too rigid. Being rigid is very different to being bulletproof. Rigid structures appear hard on the outside but can easily snap, whereas flexible structures can more readily absorb the momentum of all that life throws at them. When we are in rigid rule mode of thinking, we are tough on the outside but easily crushed when things become too much. When we are in flexible mode, we are like a tree: we can sway and flex in the harshest wind but never lose our firm rooting.

It works like this: as humans we make sense of the world by formulating things into rules. We also create rules about ourselves. These help to create the sense of a consistent self. So far this is all quite reasonable. The problem arises because these rules can easily become hard baked into something too rigid. We make rules for ourselves such as: I must always be liked; I should always be nice; I should always be the joker; and – a common one – I must always be respected.

You spot the theme. These are the *must-always* and *should-always* that we apply to ourselves. Think about an incident where the outcome was something undesirable for you when you felt it really should not have been and it is likely that it came down to a *must-always* or a *should-always* rule that was conducting things for you under the surface.

## Case Study 2.4

Mike had a short-haul London to Paris business flight. It was the middle of the day, which should have been a quiet, hassle-free time to fly. He had just enough time to polish off a couple of spreadsheets before his meeting in Paris. But Mike ended up sitting next to Mr Grumpiflier. Mr Grumpiflier saw it as a matter of pride to sit with his elbow permanently positioned, not only over the armrest, but over Mike's seat. Mike gently shuffled his arm roughly in the area of the armrest, hoping Mr Grumpiflier would move his arm, but to no avail. Mr Grumpiflier wasn't budging. Mike even asked Mr Grumpiflier if he could spare him a little room. Mr Grumpiflier harrumphed and looked affronted, shuffled his arm a little and put it back pretty much where it was.

Rigid-rule Mike reckons this guy has no right to behave like this. Mike has a right to sit in his seat and nobody has the right to steal his all-important share of the space on the seat boundary. Rigid-rule Mike spends a stressful flight in an increasingly tense game of elbow shuffle. He arrives irritable and tired, and he never got those spreadsheets done.

Bulletproof Mike also values respect, but he is capable of being flexible if it means a better outcome. Recognising the stalemate, he looks for another empty seat. He moves to it, relaxes and pops open his laptop.

Bulletproof Mike does not feel his sense of self-worth has crumbled because he left Grumpiflier to it. Who knows why it was such a big deal to Grumpiflier? Either way, it was Grumpiflier's problem, not Mike's.

Rigid-rule Mike holds the belief: 'I must always be respected.' Flexible Mike retains the essence of this, but reframes it in a way that is more flexible and therefore works better for him: 'I prefer people to show respect, but if they are really not going to, it doesn't hurt me. I'm okay.'

## Case Study 2.5

Hannah is a corporate conference organiser. She worked on one conference where – for reasons that she couldn't figure out – the atmosphere seemed fairly poisonous and Hannah felt that she was subjected to some really frosty attitudes. The harder Hannah tried, the worse the situation became. Hannah felt really low after the event and complained that she felt her confidence and sparkle had been extinguished. It turned out that Hannah was getting much of her self-worth from the idea that: I can always make people like me. This had become hard-baked into Hannah as a rigid rule: I must always be popular. When this wasn't working for Hannah, she felt helpless, as if she had no option but to continually try harder. Then Hannah changed her rigid rule to a flexible preference: I prefer to be popular, but if sometimes that doesn't seem to be the case, I am okay. She found that, as a result, she was far better able to cope in a range of situations, and was more confident going into a new situation, regardless of what lay in wait.

People often question our recommendation to be flexible about one's need to be respected. For many of us, respect is an important value by which we live our lives. But it's the *need* to be respected that can lead people to behave in a way that is, at best, counterproductive. That's why the emphasis is on being flexible. And, of course, we are not suggesting you abandon 'self-respect', but self-respect is quite different from *must-have-respect-from-others*. The former is entirely within your control. The latter is not.

We can find ourselves applying rigid rules to ourselves ('I must always') or to other people ('people should always'). The issue is the same: rigid is fragile, flexible is stronger. Again, it's the equivalent of the silk shirt under your outfit.

You have probably spotted the formula by now. Become aware of rigid thinking ('I must always') and modify it to flexible thinking ('I prefer to … but I'm okay if …').

Below are some common rigid rules. Try modifying them to become flexible preferences:

- I must always be popular ...
- I must always make people laugh ...
- I must always be respected ...
- I must always have the answers ...
- I must always control a situation ...

### Case Study 2.6

Rhina was head of accounts at a large advertising agency. Once a week she would attend the meeting of its business development team. The team tended to consider Rhina's input as trivial bureaucracy. They tended to be curt, abrasive and dismissive, but Rhina was relentlessly courteous. Her assistant Viktor pointed this out and asked Rhina why she continued to bother being polite, when the rest of the guys were so rude. Rhina pointed out that courtesy may not be one of their values, but it was one of hers, so why would she let discourteous people choose her behaviour for her.

Replace your old rigid rule with your new flexible preference. Test drive your new flexible preference for a couple of weeks (remember, you have nothing to lose; you can always go back to your old rigid rule at any time). Become aware of how your flexible preference is working. When you would normally react in a way that is driven by your rigid rule, take a pause, take a breath, and act in line with your flexible preference.

### Summary

- The rules we define about ourselves help us to create the sense of a consistent self, but we lose effectiveness when our personal rules become too rigid
- Bulletproof people don't maintain *must-always* and *should-always* rigid rules
- Bulletproof people develop flexible preferences: 'If that doesn't happen, I'm okay'
- Bulletproof people are like flexible trees, swaying in the harshest wind but never losing their firm rooting

# Don't let your cave dweller pick your fights

'I must always be respected' can be one of the most destructive of rigid rules. In the US, among the most common motives for homicide is the one termed 'altercation arising from relatively trivial causes'. How often are we left bewildered on hearing of a road rage incident that has escalated out of all proportion? How often are we surprised by the power of our own anger when someone drives discourteously? We may justify it to ourselves in terms of concern for safety but we would suggest that these primal responses have another source. It is our inner cave dweller demanding respect. It is no surprise that the 'culture of respect' tends to take root more insidiously in environments of greatest social deprivation. Where you have little else, a perceived diminution of your sense of respect can cause your universe to crumble.[8]

Let's look at an example. In August 2010, Ranjit Nankani was sentenced to a minimum of 18 years in prison at the Old Bailey for the murder of Gary Johnson. Johnson had been thrown into the air and partially decapitated when Nankani drove his 4x4 at him, hitting him full on, before crashing into a line of parked cars. As Nankani lay trapped in his ruined vehicle, the body of his victim just feet away, he was shot and injured by a friend of Johnson's called Dwayne McPherson. After the trial Mr Johnson's mother, Joyce, said: 'Eighteen years is not enough. I will never see Gary. Skye (the victim's daughter) will never know her dad.'

The reason for this particularly brutal murder? Nankani allegedly stepped on Johnson's toe in a nightclub, which started a row between the pair.[9]

The fact that humans frequently go to extraordinary lengths to settle scores, at great personal cost, with no rational benefit, is well documented by psychologists.

In the workplace, thankfully, murder is infrequent, but most of us at some time pursue a trivial slight or perceived injustice to the point of conflict. We may tell ourselves that it is a matter of principle. In reality, it is our inner cave dweller at work. The compulsion to get even, to settle a score, with no identifiable rational gain, has an adaptive explanation. It is one of those instincts that appears to be encoded in us, but which tends to be counterproductive in our modern environment.

In our ancestors' more dangerous and hostile environment, it was a wise survival strategy to give the unambiguous signal that you were somebody not to be messed with, under any circumstances. To give this signal to your potential foes, it made sense to respond consistently – even if that meant disproportionately – to the most trivial slight. To let something go would have singled you out as easy prey to a potential enemy.

Evolutionary psychologists hypothesise that this instinct is particularly prevalent among people whose ancestors are predominantly from lands most dependent on herding, and who hail from areas that were traditionally remote from the forces of law and order. It is impossible, or at least very difficult, to steal arable land, but if you are reliant on herding to feed your family, you know that your livelihood can readily be taken from you at any time, simply by virtue of the fact that your adversary is more powerful or more ruthless. In this environment, reputation is all and therefore scores must be settled. This gives rise to what is known as a 'culture of honour': an individual's honour must be maintained, which means that scores invariably need to be settled. To put it more accurately, the more we are affected by this psychological or cultural inheritance (it's still a source of contention which of these it is), the more difficult we find it not to react to a perceived slight.

It is believed by many that a strong culture of honour exists in the Southern United States, as herders from Ireland, Northern England and the Highlands of Scotland largely settled these states. In a remarkable experiment at the University of Michigan, a fake psychology experiment was advertised and students were asked to volunteer. To reach the place to which they were instructed to report, they needed to squeeze past a stooge who appeared to be filing papers in the corridor. As they brushed past, the stooge was instructed to say something insulting under his breath. Students who hailed from northern states were more likely to brush off the insult or laugh at the temerity. Students who hailed from southern states were far more likely to become visibly angry and confront the stooge. Their levels of testosterone were measurably higher as their bodies prepared for a fight.[10]

Ask yourself who you most want to be like: the students who laughed off the insult or the students who could not let it go? Allowing our inner cave dweller to choose our battles is grossly inefficient and mitigates against being bulletproof. Pausing for a moment to remind our inner cave dweller that we do not need to react is a crucial part of being bulletproof.

Try taking a breath and switching your rigid rule to a flexible preference: 'I'd prefer that guy to apologise to me for unnecessarily interrupting my presentation and making me momentarily lose my flow of thought in front of all my colleagues ... but if he is really not going to, it's not going to spoil my day.'

You can choose to live by a standard of courtesy, and that's a good thing, but you cannot control the standards by which other people live.

Matthieu Ricard, the former scientist-turned-Buddhist, points out that in order to relieve ourselves of some of the suffering we experience when someone offends or annoys us, we need us to reconsider our self-image and our ego. By way of illustration, he asks you to imagine that you're lying in a boat, floating on a lake. Suddenly another boat hits you, jolting you rudely. You leap up. Who the hell has been so stupid and careless to bang into you like this? But when you catch sight of the offending boat you see that ... it's empty. Your anger dissipates. You lie down again. What's changed your mood? 'In the first case you'd thought yourself to be the target of someone's malice, while in the second you realised that you were not a target,' suggests Ricard.

When we are working with groups of young graduates, we impress on them the importance of staying focused on a goal. As a metaphor for this, we ask them to spread evenly around the perimeter of a large room. Each person is asked to focus on a spot on the other side of the room representing his or her goal. The brief is to 'move towards that goal with absolute determination, letting nothing or no one get in your way'. People tend to mistake focus and determination for strength and toughness. They brace themselves for the inevitable collisions with others. The result is generally a morass in the middle of the room where focus and energy are lost. After a debrief they are encouraged to sustain their focus but increase their sense of flexibility. In other words, they may have to swerve slightly, speed up slightly or slow down slightly. With the new mode of working, with exactly the same number of players – and therefore the same complexity – each player reaches his or her goal with relative ease. They have learnt that staying focused on a goal is about learning when to stay flexible.

The point is not that bulletproof people are submissive or acquiescent. They are not. The point is that they pick their battle carefully. They choose their fights carefully: when the outcome is in their interest. That way they stay in control. If your inner cave dweller is choosing your fights, you have ceded control.

Richard Branson, billionaire businessman and Virgin Atlantic chief, famously said that he was not the sort of person to waste time having arguments with people. At the same time he picked the biggest fight that his industry had ever seen when he took on British Airways for its 'dirty tricks' campaign against its rivals. He knows which potential conflicts to let go and which battles to fight.

## Summary

○ Bulletproof people pick their battles wisely
○ They recognise that while their inner cave dweller has the urge to settle a score or avenge a slight, they are capable of choosing a wiser and more beneficial course of action
○ Bulletproof people calm and guide their inner cave dweller in order to make the wisest choices
○ Let the small stuff go; fight only the important battles and fight them with guile, and with a calm focus

# CHAPTER 3
## USING JUJITSU COMMUNICATION

Dealing with comments from colleagues during meetings and handling conversations that are confrontational – or even appear to the listener to be confrontational – is one of the most difficult aspects of office life. But here, too, concepts such positive thinking and reframing can help bulletproof people handle them.

We call this Jujitsu Communication because although this ancient martial art is often associated with aggression and confrontation it's nothing of the sort. 'Jistu' means technique and 'Ju' actually means 'flexible' in Japanese. Jujitsu is about flexible technique and the idea of it is to channel your opponent's energy rather than try to meet it head on.

### Case Study 3.1

As a sales executive for a small electronics firm, Charlie, 28, had always enjoyed the business of identifying new clients and then developing them. He said, 'I'm told that I'm good with people and so whenever I visit a new client or go to see an existing one I always find that we have a good chat about football or holidays or whatever. I never give them a hard sell; I'm just friendly and chatty – but I always get the business.'

However, when Charlie's firm came under pressure from a successful competitor and a new aggressive sales director took the helm, everyone felt the pressure.

'Suddenly these Monday morning meetings got a lot more competitive,' he said. 'Everyone started trying harder than ever to please the sales director. The competition in the meetings and the pressure to outdo the other people in the room was awful. People would start scoring points off each other and everyone would try to shoot down everyone else's ideas ... There had always been quite a bit of rivalry, but this was just becoming nasty – and desperate.

'Every time I told myself that I was not going to play that game, and every time the same pattern occurred, I was always the one who felt isolated. Everyone sided with the boss and I was out on a limb.

'No one ever really liked our Monday morning sales meetings, I don't think. I used to get that knot in my stomach on the way to work – even Sunday nights were always blighted by the thought of the Monday morning meeting.'

## Turn criticisms around

Being bulletproof is very much about the ability to have the presence of mind to take the heat out of the situation at the height of a verbal assault, as well as the ability to recover from setbacks or verbal assaults from colleagues, customers or bosses.

You will need to deal with comments and questions in the work-place that are either aggressive or hostile or turning up the discomfort in other ways. It is unreasonable, illogical and unfair, but it is also a simple fact of corporate life that an employee who defends him or herself when being criticised not only confirms their culpability, but adds the crime of 'defensiveness' to their charge sheet.

There are smart ways to deflect a verbal assault and live to fight another day, but mounting a defence is not one of them. To be more precise, mounting a defence that *sounds like* a defence is not one of them. And, of course, the temptation to return fire is out of the question.

Eyebrows raise when we advise people to 'never defend an attack'. However, people soon see the logic. People who are seen as high-status don't tend to invest their energies in defending jibes and brickbats from other people. They understand the importance of being seen to set the agenda. When we defend an attack, we prolong a discussion which links ourselves to something undesirable, a mistake, shortcoming or failure. We have allowed the opponent to set the agenda.

## Case Study 3.2

Charlotte and John were peers and colleagues on the same account team at an advertising agency. Charlotte stepped out of a client presentation with the rest of the account team. She turned to John and said, 'John, I have to say that the client team were really unhappy. It was clear that you weren't prepared.'

Angry and upset, John then defended himself, refuting Charlotte's suggestion as outrageously unfair and arguing that no other mortal had put in as much preparation as he had. He might have put forward the number of hours and the number of late nights that he'd spent preparing. But John had already lost. He might have refuted the assertion that he was unprepared but he had accepted the premise of the discussion. John had linked himself with being unprepared.

Richard Nixon for ever associated himself with the word 'crook' after his infamous 'I am not a crook' defence at the height of the Watergate scandal.

Imagine if John had responded by saying, 'Okay, I hear your concern. Thanks for the feedback. I need to give some thought as to what might have given that impression. I think it's always worthwhile for all of us to look at what we could do better. What about your performance? Is there anything you feel that you could have done better?'

John's use of the phrase 'I need to give some thought as to what might have given that impression' means he does not defend or attack, and, therefore, does not give his critic anything to push against. He sounds open and reasonable, but he does not accept the premise and emphasises 'impression'.

John has left Charlotte with two options: she either has to refer to her own shortcomings, or look churlish by criticising John but refusing to acknowledge that she has any shortcomings (by the way, this is not one for use with your boss).

Become aware of situations where you would normally defend yourself. Try simply taking a breath, and saying nothing about the criticism. Then move the conversation on to what you see as the most immediate forward-looking priorities.

Have you ever noticed how martial arts experts often stand on their own in parks doing the same movements over and over again when there are no assailants? This is because they understand the principles of muscle memory. Repetition is the key in committing a technique to muscle memory. This enables a technique to become more deeply ingrained, so when you need to recall it, it becomes much more automatic and instinctive. The process at work engages with the brain every bit as much as the muscles. It strengthens the relevant neural pathways.

If you keep practising Jujitsu Communication in the low-stakes situations, the techniques will more readily and automatically spring to mind in the high-stakes situations.

Jenny, a young woman executive we spoke to, explained how she had used this technique: 'Every year the public affairs department where I work becomes insanely busy as we prepare to publish the financial results. A colleague from another department and I share a secretary, and it becomes a tug of war at this time of year between the two of us as we battle over her time. This year when I broached the subject, he said, "Here we go again … you only ever think of yourself." Normally I would have become upset and told him how unfair his comment was. This time I simply took a breath and said, "The annual results aren't far away. I think it would be good to start making some plans for resources." At first he seemed completely wrong-footed and there was a moment's silence. He apologised. We came up with a really good compromise.'

If we meet the force of an assault head-on, we increase its intensity. We invite the other person to come forth with more evidence in support of their assault on us. We accept the premise and, therefore, we affect other people's perception of us. And we waste energy and lose focus.

Bulletproof people understand that – rather than fighting like with like – the most effective way to fend off a verbal assault is to take the energy out of the assault and turn it around so that it disables your assailant.

## Summary

○ Wrong-foot your opponent by not defending an attack
○ Take breath and a pause, and then move on to what you want to talk about
○ Phrases like 'I need to consider what gave you that impression' make you sound proactive but emphasise the fact that it is an impression only

# The power of the breath

There are smart ways to respond to a verbal assault and there are dumb ways. Many of us know the smart ways but too often enact the dumb ways in spite of ourselves. This takes us back to the cave dweller and guide metaphor. The cave dweller wants to go for the instinctive, automatic and emotional response, but the guide knows that there is a smarter way to handle the situation. The problem is that the cave dweller is more powerful than the guide.

Sometimes we allow the cave dweller to take over. We get emotional, we counter-attack, we lose our temper and then we tell ourselves that it was the right thing to do at the time. We say to ourselves, 'Well, just on this occasion he really needed to hear it like that.' Our minds confabulate explanations after the event to try to make us feel better about the way we acted. This, of course, is nonsense. There is never an occasion where exercising less control works to your advantage.

Nobody has found a perfect way to make sure that our rational, reasonable self takes charge in every situation, but we do believe that you can get better at it.

In all communication situations, the breath is vital. Try it right now. Take a nice easy breath into the diaphragm and breathe twice as slow on the exhalation. As you exhale become aware of your muscles relaxing. Now do it again, this time placing your hand gently over the diaphragm. As you breathe in, feel your hand move gently as your diaphragm inflates slightly. Again, take it twice as slowly on the exhalation. That good feeling that you are experiencing is your body signalling to your mind that everything is okay. You can cope. Because you are calmer, your thinking is clearer and you are in a better situation to choose the most helpful response.

Pausing and allowing the silence gives you time to breathe and to think rationally, and it gives others a moment to calm down. It also means that when you do speak the fact that you have taken a pause means that people are much more likely to really listen to you.

You cannot easily remind yourself *'not'* to respond in a certain way, under given circumstances. Our minds don't readily respond to the 'don't' command. You need to remind yourself to do something else instead. Again, this is where the breath helps. Before you respond or answer, take one of those deep, easy breaths. The pause will be imperceptible to anyone else but it will buy you an age of valuable time to choose your response. Practise the breath before responding in lower-stakes situations. Start now. You will be well positioned to think clearly and choose the best response in high-stakes situations.

Being 'attacked' during a meeting provokes a variety of strong emotions: hurt, anger, indignation and embarrassment, to name but a few. However, bulletproof people know how to identify these emotions. It's not a question of denying their existence or trying to combat them, but rather objectively noting them. As above, it's something that with practice can become automatic: a form of 'muscle memory'.

You can master this. You just pause and become aware for a moment about your thoughts and feelings.

When you feel under verbal attack, the danger is that your reflex defence mechanisms take over. This is where the 'wiser-you' can step in to help. Take a breath. Imagine that for a moment you are turning the volume down on the situation, just as you would do with a television, to have a quick chat with the wiser-you, before you respond.

## Summary
- Pause and breathe
- Do not be scared to allow a moment of silence before you respond

○ Take a moment to note how you feel during a confrontational conversation

○ Imagine you are viewing the situation or antagonist through a screen; you are free to turn the volume up or down

## 'Reflect' before responding

'How has the national debt personally affected each of your lives? And if it hasn't, how can you possibly find a cure for the common people if you have no experience of what is ailing them?'

The young woman in the audience had pitched a perfectly reasonable – but, at the same time, fiendishly clever – question to the presidential candidates in the live television debate during the 1992 US presidential election. Clinton, the outsider from Arkansas, is challenging the former vice-president, George Bush, Snr.

Both candidates are known to have considerable financial means. They appear to be left with the options of admitting that they are in no position to identify with ordinary people, or looking ridiculous as they pretend otherwise.

Bush waffles. He refers to the national and global economies. The questioner is insistent, chipping in to draw him back to the phrase that is at the heart of the question: 'you personally'. He's visibly uncomfortable and appears irritable. He tries a new tactic:

'Help me with the question and I'll try to answer it.'

Clinton's performance, however, demonstrates why he is such an intuitive communicator. Looking comfortable, yet caring and concerned, he slowly rises to his feet. Not too slowly; he is keen to answer the question but he knows how to look considered. He looks squarely and openly at the questioner. It's a look that suggests he is hiding nothing. 'You know people who have lost their jobs and lost their homes,' he says. 'Uh huh,' replies the questioner.

Clinton's tone of voice matches that of the questioner. As he talks, she nods her head.

'I am the governor of a small state … when people lose their jobs, I know their names.'

Clinton's answer was not ingeniously slick – the content was scarcely memorable – but he understood the power of being in rapport. Bush felt irritated and exposed, so he tried to take the questioner on. Clinton got alongside the questioner, so that they both appeared to be looking at the same problem together. Bringing personal experience to bear like this is extremely useful in any communication. This is the essence of Jujitsu Communication.

Clinton started by simply playing back to the questioner what she said. To be more precise, it is the bit of what she said that she clearly cared most about. This is what we call 'reflecting'. Clinton demonstrated the power of reflecting as a rapport-building tool. This is one of the simplest and most effective ways of showing that we are listening and, therefore, it is one of the simplest and most effective ways to create rapport.

By reflecting, we mean simply playing back what the other person has said. You can paraphrase (but what you do not do is to take what the other person has said and put an angle on it to support your argument). The important thing is to reflect the *feeling* behind what the other person has said. So for example:

- 'This is important to you, isn't it …'
- 'I can see you care about this, don't you …'

To reflect you need to listen out for feelings as well as facts. Reflecting is intended to show that you have listened, so each reflection must be unique, holding a mirror up to the feeling that the other person has just expressed. For this reason, phrases that will definitely not cut it are phrases such as:

- 'I hear what you say …'
- 'I understand where you're coming from …'

These are vague, generalised and overused. Immediately the listener feels that the speaker is going to dismiss them or reject their arguments.

We make a point of encouraging reflecting in customer service situations:

- 'You have been waiting for an hour and no one has spoken with you. That must be really frustrating.'

In fact, the use of the breath and the use of reflecting are two important cornerstones when dealing with any highly emotional person who is making a complaint. And here's a useful further tip. As you pause and take a breath, say silently to yourself, 'This person needs to be heard.' You will notice how it calms you and helps you to stay in control.

Reflecting is not the same as agreeing. In the case studies that we used, John, without agreeing, could have reflected by saying to Charlotte: 'You're concerned that we're going to lose this client; tell me more about that ... what else could we have done differently?'

Jenny, without agreeing with her colleague, could reflect his concerns with: 'You're worried that you won't have sufficient resources during this busy period. Okay, let's talk about that.'

As we often remind people, great conversations are built on rapport, not agreement.

### Summary
- Reflect back at the other person what they have said (and how they feel), without putting any spin on it
- Develop rapport – make it clear that you understand and share their concerns
- Make a personal reference wherever possible

## Ask for the 'thought behind the question'

People frequently ask a question when what they really want to do is make a statement. We could hypothesise why this is: maybe people feel that they do not have permission to simply state their point of view, as it seems too forthright to do so; maybe it is an instinctive defence mechanism, which stems from a desire to avoid committing or exposing ourselves; maybe it is just a linguistic convention.

Either way, if you simply take the question at face value and attempt to answer it, you miss vital opportunities to understand people's true concerns and to open up meaningful communication.

If you think that the question is important, do not leap straight to an answer. Try asking, 'What's the thought behind the question?'

We received the following email from an oil industry executive with whom we had recently worked:

> I tried that 'thought behind the question' thing that you guys talked about the other week. I was asked this really annoying question by a doubter I have on my team. Just as I was about to answer I paused and asked the thought behind the question. This opened up a whole new dialogue with the guy. We were able to talk about his concerns and in the end I was able to turn around a real cynic. It worked like magic.

We all have a basic human need to feel understood. If you can draw out what is really important to people, you have the basis for more effective communication. We have found that framing your response as 'the thought behind the question' seems to open up communication in a more helpful way than the more conventional 'why do you ask?'. Maybe it is because the notion of a 'thought' suggests something a little more substantive.

Highly effective communicators learn to create time and space for themselves when under pressure, without ever appearing to do so. This is why they appear to be so graceful under pressure and so capable of thinking on their feet. Being bulletproof requires the same skill. The key is to turn the attention back on to the interests and priorities of the questioner. This buys you vital time, while giving the impression that your main priority is to understand your interlocutor's concerns (not to mention the benefit of *actually* understanding her concerns).

The 'thought behind the question' technique is ideal for the purpose. There are variants on the same theme: 'You have clearly given this a lot of thought. Before I give my answer, can you tell me a bit more about your concerns?'

People often use a question when they intend to censure or criticise the other person. When people do this to us, it puts us on the back foot. The aggressor sets the agenda and leaves us with the feeling of scraping around for self-justifying answers. The 'thought behind the question' technique is ideal for turning around an assault that is dressed up as a question.

Here is an example: Kevin and Ray are colleagues whose teams have to collaborate each year to deliver the annual report to shareholders. Kevin is responsible for the financial data, while Ray's department do the creative and production. Each year the stress and temperature rise as the deadline looms. Kevin says to Ray, 'How do we know that your guys won't let us all down again by going over time and over budget?'

Ray could react with aggression, with self-justification, with excuses or with an apology. But just imagine if Ray were to respond like this: 'Just before I answer, Kevin, it sounds like you have some real concerns there. Could you tell me about them?'

The onus is now on Kevin to articulate things in an adult way. Once Kevin has spoken, a good follow-on for Ray would be along the lines of: 'What specific thing would you need to see in order to allay your concerns?'

In the exchange above, Ray has put himself in the driving seat of the conversation without ever needing to become defensive or aggressive. That's Jujitsu Communication.

## Summary

- Before you answer a question, consider the thought behind it. This is the real issue that the questioner is really concerned about
- Then use a question in return to tease out more details or make sure that your answer to the question addresses this thought

# Shift the focus on to the other person's underlying interest

The 'thought behind the question' (and its similar and closely related phrases) also allows you to move forward to interest-driven as opposed to position-driven communication.

For example, David says to Kim, 'I want you to take all references to Project X out of the proposal.' Let's assume Kim feels that there are important elements to keep in. So, if Kim is being position-driven, she will respond with something like, 'Well, I think it is important to keep them in.' A tug of war ensues. Kim may get her way, but she will probably leave David determined to win the next round.

Bulletproof Kim takes a pause and decides to go for the interest-driven tactic. Her response will be, 'Why is that important to you, David?'

David now feels better towards Kim as she is taking an interest in what is important to him. Kim has moved herself alongside David, rather than taking him head on, to a position from which she can far better steer the conversation to a more productive outcome.

This might be followed up along the lines of: 'David, I take your point about XYZ ... from my perspective, I think it's important that we mention ABC ... can we find a workaround?'

Just like 'thought behind the question', there is, of course, a range of variations on the 'why's that important to you' theme. The important thing is to try it out. Rather than going straight to your position, start by asking what is really important to the other person. Become aware of how it opens up communication.

## Summary
○ Do not take up a position
○ Enquire about the other person's underlying interest
○ Shift the focus on to the desire to meet common interests

# Insist on specifics

Let's go back to the example of Ray and Kevin. Notice what Ray did in his follow-up to Kevin. He invited him to be specific. Requesting specifics is a useful technique for Jujitsu Communication. Most verbal assaults tend to be vague. Breaking them down to specifics takes the toxicity out of them. The request for specifics turns the energy around, putting the pressure on your interlocutor. And here's the beautiful thing. It allows you to turn the spotlight around while remaining eminently reasonable and avoiding any hint of aggression or defensiveness. There are two ways to deal with an attack: sidestep it or turn it around.

Let's look at the following case study as an example:

## Case Study 3.3

'Everyone thinks that training course you ran about the new project management system was a complete waste of time,' Jules fed back to Jim. 'It was way wide of the mark.'

'I'd like to understand more about that. It would help to know exactly who expressed an opinion and what was said,' replied Jim.

'Well, I wasn't the only one thinking it,' Jules answered. 'Robbie said he felt that we missed some useful stuff and Sharon was shifting around in her chair throughout.'

'When you say a waste of time, could you help me out here by being a bit more specific?' asked Jim.

'Well, there was some important stuff that wasn't covered.'

'What exactly?'

'Well, it would have been useful to know something about budgeting.'

'How precisely do you mean?'

'Well, it seemed that we just skated over the budgeting software.'

Jim concluded by saying, 'Okay, so you, Robbie and Sharon would have liked to know more about the budgeting software. I'll certainly keep that in mind for next time.'

Notice how Jim summarises the point in the final, most specific and most reduced form (this will take the sting out of it).

Another way to turn the energy around is to require the person making the criticism to be specific about what she would like to see instead, for example: 'If you felt that we spent too much time on $X$ how much time would you like to spend on it?'; or, 'If we spent too little time on the budget software, what do you feel would be the right amount of time?'

And remember, if somebody makes a comment that suggests that you, your project or your team are about to screw up, the only effective response is along the lines of: 'What specific actions could be taken at this stage to allay your concerns?'

## Summary

◯ Take the sting out of hostile comments by asking for specific details
◯ Politely but firmly insist that the other person be as specific as possible
◯ Once you've identified these precise concerns, explain how you'll act on them
◯ If someone suggests that they doubt your competence to deliver something, don't defend – ask specifically what would allay concerns

# Emphasise shared values

Whatever the situation, if you're seeking to communicate effectively, it's important to secure the acceptance of your audience, says Simon Lancaster, who has written speeches for CEOs of companies such as HSBC and Cadbury, as well as senior politicians and Olympic gold medallists.

'You need to establish a degree of empathy,' he says. 'Handling a difficult question is like making a speech, in that it's a journey. You're taking your audience with you from A to B, and that means that you need to meet them at A. You need to establish common ground. This might mean explaining that you understand their concerns, even if you don't agree with them. I've written speeches for people who are quite happy to go to a meeting where they know that the audience is very annoyed with them and have a lot of valid anger. But they'll stand up there and say, "I know you're angry … I know we disagree." It really helps build a rapport because it's honest. Some people think they'd better just focus on the positives but that can simply enrage the audience even more because it doesn't sound honest and it's not addressing their concerns.'

Simon says that the ancient Greeks believed that a persuasive speaker should have ethos (that is empathy and evidence that they are of good character), pathos (they share values with the audience) and logos (this is the substance of what they're saying – the action they'll take).

In a modern context, he summaries this as EVA. 'I've heard top politicians use this approach, and it works brilliantly,' he says. 'I've advised clients to use it in all kinds of difficult situations.'

So, to put it into practice:

- *Empathy* – 'Yes, I understand that you're angry.'
- *Values* – 'Look, I want to make sure that we can be proud of ourselves because we're known for offering the best customer service in the country.'
- *Action* – 'So, I'm making some changes that will really help us deliver a better service to all our customers.'

Emotion is more powerful than logic, according to Simon. The part of the brain that deals with emotion is larger than the part that deals with logic. 'Some people think that bringing emotion into the workplace is somehow unprofessional. People sometimes say things to me such as, "I'm an economist; I'm not interested in emotion." But the point is that he was using emotion simply by saying this. He was demonstrating his pride and trying to cause me to feel shame.'

You need to use emotion carefully, of course; getting upset or cross with your audience won't achieve anything. It's more effective to inject some emotion into your communication by using stories and anecdotes. You can appeal to people's values, loves and hates and not just their reason.

We worked with Vincent, the CEO of a medium-sized packaged food company. The organisation was attempting to implement a major change, and employee morale seemed to be in free fall. We introduced EVA to Vincent. At a particularly tough brown-bag lunch meeting, Vincent abandoned his combative style, paused for a moment, looked away thoughtfully to signal that an 'off-script' moment was coming, and then said: 'There's nothing worse than feeling that you're going through change and you don't know what's going on, that nobody's listening and there's nobody you can turn to. I have been in that situation and I wouldn't wish it on anyone. That's why I commit to coming down here to talk to you face to face every Friday.'

The change of mood in the room was palpable.

## Summary

- ○ Match and reflect the *emotions* of your audience
- ○ Show that you have the same *values* as your audience
- ○ Then explain what *action* you're going to take

# Using stories in communication when under attack

Often when you're under attack in a particular situation the solution – and the challenge – is to persuade your attacker. Simply defending your actions or your point of view can often look weak and means that you're arguing on your opponent's turf.

Screenplay lecturer and consultant, Robert McKee, argues that telling a story is the most powerful and effective way in which to convey a message. This is true of a sales presentation or a pitch for funding but also when it comes to communicating effectively with a boss or a team. Whether it's persuading your boss to do what you want them to do or engaging and motivating the team that reports to you, creating a storyline which explains your position and what you're trying to do works better than simply throwing facts and figures at them.

McKee argues that there are fundamentally three ways to persuade; two of the ways have limited effectiveness, but the third pulls together all of the strands that appeal to people. 'I've given many, many lectures to business people and I've noticed that very often in a working environment their problem is one of persuasion,' he explains. 'Almost always getting out of a difficult situation involves persuasion.'

First, you can use the classic PowerPoint presentation. This is where you gather evidence of a factual nature and you compound it in an inductive argument. You go through this point, then that point and then you say, 'therefore ...' It's very familiar, but this often doesn't work because the people to whom you are presenting have their own facts, figures or evidence. Moreover, when you're thinking about persuading someone and not necessarily engaging with them, you tend to avoid negatives. However, in their minds, the audience is already hearing all the negatives, and they're thinking of a whole other argument against what you're saying. 'You're setting up an argument – and thereby inadvertently encouraging your audience to develop the counter-argument,' says McKee.

The second method of persuading people to work with you rather than against you is coercion. You can bribe them or flatter them or threaten them. This often works temporarily – people will react but in the long run this approach is going to come round and bite you on the arse. Either your audience is always going to have their hand out wanting more flattering words and promises, or, if you're always threatening them, they'll get fed up and leave the organisation or just bad-mouth you.

However, the third option, according to McKee, is to tell a story. Here, you take all those facts that you would have used in the Power-Point, plus all the negative points that you wouldn't normally mention, and you argue both sides of your case by putting it into the form of a story. By taking all of the information and dramatising it, storytelling works both emotionally and intellectually. You include the negatives in a coherent pattern with which they're all familiar but which also makes sense of them and puts them into context.

Telling a story in order to explain your point of view and outline your reasoning is a powerful way to undo an attack. You might explain the way in which your organisation, team or department is currently 'in the cave' but has plans to get out of it. You may choose to tell a story of how you or others have been in a given situation, but have won through in the end. You may choose to explain a change by bringing it to life, from the point of view of a specific individual, or 'protagonist', in the story.

The chief technology officer of a packaged consumer goods company was trying to get the heads of the different countries to buy into a big new inventory and supply-chain management system. He would tour the office with his deck of PowerPoint slides, but to little avail. Eventually we persuaded him to turn off his laptop and tell a story: Think of Mick. Currently when Mick enters the warehouse every morning, he has to count up the number of palettes manually, before getting on the phone ...'

Stories of challenges undertaken or adversity overcome are great for capturing attention. You will notice the climate in the room change as soon as your audience hears the words along the lines of, 'Let me take you back to a time, not so long ago, when ...' As McKee explains, 'The best stories entail a journey from darkness to light.'

What stories can you use, either about yourself or others, to make a point, and deflect an attack in the heat of the moment?

## Summary
○ Use the power of story to take your audience on a journey with you
○ Having a problem solved, a question answered or a challenge overcome will keep them on board and help persuade them

# The power of context

When people are particularly concerned or agitated about something, they very often lose sight of the context. We are all guilty, at one point or another, of getting things out of proportion when we're annoyed or upset about something. There are ways of putting people's concerns subtly and tactfully into context.

For example, when replying to a question, you can change the focus of the debate. Just as a movie camera will concentrate on one detail or pan back to show the whole scene, you, too, can change your focus. Perhaps you're defending cuts or an increased workload for your department. If you want to back up your case, then you could focus in on a particular example: 'I've had to cancel my summer vacation this year,' or 'I can appreciate what you're saying. We're all under pressure. For instance, Hannah's had to forego her bonus this year.'

Then again you can pan back: 'I know it's difficult right now, but every organisation is having to cut their budgets at the moment – just look at the article about the economy in the papers today,' or 'Everyone in this sector is working harder – clients are demanding more for their money. Michael over at National Consolidated was telling me exactly the same thing last week.'

Again, thinking about context to defend a decision or a choice you've made allows you to explore the extremes. Say, for example, you've been criticised for the type of IT system that you've bought for the company. You might want to start by talking about a state-of-the-art system that is all bells and whistles and does everything that your colleagues could ever dream of. Great, eh? But then you show them the enormously high price tag.

You then tell them about a very affordable system which would come in way under budget. Sound like a good deal? Perhaps, except that it's limited in the following ways …

Thirdly (and remember that in speeches the power of three is incredibly powerful), you come to your option. Having explored the extremes, this choice offers the best of all worlds.

## Summary

○ Aim to put an argument or an issue into context

○ Pan back from the issue in question to look at the whole organisation or the whole sector or even the state of the country

○ Explore the extremes – and then show why you've opted for your choice, which is the best of both worlds

# Correct inaccuracies when the storm has passed

Imagine that you're sitting in a restaurant. The service is poor. You ordered a long time ago, but there is no sign of your food. Your empty stomach is beginning to rumble. Nobody has given you an explanation; indeed, it's not easy to catch anyone's eye. Then eventually you manage to speak to the maître d'. You explain that you have been waiting for thirty-five minutes. At this point, he looks something up on a small piece of paper and fires back that according to his records you have only been *weighting twenty-five* minutes!

How do you feel now? Do you revise your view of the restaurant and feel a whole ten minutes better? In reality you probably go from irritated to incensed. This is because what matters to you is a combination of that empty feeling in your stomach and the feeling that your time had not been respected. What you really wanted was in part to have your food sooner rather than later but, more profoundly, to feel heard and understood.

When Tony Hayward, CEO of BP, responded to the Gulf of Mexico oil spill by seemingly looking for exonerating factors in BP's favour, he merely attracted greater opprobrium on to the company. In the heat of the moment, there was one thing and one thing only that the wider community cared about: clean up the ocean! Hayward needed to show that he really understood this before correcting inaccuracies. Never correct an inaccuracy in the heat of the moment. It will not lessen the criticism but it will almost certainly raise the temperature. When we correct an inaccuracy, it suggests that we have failed to hear what is truly important. Far from exonerate you in the eyes of others, it encourages an escalation of evidence slinging. This doesn't mean that you accept or agree with the inaccuracy, it means that you let it pass, for the moment.

Letting an inaccuracy pass unchallenged, particularly when you are under fire, understandably sticks in the craw. You also feel that, when you're under fire, every little thing you can do to protect your reputation is going to count.

The first rule of correcting inaccuracies, in another person's criticism of you, is never to do it in the heat of the moment, when emotions are heightened. The second rule is to make sure that you are seen to have heard what is really important to the other person – and this is where reflecting helps.

The best way to correct an inaccuracy is to avoid appearing to cover your own back and to ostensibly show concern for accuracy or information and fairness to others.

### Case Study 3.4

Mike's department had been criticised for its service levels. The issue of late submission of reports has been highlighted, but Mike's critics had exaggerated the extent of the tardiness by a good forty-eight hours. Bulletproof Mike assured his critics that he grasped the real issue and was on the case, but corrected the inaccuracy once the initial storm had passed and feelings were more stable.

'The important thing is to make sure that all reports are submitted on time in future and we are taking steps to make sure of that ... I am just keen to make sure that everyone has information that is as accurate as possible here. Our records seem to show that it was submitted at 5pm on Tuesday – do you know how Pat was given to understand that it was Thursday? I'm keen to know if there's anything we can do to make sure that everyone is working from the same information in future.'

Show that you have heard what's important. Show that you are taking steps to fix it. Then, show that you are primarily concerned whether there is anything that you can do to make sure that everyone has the same accurate information … or that the risks of misunderstandings are reduced in the future. At this point, you will be likely to receive an apology from your critic for any inaccuracy.

### Summary
○ Don't correct an inaccuracy during the heat of the moment – wait until emotions are more stable
○ When you do correct an inaccuracy, acknowledge that you in no way diminish the underlying issues and the feelings caused

## Show concern for your assailant

### Case Study 3.5
Mary and Jacques were assigned to work on the audit of a major client. It was a long and involved assignment that required long hours at the client's headquarters. Jacques was unaware of any problem until he received a telephone call from the senior partner. Mary had expressed that she was unhappy working with Jacques. She felt that he was not acting like a team player, he was not communicating and sharing important information, and he would often dump work on her, relying on her good nature to pick it up.

At this point, there are two possible outcomes: Jacques allows his inner case dweller to kick in; or he uses Jujitsu Communication to handle the situation.

Jacques' cave dweller feels a compelling urge to protect his reputation, to launch a counter-attack on Mary, and to draw attention to Mary's lack of professionalism in not coming to him first.

But Bulletproof Jacques is smarter than this, and he is adept at calming his inner cave dweller. He says to the senior partner: 'It's interesting that you say that. I am obviously concerned that Mary feels that way. I know she is feeling under quite a bit of pressure at the moment. She's working long hours and I want to do all I can to help her through this time. I'll call her right away to see exactly what I can do to make sure the way that I work with her works better for her.'

The senior partner thanks Jacques and goes away relieved that the conversation went well: Jacques heard the message, and in Jacques he has a professional and caring colleague. Jacques has successfully positioned himself alongside the senior partner and refocused the spotlight on Mary. Jacques didn't put forward his defence and he did not attack Mary; the senior partner was spared the invidious position of having to act as judge between two employees.

Most self-help books advise that we should draw attention to the unhelpful behaviour of a co-worker. They tell us that we should point out the behaviour and explain how it caused us to feel. Now, there is certainly a time and a place for this, but we suggest that you limit this to extremes of intolerable behaviour. The simple fact is that too much talking about how your feelings have been hurt will not endear you to co-workers. Nobody wants to work with someone who appears unduly sensitive and emotionally high-maintenance.

When someone behaves in a way that you feel is undesirable, a smarter strategy is to turn the focus on the perpetrator of the behaviour, rather than making the situation mean something about yourself.

- 'Tom, I noticed you ...'
- '... has something angered you?'
- '... is there anything that I can help you with?

Consider the following dilemma: Dick and Don are both competing for the next available opportunity to become partner at a law firm. They both started on the same day, some years ago, but the underlying sense of competitiveness has escalated. As the other lawyers gather for the address by the senior partner, Don takes up a prime space in the circle of seats directly in the sightline of the senior partner. Dick arrives late, with no available seats left. He picks up a chair and places it directly in front of Don, blocking his view of the senior partner. Don now either spends the meeting looking at the back of Dick's head or he asks Dick to move.

The latter tactic raises the stakes; it draws attention to the fact that Don is feeling slighted and he loses face publicly if the chair remains where it is.

Bulletproof Don uses Jujitsu Communication. Ostensibly he shows concern for Dick. Standing up, he places his hands on Dick's shoulders and says, 'We all sat down without leaving a seat for Dick. Could we all shuffle along slightly so that we can all see each other face to face?'

Body language experts recognise that it is the higher-status individual who invites the other person to go through the door first. This is the essence of Jujitsu Communication.

### Summary
○ Showing concern for the person who might be seen to be attacking is often more effective than counter-attack

# Outflanking

Have you ever been in a situation where you have started off angrily making a customer complaint, and ended up reassuring the person to whom you were complaining that is wasn't such a big deal after all and that you fully understand that 'these things happen'?

If you have, the chances are that the complaint handler was very effective at using the outflanking technique.

If I am hungry and that room service I ordered is very late, when I call down to reception I want to feel cared for and understood. If the apology doesn't quite match up to how I am feeling, then I feel that I have still got some work to do.

On the other hand, imagine if, on my pointing out that I am a little annoyed, the complaint handler responds, 'Sir, you have every reason to be annoyed. I would be more than annoyed; I would be furious. We have let you down and that is completely unacceptable ...'

You might be familiar with the *Monty Python* sketch about the diner who casually complains to a waiter that his fork is slightly dirty. The horrified waiter immediately brings the head waiter who explodes with indignation and explains that the entire washing-up staff will be sacked. With *Python*-esque absurdity, the situation spirals out of control. It's a completely ridiculous situation, of course, but what is realistic is that the diner who made the complaint starts protesting that the dirty fork really doesn't matter.

When someone makes a particularly heartfelt apology or outflanks our concern, we naturally want to restore the balance and reassure the other person of our reasonableness. The principle goes beyond complaint situations to virtually every walk of life.

Counsellors who help people with addiction problems, for example, may use this technique. Before committing to a programme of recovery, an alcoholic may argue that there is not a problem and nothing needs to change. Counsellors discovered that if they took this view head on, they would simply increase the level of resistance. A far more effective strategy was to establish a sense of rapport and then ask, 'Are you saying that you are absolutely happy with everything in your life and nothing at all needs to change?'

To this, the other person will almost invariably acknowledge at least some aspect of his life that would benefit from change. There is a small opening, but that is all that the counsellor needs to start moving the conversation in the direction of the case for change.

Outflanking is about overstating the other person's point of view to the extent that – and we all like to see ourselves as reasonable and flexible – he or she will restore the equilibrium by coming back towards your point of view. (It can only be used once you have managed to set up a state of rapport. If you attempt the outflanking technique before you are in a state of rapport, the other person will smell manipulation and the defences are likely to spring up.)

Imagine David is making the point to Kim that he really dislikes Proposal 21. If Kim scours the proposal for bits that might change David's mind, David remains in the same position; he is in the habit of saying no and shooting things down, so, of course, he may as well stay congruent and consistent in his reactions.

Bulletproof Kim will get alongside David and use the outflanking technique: 'Thanks for sharing your thoughts, David. Just so that I understand, are you saying that there is absolutely nothing you like in Proposal 21?'

David, because he wants to see himself as open and reasonable, will almost certainly respond by finding something he likes: Kim has the basis for conversation.

**Summary**
- Establish rapport by listening and reflecting concerns
- Once you are in rapport, play back the other person's issue or concern, but make a point of overstating
- If your best option is to apologise, it is better to over-apologise than risk being seen to under-apologise

# Use the power of reciprocation

If you have ever found yourself in a kasbah in a North African country, the likelihood is that someone has thrust a cup of mint tea and a pastry in your hand before broaching the subject of his beautiful hand-woven carpets. This is because the salesman understands the psychological power of reciprocity. It may seem preposterous that a cup of mint tea might make you more likely to buy an expensive carpet, but the salesman knows that it does. Reciprocity is an important driver in human interactions, and small favours, concessions or good deals can lead to reciprocated actions that are out of all proportion to the original act.

Here's another example of people's innate desire to reciprocate: Robert Cialdini, Regents' Professor Emeritus of Psychology and Marketing at Arizona State University, sent a Christmas card to a large number of complete strangers – and promptly received cards back from many of them. They had no idea who he was but they were sent a card and so they reciprocated.

Reciprocity can help you create that all-important opening when you find yourself at loggerheads with someone. The key is to acknowledge one specific area in which you are willing to accept and acknowledge that your adversary may have a point. Almost everybody will then reciprocate by acknowledging the validity of your view on a certain point. The door of communication starts to open and you have movement.

Consider this dilemma: Roberta, who is head of finance, finds herself in a stand-off with Matt who runs IT. Both believe that the other is trying unfairly to deflect blame for an error on to their own department, but Roberta knows that a vacuum in communication is bad news. She and Matt will need to work together to solve this problem and make sure that it doesn't happen in future.

Bulletproof Roberta uses Jujitsu Communication. She re-establishes communication by saying, 'Matt, I read over that email that I sent you in the heat of the moment, and, in fairness, you had a point. It did sound like I wasn't taking into consideration the pressures your department have been under. I can understand why you felt how you did. I should have been more balanced.'

### Summary

○ Giving ground over a small issue and accepting a point that is obviously of concern to your opponent establishes a rapport that improves communication and helps you win the bigger battle

## Preparing for a presentation

It seems that in most corporations *the presentation* has taken over from the conversation as the communication mode of choice. At the time of writing, pharmaceutical giant Glaxo has announced to the press that its scientists will have to make *Dragon's Den*-style presentations to its

– presumably sceptical – senior management, in order to win support for the pipeline drugs that they are championing. For those not familiar with the reference, *Dragon's Den* is a TV show where a series of hapless entrepreneurs pitch their ideas to a panel of cynical and hard-bitten venture capitalists in the hope of bringing a partner, and their finances, on board.[11]

The presentation, for the majority of the time, is a remarkably inefficient mode of communication. *Report writing* requires us to organise our thoughts. *The conversation* promotes a generative and developmental mode of communication. On the other hand *the presentation* promotes a sit-back-and-judge mentality. Nonetheless, we need to deal with reality as we find it. It appears that many corporations feel that *presentations* provide an ideal platform to pick out the shining talent of the future. Excelling at presentations is an important part of being bulletproof.

You may hear the old chestnut that for most people fear of public speaking ranks higher than fear of death. We have never come across any robust data to back this up. It may be that public speaking is more avoidable than death, but even there the difference is becoming marginal. In today's corporations you need to be able to cut a dash in the presentation stakes.

The principles of Jujitsu Communication apply to the presentation every bit as much as the conversation. The presentation is basically a performance. No martial artist – or athlete or actor or musician, for that matter – would step out into the performance arena without the appropriate preparation ritual for mind and body. These things only take a few minutes, but, based on our observation, the majority of presenters in the corporate world use no form of preparation ritual. If anything, the vital minutes prior to a performance are spent making compulsive last-minute changes to the PowerPoint slides. Let's be clear: people do not buy your argument because of what is on your slides; they buy your argument according to the confidence that they have in you.

If you are about to perform, your body should adopt a state of heightened alertness. Professional athletes understand this and actively seek out this feeling, hence 'getting in the zone' or 'getting psyched up'. They understand that if they are not feeling these sensations, they are likely to lack focus and underperform. Evidence suggests these physiological or 'autonomic' responses are fairly common across all of us; indeed they do not vary much between people who are highly confident and people who consider themselves shy and nervous. What varies hugely, however, is the way in which people read these signals and the interpretations that follow.

Studies show that people who are less confident have a greater tendency to interpret their body's autonomic responses as a problem. To this group, the speeding heart, dry mouth, clammy hands and churning stomach are signs that something is wrong. These signs then feed into a cycle of anxiety. Indeed, as Dr Amy Silver puts it, 'It appears that a misreading of our bodies' natural signals is one of the greatest sources of performance anxiety.'[12]

For the confident group, measures of their physiological changes show that their bodies are doing pretty much the same thing, but the language that they use is markedly different. They are more inclined to describe themselves as 'calm', 'relaxed' or 'focused'. It is not that the latter group are deluding themselves. It is more likely that they have learnt to read and interpret their body's responses in a way that works for them.

As acting coach Peter Nicholas puts it, 'The key is to welcome those sensations in your body. Practise becoming aware of them. Be glad that your body knows what to do. In a physiological sense, being nervous and being excited are the same. Stop telling yourself that you are nervous. Start telling yourself that you are excited. You cannot get rid of those butterflies in your stomach, but you can get them flying in formation.'

A simple physical and mental ritual helps. Tongue-twisters not only relax the facial muscles and tongue, they refocus your attention:

- Unique New York, New York's unique.
- Peggy Babcock's mixed biscuits.
- Nine men in a mini is too many men in a mini.

Humming also helps. It is surprisingly simple but effective. With feet several inches apart, and your knees nice and relaxed, as you hum picture the sound moving up and down your body in a 'figure of eight': low, bass down towards the groin and higher pitched towards the crown of your head. This will loosen your mouth and facial muscles and relax your body.

As all sports performers know, gentle muscular stretches are an ideal way to release tension in your body. Become aware of your breathing, and slowly and effortlessly increase the depth of breath in an easy sensation down to your diaphragm, and slow and easy on the exhale.

### Summary
- Remember – those nerves are there to help you, to improve your performance, not to make life more difficult
- Become aware of your body gearing up for a performance; remind yourself to welcome the sensation
- Learn to recognise the feelings that are evoked, so that you begin to view them as natural rather than a sign of weakness
- Visualise the butterflies in your stomach lining up in formation, as if they mean business

## Practise drawing on different levels of confidence

It may appear self-evident that bulletproof people are confident. In his work as a confidence coach, Peter Nicholas has observed a common misconception about confidence. 'People generally tend to talk about confidence as if it were a fixed quantity doled out at birth and then remaining unchanged throughout life. All my experience tells me that this assumption is false and that confidence is something that any of us can learn.'

When people meet their heroes from any field of performance, one of the things we commonly hear is a sense of surprise at how unassuming this particular superstar appears to be. That is because top performers do not constantly function as if they were constantly stepping out in front of an audience of thousands. They learn how to 'turn it on or off', or, more precisely, they know how to select the level of confidence that they need to operate and readily switch on to that level, like a driver selecting a gear.

Central to Nicholas's idea is that we have a full range of confidence levels within us. Science seems to be bearing out Nicholas's intuition. It makes sound adaptive sense, in evolutionary terms, to be able to move between varying levels of confidence.

Research into testosterone shows that levels increase as we gear up for a competition. This is understandable. Testosterone is associated with aggression and competitiveness – precisely what we need to prevail in a competitive situation. But research among sports people shows that testosterone's greatest surge comes *after* success has been achieved. If you ask people to cite a time when they have felt at the most confident, more often than not they will mention a feeling directly following some victorious achievement.

This makes sense for our ancestor. A good time to go and pursue more of the same is following a success, so our bodies fire up the chemistry set to go and do so. Success is a positive feedback cycle.

Conversely, a similar cycle occurs for failure and setback. On these occasions, instead of testosterone, our bodies flood with cortisol, which is a hormone more readily associated with withdrawal and avoidance. If our ancestor has just suffered a defeat, it makes sense to get away and live to fight another day. Watch how soccer players' 'heads drop' when they concede a goal.[13]

Winning and losing streaks are real; they have a sound physiological basis. But like any physiology that affects our levels of resilience, we can influence it to work in our favour.

Peter Nicholas believes that we all have the ability to function at the entire range of levels of confidence, but most of us get stuck at a certain level. That becomes our default setting. Nicholas feels that a vital starting point is to recognise all of our varying levels, and to familiarise ourselves with them, without judging.

'I ask people to think of their range of confidence as levels, numbered from one to ten,' he says. 'I then ask them to walk around in a space. As they walk I shout out a number, and they are then required to walk as they would walk at that level of confidence. I ask them not to act it, but to *be* it: to become aware of how they move, how they think, how they feel inside, how they tend to see that world, at that moment. I call out a series of numbers, so that they get used to the feeling of transitioning between one and another. I ask them to breathe out the level that they have and breathe in the new level.'

As we develop a sense of awareness about our confidence levels, we can also experiment with them: practise breathing out the current level and breathing in a new level. As we do this, we practise extending our influence and control over our levels of confidence.[14]

The memory is the primary agent of confidence. Our ancestors' surge of testosterone happened because the recent victory was still imprinted on the mind. Doubt creeps in when thoughts of recent failures plague our minds. Our mind draws on its sense of the potency and recentness of past events to gauge the appropriate level of confidence.

However, we now understand more and more about the human memory and what an intriguing phenomenon it is. It seems that the accepted metaphor of a library or archive is misplaced. If we cast our minds back to a memorable event, our intuitive sense is that our mind is plucking it out of the movie library and replaying it for us. A more accurate metaphor is that our mind is re-shooting the movie, sometimes with some big changes in the plot and script. Our memory does not so much recall as recreate. And each time it recreates, the pathways in our mind become deeper, making associations and, in turn, altering our thoughts and feelings.

The thoughts that we have create observable physical changes in the brain. Alvaro-Pascual Leone, Harvard Professor of Neurology, explains this via the metaphor of snow on a hill. The shape of the hill may change little, but imagine someone taking a sled ride down the outside. The sled ride represents a thought. After it is completed, it leaves a trace in the snow. If another sled takes the same path, the rut becomes deeper. Because it is deeper, it becomes a root that future sled rides more readily follow as they go with the path of least resistance. By choosing the thoughts that we have, we can help to make those deeper sled runs in our minds more positive and helpful. As we do so, the less helpful ones become less used.[15]

Peter Nicholas points out that we all have our 'ten moments' in confidence (when the individual feels at his or her highest level of confidence). They are, by definition, personal and unique to each of us. The moment may be something that would seem insignificant to a third-party onlooker, but it is the personal nature of 'ten moments' that gives them their power. The key is to make a habit of revisiting them, recreate the movie in your mind over and over. The more vivid and intense you make each aspect, the deeper that pathway for the sled to travel down in future.

Experiment with this now. Choose a 'ten moment' from any aspect of your life. As you run the movie in your mind, experiment with turning up the colour, the contrast, the brightness and the volume. Move around and see it from a range of different perspectives. Practise picking out a detail and focusing your attention on it; it might be the sound, smell, colour or texture. Select a detail that is going to serve as your trigger to take you back into that thought when you need it. Let your attention rest on it for a while. Picturing that detail will now give you a ready trigger when you choose to access this level of confidence.

Research among elite hockey players from the University of St Catherine's, Ontario, shows that they experience a surge in testosterone when they view video footage of one of their past victories (with no change when they view neutral footage).[16] Testosterone is the get-out-and-compete hormone. You will be unlikely to have a movie of one of your past successes when you need it, but this is why you create the 'movie' in your mind.

Of course, your movie does not have to be a past event. Sports people learn to picture themselves experiencing 'ten moments' when they need one: at the height of a competitive performance. Go through the exercise again for a current event or one that is about to happen in the near future.

Nicholas points out that the most crucial thing is to be comfortable with moving between levels of confidence when you need to. A professional performer may do all of the correct mental preparation, but may occasionally still feel confidence fall at the crucial moment. Prepare for the drop, so that if you feel it you know that you are going to be okay. Remind yourself that these things happen, breathe out the current level and breathe in the level you want to play at. Notice your confidence start to rise again.

If you have a tough presentation coming up, ask yourself how you want to be in that presentation: what do you want to feel and look like? When was there a moment in the past when you found yourself feeling and looking like this, and operating at this level of confidence? (It can be a seemingly small incident – the important thing is that it means something to you.) Focus on that moment. Turn up the contrast, the colour, the volume for each detail in your mind. Now, picture yourself in the presentation operating in just the same style, first as a third-party onlooker, and then seeing the situation through your own eyes. Then imagine a drop in confidence – for example, you're thrown a very difficult question, or your audience appears very taciturn – and practise breathing out. Then picture yourself simply breathing back in your restored, high level of confidence … and carry on.

## Summary

O You have the full range of levels of confidence within you
O Become aware of what you are like at each level and practise moving between them
O Think of moments when you were at a 'level 10' and play the movie in your head whenever it helps
O Sometimes you'll be aware of a drop in confidence. Remind yourself that that's fine
O Take a breath and imagine yourself 'breathing in' a higher level of confidence

# Create an ally among your audience in advance

Bulletproof people boost their confidence by drawing on their bank of 'ten moments'. They also practise being comfortable moving between levels of confidence, so that if they feel a drop at any stage they know that it will not be a problem. However, there is a further tactic. Bulletproof people do their groundwork and seek out an ally in the audience.

## Case Study 3.6

Samantha recognised that mental toughness in front of a potentially hostile panel is essential, but in itself is not enough. The key is to win over the panel. To do this, she put in a telephone call to Alexandra, who she knew would be part of the panel. Flattering Alexandra, she pointed out that she appreciated how precious the panel's time was and she wanted to make sure that she did all that she could to make sure that she used the panel's time as effectively as possible. Alexandra was impressed by Samantha's thoroughness, and, of course, she was then inclined to warm to Samantha, and even passed on some practical advice about what worked well for this group (such as use of humour, degree of formality, whether they were PowerPoint junkies or not ...).

Asking advice builds relationships in two ways: firstly, it flatters the person whom one is asking, as it suggests that we value that person's expertise; secondly, when someone does us a favour or gives us something, they tend to like us more.

This second phenomenon is sometimes referred to as the 'Benjamin Franklin' effect. During his time in the Pennsylvania Legislature, Franklin quickly needed to befriend a hitherto political foe in order to win his support in a crucial vote. When Franklin heard that his rival possessed a 'very scarce and curious' book, he wrote to him requesting that he lend Franklin the book. The rival legislator obliged. Franklin wrote back expressing his gratitude and emphasising his sense of the favour. Franklin won the friendship and support of his rival. He appears to have had an intuitive understanding of the way in which our minds deal with cognitive dissonance. Because our minds like consistency and congruence between our thoughts and actions, if we show someone a kindness or do them a favour, our minds then realign our attitudes – we tend to like them more. If you want to get along with someone, ask a favour – and make a point of expressing gratitude for the favour.[17]

But it goes further. Once Alexandra has given advice to Samantha, she has a stake in Samantha doing well. She feels Samantha's performance reflects on her: if Samantha does well, it fits with Alexandra's self-concept as someone who reads situations well and gives astute advice. Samantha has created an ally in the audience – someone who is rooting for her.

Before a presentation, to whom can you speak in advance, asking advice and thereby creating an ally?

## Summary

- ◯ Boost your confidence by creating an ally
- ◯ Asking advice builds relationships; the advisor has an invested interest in your success
- ◯ If you want to get along with someone, ask a favour of them – and make a point of expressing gratitude for the favour

# CHAPTER 4
## HANDLING TOXIC BOSSES
## AND OTHER DEMENTORS

It's not just Harry Potter who is at risk from soul-sucking monsters. These people are lurking in every organisation. Our immediate instinct might be to attack them full on but that will just make the situation worse. To be bulletproof against dementors, we need to use an array of strategies.

### Case Study 4.1

Shelley enjoyed her job in the research department of an investment bank. She had been looking forward to meeting her new boss: a younger woman who had been brought in from another organisation. Shelley was naturally slightly nervous but keen to work with someone new. However, the first thirty days did not go as planned. Shelley felt ignored by her boss.

'It started off that I had to ask for a time to see her rather than her arranging to see me,' said Shelley, 'but I assumed she was just busy, and anyway I thought it'd look good if I took the initiative. And she was very nice when we first met – pleasant, and keen to know what I'd been working on.'

But after this initially positive meeting, Shelley continued to feel ignored as her emails and phone messages went unanswered. When she was finally called to a meeting, Shelley believed that things were finally about to change. They would now get to know each other and she welcomed the opportunity to discuss her exciting new projects.

'I arranged a catch-up so my boss could see the projects and the initiatives I'd taken recently. I also wanted to ask what else I could do for her. But in some ways I wish I'd never bothered.'

Clearly annoyed at having Shelley take up her valuable time, the new vice-president told her to stop wasting time on pet projects and focus on things that really created shareholder value for the company. Shelley was told she was a poor communicator and a poor report writer. Her boss had heard critical reports that Shelley's commercial grasp of the company was inadequate. In the new financial climate, Shelley's concern with 'soft' issues was no longer appropriate. The younger but more senior woman implied that Shelley was part of an era in the company that had passed.

'By now I could see her lips moving, but couldn't hear what she was saying any more,' recalled Shelley. 'Later, I began to be excluded from circulation lists and meetings were taking place that I didn't know about. Budgets were suddenly pulled for all my projects.'

As Shelley failed to make internal-position shortlists, even though she was well suited, her confidence hit rock bottom. Basic tasks that she once would have taken in her stride seemed beyond her.

'This woman was a looming shadow over everything. I couldn't understand why she behaved the way she did towards me,' Shelly said, smiling sadly. 'I just wanted to know why she didn't like me and what I'd done to her to bring about this reaction.'

Part of Shelley wanted to shout at her new boss, and give vent to her anger, while another part wanted to beg this woman to back off. At home, relationships were suffering. Shelley was soon suffering sleepless nights and began snapping at her husband and children. She felt an inner anger, but did not want to exacerbate the situation by letting it out. Shelley thought about getting a new job, but her confidence was at such a low ebb that she could not see how she could possibly do well at interview.

## Don't let your boss's problem become your problem

There's a saying, borne out by a wealth of research, that people do not leave companies – they leave bosses. Who hasn't had a 'toxic' boss at some stage in their career? We have seen people's entire persona appear to change with the change of boss. And despite the innumerable books on leading others, the vast majority of most of one's career is primarily concerned with how to deal with one's boss. Abasing oneself at the boss's power will encourage more of the same behaviour. Seeking to be the boss's friend will simply irritate. 'Standing up to' and 'speaking truth to power' will make you a martyr but it won't help you. And the leadership courses that maintain that your relationship with your boss is no different from your relationship with any professional colleagues are simply wrong.

Bosses, like customers, are not exceptionally virtuous or exceptionally malevolent. Their profile matches the population as a whole. About one in thirty would be a diagnosable sociopath, if they ever bothered to be diagnosed. Other than that, your boss is a fallible human being with the usual bundle of insecurities. If you have a boss who appears to have aspects of a dysfunctional personality, you will not change their behaviour with a heart-to-heart, clear-the-air conversation. It is fatal to get on your boss's radar as an emotionally high-maintenance or oversensitive employee. (There may be a time when it's right to confront your boss with a conversation to tackle things that need to change, but it is not necessarily the right approach and can be counterproductive.)

On the other hand, if someone acts towards you in a way that you perceive to be derisory, disrespectful or bullying, your temptation may well be to start plotting a victory against the person. Forget it. Is this really a worthy focus for your talents? There are far smarter ways for you to come out on top in the longer run.

Here again, mindfulness helps. For many people their progression through life is a series of emotional reactions to the machinations of others. This is inevitable if we lack the faculty to step back from our emotions and dispassionately become aware of them. If we do not practise stepping back, becoming aware and making choices, we end up being complicit in the other person's drama. By default we take on the role in which the other person has – intentionally or unintentionally – cast us. Awareness leads to choice.

As with most tough situations, there is the risk of slipping into the 'about-me' thinking error here. To start thinking 'I must be an unworthy person, look at the way I am being treated' is understandable but not helpful. The way in which your boss behaves is down to their choice – it's not about you. You do not *make* anybody treat you in a certain way.

You may not like the way your boss behaves, but the odds are they are not plotting against you. Remember the Barry Manilow experiment from chapter two? You almost certainly do not loom as large on your boss's scan of the landscape as you assume. Bear in mind the mind-reading error: we are inclined to make assumptions about other people's intentions and we are inclined to overestimate the extent to which we feature in those intentions.

Your boss behaves in a certain way because he is a fallible human being. He may be considerably more fallible than most. His behaviour may be unreasonable. Our sole aim is to help you to reach the outcomes in a given situation that work best for you.

Ask the 'how am I feeling when *I* behave like that?' question. The answer is probably 'I almost never behave like that'. But 'almost never' is not the same as 'never'. Asking yourself this question will not change your boss's behaviour but it will remind you that your boss – like you – is a fallible human being.

It may be that what you observe within your boss is a relatively stable trait. In other words, it is not specific to you, but it may appear that way as the aspects of this behaviour that are directed towards you will draw more of your attention. If people behave in a cold or hostile way towards us, it is often because they sense – regardless of whether we have done anything to justify the impression – that we do not like them.

Shelley is clearly giving her boss too much power and influence over her. Her thoughts and her horizons are getting smaller as she focuses on this woman. It may be that Shelley is applying a rigid rule – 'my boss *should* like me' – so she could change her thinking to be more flexible. Of course, she wants to be liked by everybody, but she could ask: 'What actually matters if my boss doesn't like me? I can still carry on doing my work, even if there isn't a great relationship between us.'

Change that 'should' rule into a flexible preference, such as, 'I prefer to get along with my boss, but if that's not happening right now, I can still function.' The behaviour that you observe in your boss may not be good or pretty, but remind yourself it is because she is a fallible human being.

We spoke to a woman called Karen who was convinced that her boss did not like or respect her and was looking to oust her from her position. An experienced PA, Karen had recently inherited a new boss: a charismatic woman, who Karen informed us 'has a problem with other women'. Karen 'knew' her boss did not respect her because she did not respect her time or her personal life. Karen felt that her boss had set out to make her life intolerable.

When we pressed Karen for the hard factual evidence of this, it seemed to centre on the fact that her boss regularly gave Karen work to do at very short notice with unfeasible deadlines, meaning Karen would feel obliged to work way beyond office hours. Karen's boss's behaviour could not be disputed, but what about the intention? Could there be an alternative explanation and, if there was, could Karen find a way to deal with it? We left Karen to ponder. When we met Karen again, she seemed like a different person. Karen had experimented by replacing the thought 'my boss doesn't respect me' with the thought 'my boss is disorganised'. Karen had helped to organise her boss by going through her workload at the start of each day. The relationship was transformed.

Freddie's relationship with his boss was also fraught. Freddie was an account executive at a larger marketing services firm. When Freddie went on a sales call with his boss, the sales director, his boss would insist that they went in his Jaguar. At the end of the day, Freddie's boss would leave him hanging around until well into the evening, while he tended to business, often taking an office at the client's premises after hours to do paperwork. Freddie would get home late in the evening.

'It's a power trip for the guy,' Freddie told us. 'He leaves me hanging around every evening to show that he can.'

After examining alternative explanations, Freddie explained to his boss that he had a young family and it suited him not to be home too late in the evening. He requested that, if they were likely to be out late, Freddie could travel independently. The sales director was happy to oblige. It turned out the sales director had no family and he enjoyed being out on the road; he assumed everybody else did, too. He didn't have family obligations himself, so these were a blind spot to him.

Clarify three things in your mind:

- The behaviour that you see
- The way in which you *interpret* that behaviour
- The *feelings* that you have when you witness the behaviour

The first is fact, the second is interpretation and the third is feeling. (If it helps, write them down.) What thought do you have when you witness this behaviour? What other explanations are there for your boss's behaviour?

Is there another way to interpret your boss's behaviour? Are you assuming some sort of intention behind your boss's behaviour? If so, it is worth reminding yourself that this is your assumption – it is not fact. Reminding yourself of this may well help you to think of more practical ways to deal with the behaviour.

## Summary

○ Bosses aren't exceptionally virtuous or malevolent – they're actually fallible humans with all the usual insecurities
○ It's unlikely you loom as large on your boss's radar as you assume
○ Your boss's behaviour may not be specific to you only
○ Bulletproof people are able to step back from their emotions about their boss and become more dispassionate about how they feel
○ It's easier for you to change your behaviour than for you to change your boss's

## Make your boss a customer

They might have authority over you but your boss is not analogous to a parent or a teacher. Your boss may or may not take an interest in your career. Your boss may or may not choose to look out for you. Yes, these things might happen but none of them is the primary purpose of your boss. Your boss is someone with whom you interact to meet her needs and your needs – and they're looking after themselves.

Your boss is first and foremost a customer. As with any customer, it's important to find out what motivates them, what their priorities in life are – and to focus on those. They might not be what you consider important but sometimes it's important to be pragmatic rather than be preoccupied by your own needs. Challenging your rigid rules is relevant here, too. So with a boss who seems determined to have things his or her way and to turn everything into confrontation it might be necessary to say, 'I'd prefer to stand up to people, but I'm okay if they have their way once in a while,' or 'I'd prefer to do things this way, but I'm okay if we do this bit of the project that way.'

Again, choose your battles.

So, back to Shelley. We asked her to identify a time when she had worked successfully with an individual who had a difficult manner, who did not readily seek rapport or who appeared to be high-maintenance. During her previous role with a consulting firm, Shelly had taken real pride in her ability to navigate difficult or high-maintenance customers. The breakthrough for Shelley came when she started viewing her boss as her customer: a relationship to be navigated in order to meet the needs of both parties.

Bosses are also like customers: they are transient. (Remember the temporary-versus-permanence test, and ask, 'Is this really the way things are going to be, or can I expect things to change before too long?') Your strategy is to navigate the relationship so that both your needs are met, until you are in a position to move forward to a boss who works better for you. Ask yourself whether or not you have higher emotional intelligence than your boss. If you do, then you are in a strong position to navigate the relationship. And, of course, remember the temporary-versus-permanence test. It is tempting to think that you are lumbered with this lousy boss in perpetuity. You are not. Like a customer, a boss is both transient and manageable.

Viewing your boss as a customer works because it implies a healthy distance, which takes some of the intensity out of the situation. It emphasises the fact that you have more control and latitude than you have been assuming, and it shifts your thinking from problem-focused thinking into goal-focused thinking.

- *problem-focused thinking* – my boss is difficult and unreasonable
- *goal-focused thinking* – how am I going to manage this difficult customer to achieve a successful outcome? What would work well? What strategies can I think of?

If your boss was a customer, your starting point would be to look at your 'customer insight'. What do you know about her? What are her likes and dislikes? Adapt your approach just as you would for a customer. Take pride in your ability to be flexible and adaptive. If you do not see a pay-off in terms of a change in your boss's behaviour, don't worry, and stick with it. You can't control the way someone else responds.

### Case Study 4.2

Simon was head of PR at a financial services company. One day he was introduced to his new boss, Amanda. Amanda was vice-president of marketing and would report to the chief communications officer, whom Simon used to report to before Amanda's arrival. As time went on, Simon, who already sensed that he had moved down in the pecking order, felt that Amanda seemed to barely respect his seniority and experience. Relations started to deteriorate.

Simon felt his status under threat so he responded with strategies intended to reassert his talent and importance. Simon had to work directly with the CEO on the annual statement to the shareholders, and he would often drop the CEO's name to Amanda. When we met Simon, he appeared to be at the end of his tether. When he achieved some significant press coverage, he would not mention it directly to Amanda; instead he would leave it for other senior people to spot the coverage and congratulate the department. The deterioration in Simon and Amanda's relationship accelerated. Amanda became increasingly angry and manifested this in her behaviour towards Simon, which he took as demeaning.

'We rarely communicated, other than with the odd email, and I could hardly even bear to look at her in meetings,' he told us. 'I'm sure other people noticed. I was getting pretty worried about my career at the company.'

However, when we caught up with Simon some time later, he could not have been happier. The relationship had diametrically reversed; he told us, 'I've got all the time in the world for Amanda now.' So, what made the difference?

'I learnt how Amanda likes to be communicated with,' Simon explained. 'I was getting great press I thought she would be delighted about. But Amanda hates surprises. When the CEO called her up to say "Great piece in *The Times* today," far from it being a pleasant surprise, she felt exposed and undermined. Now I'm meticulous about keeping Amanda informed. That works for her and gives her confidence.'

Simon also realised that Amanda liked systems and lists. 'Like a lot of people in the media, I tend to work fast and go with my instinct – my desk is always awash with Post-it notes and I prefer to have a quick chat with people about things rather than send memos and reports. I get the work done and I'm efficient, but that's just how I operate. But when I realised that Amanda likes to have everything written down with plans, spreadsheets and tick boxes, I started to produce those for her. It's not my way, but if she wants it and she's my boss, then I'll do it for her. It also means that I'm in a better position to try to persuade her about something that's really important to me.'

Simon had turned Amanda into a customer.

One of the best pieces of advice to anyone at the start of their career is: seek customers, don't seek bosses. A seemingly toxic boss is simply an emotionally high-maintenance customer. Your boss may have unresolved emotional issues that play themselves out in the workplace. That's fine. That's his right as an imperfect human being.

## Summary

○ Your boss is first and foremost a customer – knowing this implies a healthy distance

○ Your boss is transient – you need to navigate this relationship until you can move on

○ Bulletproof people put themselves in the driving seat by creating options for themselves

○ Identify the extent of control and influence you have and use it to the maximum

# Life can't always be fair

In our observation, the other reason why people so often continue to push down a dead end is because of the innate desire to see fairness. This so often leads to unproductive behaviour. When in discussions, we frequently help an individual identify a more productive route out of an unhelpful situation; the instinctive response is along the lines of: 'But that's not fair. Why should it be me who moves/changes … surely he/she should … etc.'

Fairness is an exceptionally strong human value. Just look at any newspaper or news programme: stories of injustice – whether it's people cheating the social security system or being cheated themselves by large companies – are always good copy. No surprise there, from an evolutionary point of view, except that research shows repeatedly that we have a powerful drive for fairness, even in scenarios where we personally are not involved and stand to make no gain or suffer no loss.[18]

The demand for fairness when it yields us no direct personal gain and may even cost us is commonplace and probably stems from way back in our evolutionary past. During our research, we've observed many people stuck in unproductive cycles of behaviour because their inner child is crying out for fairness and won't let them walk away and choose a more productive alternative.

When we put this idea to Mal, a 56-year-old engineer, he nodded but looked uncomfortable. Mal was a rocket scientist; he had been an engineer at NASA and had one of the highest recorded IQs that we had ever come across. He had been doing a coaching course that had emphasised the importance of identifying, and sticking with, your core, irreducible and unshakeable value. For Mal, this was fairness. He saw the inherent sense in what we were saying, but went on to say, 'It just feels like, well … if I'm not all about fairness, then I'm not all about anything.' Mal rightly valued fairness but he had hard-baked this into a rigid rule. Mal carried the rule in his mind: 'Things around me must always, always be fair, come what may.'

It turned out that this rule had got Mal into a number of unhelpful situations, one of which was ongoing. He was seen as stubborn and naïve, as he refused to sign off on a project because he thought one of the teams involved had been treated unfairly. Colleagues felt that he was jeopardising people's jobs over a point of principle.

Almost a year later, Mal told us how relationships at work had been transformed. He felt relaxed, confident and better about himself. He had modified his rule about fairness to make it more flexible: 'I very much prefer things to be fair, but if that's really not going to happen in a situation, I'm okay with that.'

Shelley, who you may recall had had a similarly strained relationship with her boss, had a similar insight. Part of the breakthrough for Shelley came when she recognised that she was carrying a rigid rule in her mind concerning her boss. Modifying this and making it more flexible helped Shelley to move on: 'I would prefer [my boss] to recognise my good work and that she has been treating me unfairly, but I understand that this is not likely to happen. I am okay with that and I can move on.'

If you feel your inner cave dweller shouting, 'But it's not fair!', calm down and reassure the poor soul with: 'Sure, it's not fair, and it would be nice if it were, but I'm okay, I can live with it.'

## Summary

○ People often end up in a dead end by being determined to satisfy their innate desire for fairness

○ A strong belief in fairness can often lead to unproductive behaviours

○ When 'it's not fair', calm your inner cave dweller. Bulletproof people say, 'I'm okay and can live with it'

# How to communicate with a toxic boss

You may choose to have a formal conversation with your boss in order to draw his attention to the behaviour that you find unacceptable. There are two risks to be aware of here:

● If the effect of your boss's behaviour is what he intends, by drawing attention to it you confirm that it is having the intended effect and, therefore, reward and reinforce it

● If your boss is apparently impervious to the effect of the behaviour then, let's face it, emotional intelligence is not his or her strong suit. Having their attention drawn to the emotional parameters of the relationship will probably irritate them. You don't want to be seen as an emotionally high-maintenance employee

You may feel that your boss *should* show more emotional intelligence, but how realistic is it that this particular wish of yours will come to fruition? So, let go of *'should'*. Remember *'should'* is often accompanied by its best mate, *'isn't going to'*. After all, your boss is a customer. How much time and energy would you normally invest in the belief that a customer *should* be more emotionally intelligent?

There are some effective things that you can do when communicating with a toxic boss. But, of course, in line with one of the key themes of this book, it is one thing to *know* the right thing to do, it is quite another to *do* it in the heat of the moment. Remember the power of the cave dweller. Your boss might behave to you in a range of passive-aggressive or aggressive-aggressive, verbal or non-verbal ways. You will know the right thing to do, but your mind will automatically be processing the under-assault sensation. The cave dweller will have been prodded with a big stick.

There is a technique that you can use to make sure you choose the right response in the moment. Again, it comes down to being mindful. It's the breath that creates that all-important space to think clearly in the moment. Deep, relaxing breathing has a remarkable physiological effect on us. Just as brief shallow breaths tell our heart to start pumping because we are in trouble, deep, easy breaths tell the brain and body that we are okay.

In the next couple of conversations that you have, remember the breathing technique we mentioned earlier and make a point of taking one deep, easy breath before you respond to anything that somebody says to you. In the first instance, simply become aware of how it feels. The breath will be imperceptible to the person whom you are talking with, but to you it means awareness, choice and being in control.

The golden rule when dealing with a relationship that features behaviour that you find undesirable is simply not to reward it. Rewarding the behaviour means showing that it is having a significant effect on you. So, minimise any sense of drama. You are only drawing attention to the behaviour because it is a temporary hindrance to getting the job done. And remember that bad behaviour is always the responsibility of the perpetrator of that behaviour. Keep that the focus – not your emotions. The tone should be adult and businesslike. Below are just a couple of good examples of how to achieve this:

- 'Brian, I want to work with you on this but I can only do so if you talk to me in a civil manner. Now, let's start again, shall we ...'
- 'Brian, I'm looking to help here, but it doesn't help me to help you if you raise your voice ... let's start again ...'
- 'Brian, it doesn't serve either of us well to get side-tracked into personal abuse. Let's start again ...'

The message is always about the perpetrator of the behaviour, not about the recipient of it. So, avoid responses like:

- 'How could you treat me like that?'
- 'How dare you talk to me like that?!'
- 'That really hurt my feelings.'

It is far better to say something along the lines of:

- 'Are you having a bad day?'
- 'Did something I said or did anger you?'

You may also need to deal with bosses who don't shout and get angry, but who are surly, quiet and passive-aggressive. Using long silences is a ploy that people use to unnerve others. The key is to draw attention to it. You can readily puncture this ploy via the telephone by simply asking, 'Are you still there … ?'

When it is face to face you can say something like, 'I notice that you are not responding. Should I take it that this is because you are unhappy about something?'

A toxic boss will often signify his vague unhappiness or discontent without being specific. Remember, it is the responsibility of the one signalling discontent to be clear and specific about the alternative that he wishes to see. By putting the ball in his court to articulate a clear request, it will cause him to think more carefully in future before signifying vague disapproval. Try phrases like: 'I sensed you were unhappy about that. What would work better for you?'

If you feel that a toxic boss or co-worker is encouraging you to take up a role to play in the scenario that he has set up, do not reward him by taking up the role. A clear break in rapport helps. When we want to be in rapport with someone, we mirror body language and match voice tone and intonation. Doing the reverse breaks rapport in a way that signals you are not participating in the game or drama.

We observed one highly efficient office manager deal with a co-worker who arrived back in the office after a boozy boys' lunch and started to bait her with a nickname. She finished the job she was doing, turned to look at him, emotionless for a moment, and then simply said: 'Can I help you with something?'

Oh, and then remained silent.

Rapport severed. Behaviour unrewarded. Message received.

On the other hand, if you want to convince your boss of something it is worth remembering that bosses tend to be sensitive souls with fragile egos. They may feel out of their depth. Perception of others tends to be important. Either way, the golden rule is never to make it appear that you believe that your boss's judgement was wrong. If you want to persuade your boss of something or change his mind, go for the 'new information approach'. In other words, whatever your boss's judgement was, it was right at the time – but, of course, now new information has come to light. For example, you might say: 'Of course, supplier X has always been the best company for the job, but given that things have changed …'

In life, as in the movies, understanding more about the 'villain' – which in this case might be your boss – instead of just damning them immediately, is a more realistic way of viewing the world. Robert McKee says, 'Try and see things from the villain's point of view. Instead of just telling yourself and anyone who'll listen that the guy is a dick, talk to him and show you understand him. Start the guy talking about his life and then repeat his life back to him, but starring him. You can lead him like a child. From our time as children we've listened to stories so tell him, "I see what you're up against." He'll start to think: "This person really gets me." Once you can get this guy to realise that you understand him, then life becomes much easier.'

## Summary

- Avoid drawing attention to your boss's behaviour – avoid becoming an emotionally high-maintenance employee
- In conversation with a toxic boss, take a deep, easy breath before responding

○ Puncture a person's silence ploy by drawing attention to it – 'Are you still there?'
○ Bulletproof people minimise any sense of drama by keeping their tone adult and businesslike
○ Bulletproof people don't take the set role another person is nudging them to play – they know how to break the rapport
○ If you want to change your boss's mind about something, don't suggest that her initial judgement was wrong; suggest that the situation has changed or new information has come to light

## Create options

If you want to reduce stress and therefore feel and act in a more resilient way, look at how you can increase the ways in which you exercise your own control, freedom and latitude to make decisions in a situation. In the modern office, what we do and the way that we do it is often predetermined by someone else. It often feels that we work at the behest of an omnipresent boss.[19]

It goes further. Research conducted within the civil service in the United Kingdom measured the levels of cortisol – the stress hormone – in workers at different levels in the organisation. The findings exploded the myth of the stressed senior executive. One might assume that the most senior grades, encumbered by all of that day-to-day responsibility, would show the highest levels of stress; in fact, the reverse was shown to be true. Those further down the organisation were significantly more likely to suffer ill-health associated with stress. For them, stress comes less from the demands of the job, and more from the degree of control that the individual has when delivering against those job demands.[20]

So how can we increase the scope of control that we are able to practise in any given situation? Feelings of stress and unhappiness at work are likely to be accompanied by feelings of helplessness. Confidence falls, cortisol increases and, of course, cortisol is there to say to you 'stay out of trouble, hide, keep your head down'. Under stress, our minds tend to narrow their focus. This mechanism has a useful evolutionary purpose. Narrowness of focus in our evolutionary past may have been the most useful way to concentrate our energies to ensure safety, but it does mean that when we are feeling low or stressed we are typically at our least creative, inventive or imaginative about the full range of alternative options that might be open to us.

We are at our least stressed, happiest and most personally effective when we have control. Control is about choice. The first step is to challenge yourself to identify aspects of the current situation where you have choice. Then start to exercise choice in those situations. How might you prioritise? What are the things that you could choose not to do? Whose help could you call on in the current situation? How could he or she help you?

A significant breakthrough comes when we ask people whether they really need to remain in the situation. The answer that frequently comes back is along the lines of, 'Well, you can't choose your boss.'

When we stop and reflect, we realise that we are, of course, free to exercise more choice – in more ways – than we typically allow ourselves to consider.

A follow-up question goes along the lines of: 'If the current situation doesn't improve, what alternative options could you create for yourself?'

This is followed by: 'What could you start to put in place right away, so that you are in a position to exercise those options if you need to?'

Those stressed civil servants would be far less stressed if they had the latitude and control that comes about from knowing that you can step into an alternative job, if you need to do so. Even if they stayed in the same role, just knowing that they had the option of stepping into an alternative role would reduce stress. In our view, people become blinkered when they find themselves in a high-stress situation. This means that they are less likely to look at their full range of alternatives and less likely to create options for themselves.

And remember that, like any good supplier, you have a product that people want. There are other potential customers out there. Just as you have some latitude to choose the customers with whom you do business, you also have some latitude to choose your boss. There are plenty of other bosses (customers) in the marketplace, who would appreciate your skills. You may not like the idea of leaving your current job or your current employer, but it is always an option that you have. Put yourself in a position to be able to exercise this option if you choose. Brush up your résumé, hone your interviews skills, use your network of contacts, even start early, informal conversations with other employers (customers) who might be in the market for your talents. Once you create alternative options for yourself, you put yourself back in the driving seat. Any smart supplier scans the horizon for potentially more fruitful customers.

Many people are uncomfortable with our suggestion that you should consider leaving the role because of your boss, but a supplier is far more effective if he has also explored the possibility of working with other customers who have expressed an interest in his talents. This is not a case of running away from situations. The power comes simply from the act of starting to exercise choice and create options. You may or may not exercise the options but it is having options available that lowers stress and increases confidence to deal with situations. The process of identifying choice, exercising choice and creating options soon becomes a habit. Once you start doing it and feel how personally empowering it is, you will find yourself doing it instinctively in situations that may have seemed hopeless to you in the past.

## Summary

- Stress at work is often accompanied by feelings of helplessness as confidence falls and our focus narrows
- Stress comes less from job demands and more from the lack of control we have when delivering against those job demands
- To reduce stress and become more resilient, consider how to increase your own control, freedom and latitude to make decisions – create new options for yourself
- You do not need to use them – just having them empowers you

# You have more control over your relationship with your boss than you think

As we've said, it's important to understand that, given your boss's seniority within the organisation, in many ways they have more power than you. It's also easier to change the way in which you work, rather than trying to make your boss change their habits. But bulletproof people do not allow a difficult boss to create feelings of helplessness and impotence within them.

You might not be able to control your manager but you can control the way you think about them and even the way in which you relate to them. When it comes to making the most of a difficult boss, it's interesting to look at the work of Dr Suzanne Kobasa Ouelette, a researcher in stress at City College, New York. She believes that people who cope effectively with stress have three particular traits, which she calls 'The Three Cs':

- *Control* – successful copers feel in control of their lives and decisions. They feel they can influence and have an impact on events and their surroundings, and they can make things happen. They have an internal locus of control, rather than an external one. They feel powerful, rather than like a victim who allows circumstances to dictate their life's outcomes. They feel in the driver's seat of their own lives in making choices. Remember, you don't have to cede this right to your boss. You are a supplier and you have choices. Can you change things or reorganise things at work so that they work better for you, like Karen and Freddie did in the previous examples? Challenge yourself to think where and how you can exercise choice in this situation – it may be over something big or something small; either way it will help.
- *Commitment* – successful copers have a strong dedication, involvement and commitment to whatever they do, and put their heart into it and give 100 per cent. They are curious about the world, rather than feeling alienated from people, their workplace and the

environment. Bulletproof people don't let their difficult relationships with a boss damage their working relationships with other colleagues and their overall commitment to their job. If you are going through a tough time with your boss, make sure that you increase, rather than decrease, your commitment to your work.

- *Challenge* – successful copers treat a problem as if it were a challenge from which to learn, grow and test their strengths and abilities, instead of feeling afraid, burdened or threatened. As the Japanese saying goes, 'The end of the world for a caterpillar is the beginning of a whole new life for a butterfly.' It's worth remembering that what you learn from dealing with this difficult boss will be useful for handling bosses and colleagues in the future; see your boss as a customer and take on the challenge. You can't change your boss's behaviour, but you can focus on being the best possible, most resilient and flexible supplier you can be.

Of course, your boss is important, but often it is your boss's boss who is *really* important. As with any customer relationship, you also need to know who's the ultimate decision-maker and purse-string holder. And, in many cases, that person is your boss's boss. That is why he may be important in helping you to find a new 'customer' (a new boss).

What leverage do you have with your boss's boss? Are you on his radar? Do you have a relationship with him? Aim to build your 'leverage'. Any entrepreneur knows that they need to have a 'USP' (unique selling proposition). Determine what it is that you can do better than anybody else – something that is a high priority to your boss and your boss's boss. Keep getting better at this and making sure that both your boss and your boss's boss are aware of it.

Don't flaunt it. Anything that suggests you are throwing down the gauntlet to your boss will worsen the situation. A toxic boss is most lethal when feeling insecure. Just quietly get on with it. Use the three Cs. View building leverage and a relationship with your boss's boss as a challenge. Commit to it. You will increase your sense of control.

## Summary

○ You have power over the way you think about and relate to your boss

○ Challenge yourself to identify any aspects, large or small, in the current situation over which you have control – and take action

○ Consider dealing with them to be a challenge and an opportunity, rather than a hopeless task

○ Increase your commitment to your work

○ Don't let the problems you're experiencing with them damage your relationships with others

# Find a mentor

Dr Karen Reivich is co-author of *The Optimistic Child* and a world-recognised authority on resilience. In her research, she notes that resilient people are not the tough individualists going it alone that many people assume them to be. On the contrary, she finds that most resilient people are those who have no qualms about reaching out for support as and when they need it.

'Contrary to some of the myths around resilience,' Reivich explains, 'resilient people don't go it alone. When bad stuff happens they reach out to the people who care about them and they ask for help.' Empathy is vital as it 'is the glue that keeps social relationships together'.

Bulletproof people are unafraid to go out and enlist the help of others. In fact, they actively go out of their way to do so. They probably recognise that, far from seeing us as weak, needy or indebted to them, the people from whom we ask for help tend to feel flattered and tend to like us more. (Recall the Benjamin Franklin effect: when we do someone a favour, we tend to like that person more. We have invested in that person, so our minds want to make sense of our behaviour by looking out for good things about that person.)

If you seek out a mentor, you will not only have the direct benefit of a wiser and more experienced guide to help you through tough times, you will also have created an ally. While there is clear evidence for the benefits of having a mentor, the reasons for these benefits are less clear. However, we would put forward two strong hypotheses:

- Because our mentor has presumably been around longer than we have and has attained some level of career accomplishment, our mentor symbolises to us an important principle of being bullet-proof: the principle that whatever we are going through now, we come out the other side
- By externalising our thoughts as if describing them to another person, we gain greater clarity, calmness and perspective around a situation, and, therefore, we make better choices. Even if we don't have the conversation, the process of thinking through the conver-sation is what helps. This may help to explain another curious phenomenon about mentoring – the fact that even when the mentor does not do very much at all, there still seem to be meas-urable benefits[21]

Choose a mentor. If your company does not have a formal mentoring scheme, find someone to be your informal mentor (someone you know, but not too intimately, to allow for a little reflective distance). If you are unable to find anyone suitable, create an imaginary mentor. Even an imaginary mentor will help to deliver the two benefits of mentoring that we mention above. And, of course, like so many of the ideas in the book, thinking things through as if you were talking with your mentor will strengthen those more helpful pathways of thought in your brain maps.

## Summary

- ⭘ Bulletproof people are more resilient and have no concerns about reaching out for support when they need it
- ⭘ Bulletproof people externalise their thoughts by describing them to another person – even imaginary – to gain perspective and make better choices
- ⭘ Find a mentor – even an imaginary one

# CHAPTER 5
## TURNING REJECTION INTO A SPRINGBOARD

Being rejected, or suffering a series of knocks, can feel like being in the wilderness. You're lost without a map and can't see any way to get back to normality. Anyone who has succeeded in any field has almost invariably had to survive knocks and setbacks. Taking stock, being honest with yourself, identifying what strengths you have and putting things into context by thinking of them being part of the storyline of your life, will also help. As we will discover, every hero spends time in the wilderness.

### Case Study 5.1

'I used to have a spring in my step. Now I can't even get out of the car at a sales call,' Bob told us. He once had the highest figures in the department. He had been sales person of the month on more than one occasion. He knew sometimes you hit a lean patch. So why did it feel different this time?

'Now, when I am talking to a prospective customer, I feel like I've got "reject me – I'm desperate" across my forehead,' Bob continued. 'Even my best customers don't return my calls any more.' Bob looked like a man whose reserves of positive energy were running on empty. He was starting to show physical signs of stress and he could not help fearful thoughts about the future from entering his mind.

### Case Study 5.2

Andrea knew the statistics: one of fifty bids for start-up financing is successful. So why did this latest rejection leave her feeling floored, more so than any of the others? When Andrea left her job with a global fashion brand at the age of 31 to set up her online fashion company, she felt convinced that she had the character and talent to be an entrepreneur. Self-belief was one of her major assets. Maybe that is why she felt so affronted when the latest presentation of her business plan was rejected in a way that not only asked questions of her plan, but also left her doubting her own talent and judgement.

A business studies graduate, she had also been studying the mid-range fashion market during evenings and weekends. 'I'd spotted a gap in the market,' she said over coffee. 'Women in their 30s want something relaxed but fashionable, which they're not going to see all their friends wearing,' she explained. 'I know of lots of smaller labels and new designers who are looking for an outlet.'

Having produced a detailed business plan and joined a number of women's networking groups, she began to look for financing.

When the first angel investors she presented her ideas to said no, she was naturally disappointed but not disheartened. 'They were polite and listened, but then said no to me pretty quickly. They just said it wasn't right for them at the moment.'

She sighed and then began to list the other investors who had rejected her idea. 'Some were helpful but others were just plain rude. I remember during a meeting, one of the guys I was supposed to be talking to never even took his eyes off his BlackBerry. And after another meeting, as I was leaving the room I heard them laughing.'

These experiences left her doubting her own talent and judgement. 'I started to notice that I didn't even want to get out of bed in the morning.'

## Case Study 5.3

When Graham, then a 48-year-old senior sales manager, was asked to see the sales director one Wednesday morning, he grabbed a pile of spreadsheets showing the last month's sales figures and headed down the corridor, ready to discuss with his boss why some regions were doing less well than others.

'I'd been giving it some thought and I had some theories and some suggestions to sort the situation out,' he told us. But he never got the chance to discuss his ideas. 'I was stunned when he asked me to sit down, told me that there was no easy way to say this and explained that due to a major restructuring of the department I was out – redundant.'

The father of three returned to his office and stared at the wall for what seemed like hours. Then he picked up the photographs of his children from his desk, put on his jacket and went home.

'For the next few days I just felt numb. Then I began to get angry. It just seemed so unfair. I kept thinking "Why me?" and ruminating about who could have done the dirty on me.'

Graham visited various recruitment consultants but found the experience uninspiring at best. The few job interviews he had came to nothing. Eventually he realised that his anger and negativity were obviously apparent during these meetings. He began to take some time out to think about his options and think about the anger that he was feeling. That anger was understandable but it wasn't helping him to move on, he realised.

Writing about his experiences was part of this process. He started from his time in his first job, writing about the highs and lows, the people that he had enjoyed working with and those he'd found difficult.

'It wasn't Shakespeare but it really helped to get it all down,' he says. 'I was pretty disciplined about it, too. I tapped away at my laptop on the dining-room table when the kids had gone to school and my wife was out at work. Even the discipline of sitting down at nine and not moving until II, when I allowed myself to go off and do something else, was good.'

After a couple of weeks, Graham gave it to his wife to read. She questioned some of his assumptions while she could completely agree with other observations about himself and his working life. Coming back to his professional life story later, Graham found that some of what he had written simply didn't ring true while other bits really struck a chord. 'It was as if I was reading the life story of a stranger in places,' he said. Being honest with himself by writing about his faults and admitting where he had, perhaps, been unreasonable or at fault on some occasions, as well as giving credit to people who he hadn't liked, helped him to gain some vital insights and perspectives.

'I realised that I wasn't really happy with big companies, even though I'd worked for them all my life,' he told us. 'I also realised for the first time why I'd gone into sales – I'm actually quite a bit more competitive than I'd actually thought. That means that sometimes, looking back, I felt resentful of other people's successes, I had to admit.'

Once Graham had finished writing his story so far, he went on to write a 'credibly optimistic' ending. This meant that with a new sense of self-awareness, and with the perspective that he'd managed to gain on his career so far by writing its narrative, Graham realised that working for a smaller company at an earlier stage in its development where he had more scope to do his own thing might work better for him. He'd even been willing to take a pay cut or commute further to find it.

Six months after this writing exercise, and thanks to some renewed determination, he contacted us to say that he'd found a job that just about fitted that brief.

## Teach yourself to be resilient *before* you need it

After initially training as a psychologist, and having spent many years as acting tutor at the Bristol Old Vic theatre school, Peter Nicholas is now best known for transferring the principles he developed – to help actors to perform better – into the workplace, helping leaders to deal with the challenges of corporate life.

Peter's crucial moment of insight came early in his career as an acting coach. He was looking at an eager new class of undergraduates and it dawned on him that there might be one or two outliers who would get lucky and sail through their careers. On the other end of the bell curve, there will be those who will never make it. But for the cluster in the middle, their ability to deal with repeated knock-backs would be as important as their talent in determining their success.

He decided that it made sense to teach resilience early in their careers; having never seen any evidence that resilience is entirely innate or unchangeable, he believes that to a large degree it can be learnt, and further strengthened.

Rejection comes very much with the territory in the acting world, says Nicholas, but with acting rejection is much more personal than it is with most jobs. Very often, it's less about your CV or your skills, and more about how you look. It's that your face simply doesn't fit – and there's nothing you can do about it.

Nicholas's main thesis is that most of us only think about strengthening our resilience *after* we have had the knock-back, which isn't too late, but he suggests imagining how much more effective you could be if you were to work at your resilience *before* the knock-back; this is what bulletproof people have done.

He describes how he wrong-footed a class of aspiring drama students on their first day. He asked them to take out pen and paper, and then told them: 'Write a letter to yourself now from the you of ten years hence. You might want to say something like, "I know you were bitterly disappointed and it seemed very unfair and that you thought you'd never recover but actually in the long run it worked out."' Nicholas explains that the task gave them a sense of perspective. As a result, from day one they realised that tenacity was a quality that they would need, and thus their resilience was strengthened.

Nicholas advises his graduates to repeat the exercise whenever a sense of rejection is weighing heavy on them, as it helps them to realise that you get through tough times and come out the other side.

If you are going out to sell a new product, or an idea, or even yourself, start by preparing yourself to develop the resilience that will see you through. Sit down and write your letter at the outset. It is *from* the 'you' who has come through to the light at the end of the tunnel *to* the 'you' who is starting on the journey. Why is it worth sticking at it? What qualities have you got that will pull you through? And don't forget – where have you already shown those qualities?

## Summary
- Resilience can be learnt – you can develop and strengthen it
- Bulletproof people strengthen their resilience *before* they have a knock-back
- Write yourself a motivational letter to support you on your journey

# Get positive

Positive psychology is a new field of psychological research. Until relatively recently, almost since it was taken seriously as a social science, psychology had largely been concerned with negative issues. Psychologists have traditionally focused on feelings such as fear, depression, aggression and anxiety, the effects that these basic, animal emotions have on the mind, and the way in which we view the world and react to events.

Scientists have long talked about how emotions trigger what they call 'specific-action tendencies'. For example, fear leads to an animal's 'fight or flight' reaction, anger prompts the urge to attack, while disgust leads us to steer clear of something that would probably be bad for us. These psychological and physical changes in the body are essential for our survival as they protect us from danger – but all are entirely negative.

However, Barbara Fredrickson, who is Kenan Distinguished Professor of Psychology and principal investigator of the Positive Emotions and Psychophysiology Laboratory at the University of North Carolina at Chapel Hill, is concerned with positive emotions. Along with colleagues in the US and from around the world, she has been investigating the effect of feelings – such as joy, peacefulness, enthusiasm, love and an interest in new things – on the human brain and physiology.

The idea of being positive and of having an upbeat view of the world might sound lovely and warm and fuzzy; let's face it, who could argue against such things? But there is now solid statistical data supporting this new positive psychology and exploring how it can help us handle difficult or hostile situations, in order to help us survive and prosper.

For decades scientists struggled to explain why we experience positive emotions. Some suggested that feelings of joy make us want to do anything as we feel a kind of euphoric optimism, while others have suggested that, on the contrary, such emotions simply make us want to do nothing because we feel relaxed and content. To a growing number of psychologists, neither sounded like very convincing or comprehensive hypotheses.

Barbara Fredrickson and her colleagues have developed a theory that they call 'broaden and build'. Whereas negative emotions narrow people's view of the options in any situation, positive emotions broaden their viewpoint. With a positive view of their surroundings, people become more creative and receptive to new ideas.

The main positive emotions include joy, gratitude, serenity, interest in new things, hope, pride in an achievement, amusement, inspiration, awe and love. We all experience these emotions – the trick is to make a conscious effort to identify and cultivate them, even when we feel that the world is treating us unfairly. It's actually much easier to switch these emotions on and off than you might think.

Try this little experiment now: start by switching on your positive emotions. Take a few deep breaths and focus on the here and now. You might want to close your eyes or just look at something near you, such as a table or a wall. Then ask yourself: what can I feel grateful for at the moment? A roof over my head? My friends and family? A job that pays me well enough to allow me to have regular holidays? A colleague in the office who's become a friend? You might not be able to tick off all of these good things but, then again, you might be able to add a few more of your own. Either way, it's a fair bet that if you stop and consider it, you've actually got more to feel grateful for and positive about than you might ordinarily think.

Now, try turning off those positive feelings. What's annoying you in the office at the moment? Who's said or done something irritating or unfair to you at work? What's recently gone wrong in your career? Take a few moments to feel how your spirits are drawn downwards. It's actually surprisingly easy to affect your mood and your attitude by bringing such thoughts into your mind. By the way, you might want to take a moment to reflect on those good things again before you get too depressed!

But specific thoughts such as these – whether they relate to work or home life – act as levers that you can use to increase your positive, optimistic feelings whenever you want to. As with many things, the more you try it, the easier it will become – even when you're feeling threatened or depressed by something that is happening to you.

Fredrickson has identified what she calls a 'positivity ratio'. Her research has revealed that those of us who have a ratio of positive thoughts and emotions over negative ones – and very often this involves training and cultivating our minds to have them – of around three to one, are more resilient and optimistic. Not only this, but her research has shown such people are more creative, better at problem solving, more effective at leading teams and better able to see opportunities available to them.

It must be stressed that having a good positivity ratio does not mean wearing a suit of armour and being immune to negative thinking. 'The whole point of the positivity ratio,' Fredrickson says, 'is that it's important to also experience genuine negativity when circumstances warrant. Being resilient means being open, which also means being vulnerable. Which means the bullets will sometimes get through your defensive armour.'

This positivity ratio does, however, mean that there is a tipping point in our approach to life that can either cause us to enjoy an upward spiral of positive emotions and experiences or, sadly, draw us into a downward spiral of fear, depression and negative attitudes. Some people spend a lifetime in one camp or the other but, for most of us, as dynamic entities constantly reacting to what life throws at us – good and bad – we constantly move upwards or downwards in these spirals. But Fredrickson has identified ways in which we can consciously take the positive, upwards path more often than being dragged downwards.

So how can you raise your positivity levels and benefit not only from the increased resilience it offers but also from the idea of a 'broaden and build' approach to life, which can allow you to become more creative and receptive to new ideas?

- *Be open* – this is especially useful when you're anticipating a difficult meeting or when a new boss comes in and makes you feel unwanted or under threat. Become aware of any judgements or assumptions that you are making about people or situations, and picture yourself temporarily putting them to one side

- *Be kind* – you might not feel particularly charitable when you're under attack but research[22] shows that altruism makes people feel more optimistic and open to opportunities around them
- *Develop distractions* – go to the gym, go to the cinema, read a book, arrange to see friends

## Summary

- ○ Switching on positive emotions, especially after a knock-back, is difficult
- ○ Being positive doesn't mean ignoring your negative feelings; it means putting them into context
- ○ Using certain thoughts as levers will improve your feelings of optimism and positivity

# Do a stocktake of your strengths ... be an advocate for your success

There are a number of other techniques that can boost resilience. One is to stocktake your strengths. Look at your life so far and make an inventory of your successes, with none being too small, and list them. This could be your last promotion or it could be when a colleague thanked you for your help with something. It might also be when you made an important contribution to a project or helped to win some new business. Perhaps you gave advice to a junior colleague or trainee who had a problem. It could just be a 'thank you' email from a client you helped.

You may find it hard going at first, particularly if you are feeling a bit low, but remember, they do not need to be in chronological order and no success is too small to be listed. You will find as soon as you start to think of one or two, your memory of successes starts to flow.

(And remember, it's a stocktake, not a gap analysis; you only need to focus on what *is* there, not what's *not* there.)

Peter Nicholas recalls the story of Bruce, who was made redundant from a senior position at a global energy company. Bruce had been high up the tree there, with all of the trappings of seniority, but he had been a one-company man; he had not had to search for a job since graduating and, in his mid-fifties, he was sure that it was all over for him.

Bruce came to Nicholas to help build his confidence at interviews, but Nicholas recognised that he needed something more: he needed to bulletproof his mind.

'I encouraged Bruce to list his successes, no matter how seemingly infinitesimal. I encouraged him to give himself permission to list anything. He then listed the qualities he had that had given rise to these successes. We also did the "advocate-for-your-success" techniques. Bruce listed all of the evidence that he could muster to argue why his current situation should end in success.'

The 'advocate-for-your-success' exercise is similar to the stocktake of your strengths. Imagine that you have an inner lawyer, whom you hired to search out and present every possible shred of evidence that supports the view that you will succeed. List the evidence – every last shred of it.

Of course, success is never guaranteed, but by boosting both his confidence and his self-esteem, this radically improved the odds for Bruce. When we last heard from him, he was a vice-president at another global multinational.

Bruce was using evidence to dispute his critical thoughts. In doing so he was preventing the catastrophising and the universalising aspect of his thinking to get a grip.

As you list the successes in a column on the left-hand side of the page, list on the right the attributes or personal qualities that brought them about. Be realistically generous to yourself. Then read through both columns and dwell, for as long as you choose, on how you feel when you do so. Repeat the exercise any time you need to boost your resilience. Also do the 'advocate-for-your-success' exercise. And remember to give yourself permission to include any strength, quality or piece of evidence, no matter how seemingly small.

**Summary**

○ Bulletproof people regularly de-catastrophise by doing a stocktake of their successes

○ No success is too small to add to the stocktake

○ Remember the 'advocate-for-your-success' list – look for evidence of why future success will happen

○ Bulletproof people improve their odds by boosting their own confidence and self-esteem

# Keep separating the facts from the story

With his experience of coaching and mentoring actors, Nicholas vividly observed one aspect in particular among the emotions engendered by rejection: as actors we love drama. We love to dramatise, and so it's quite easy to focus on the cruelty and unfairness of this rejection and the effect it's having on our psyches. Since working in the corporate arena, he's seen lots of other people in all walks of life act out these feelings, too. Drama in life isn't exclusively about actors. When people are hit by sudden bad news, such as a rejection, it's natural to turn it into a drama or our own personal tragedy, however level-headed we think we are.

However, this need not be the case as you have a choice: you can choose to make this a drama about how you're suffering because of a cruel world, or you can choose not to. You can work to get this rejection into perspective. For example, you can avoid catastrophising language, such as 'That was a *disaster!*', or 'I was *terrible!*', or 'I came *so* close'. Did you really? This kind of thinking can become addictive.

Be aware of facts and stories, too. Our minds constantly look for interpretation and meaning. It is natural to make sense of what happens to us by weaving it into some sort of story. It may be natural but it is not always helpful.

The facts are what happened; the story is what we make it mean. It seems that too often our minds conflate the two. If you're rejected at an interview, the two most common types of story that one creates are stories about 'me' and stories about 'the world or people around me'. The former is along the lines that this proves that I am not cut out for this. I should never have tried it. Stories about the world construct a view that – because I got rejected – the world is, or people in general are, capricious, mean and unfair.

If an actor has had a particularly harsh knock-back, they often sit down to separate out the facts and the story, before the story takes hold and starts to contaminate other possible outcomes for that person. Nicholas says it is the same with business people. Taking the drama out of the situation, looking at it as dispassionately as possible, and sifting out the facts from the stories, impressions and interpretations of events, is very important when it comes to moving on from a bad experience and learning from it, while maintaining a positive outlook. Instead be practical and try to get some perspective. If necessary, think numbers – in this case, how many people were going for that audition? What realistically were the chances? How many people were up for the post? Was it simply not your turn this time around?

Joe put this into practice. As a 28-year-old solicitor, he had long been viewed as a high flyer. 'I basically walked into my first job at a City firm and was immediately involved in a hostile takeover bid,' he says. 'We won the case and I was singled out for my work. From then on, I was the golden boy on the fast lane to becoming a partner.'

But that didn't happen when he was led to believe it would, and when he was told that he would have to wait at least two years Joe felt bitterly disappointed. 'I was devastated. It was a terrible thing to hear – I felt that I'd had my hopes raised and dashed.'

Looking at the story objectively and stepping aside from his dramatic language, Joe began to explore why he hadn't been made a partner. 'I had a chat with a lawyer who worked at another firm, who was just a few years older than me. We realised that, actually, I was still lacking some essential experience needed in a partner – and, statistically,

I was far too young. I realised that my goal was still attainable, I just needed to keep working at it. I also realised that I had felt so upset partly because I'd been concerned about what other people in the firm would think about me not yet becoming a partner, after all. I had to remember that their opinions really don't matter.'

## Summary

○ It's natural to look for interpretation and meaning – but it isn't always helpful

○ The facts are what happened – but the story is what we make them mean

○ Bulletproof people are clear not to confuse fiction with fact

# Don't make 'no' mean more than it does

For those clustered around the middle of the bell curve of talent, like most of us, there will be some factors of success that can be identified or changed, and there will be some that are random, and down to chance. If we assume that, in the long run, chance is reasonably constant, simple tenacity in the face of rejection becomes a major predictor of success.

Nicholas believes that the most successful people are those who understand the nature of probability. 'Sure, review, learn and make changes, but understand that there is a major chance element to success. You cannot change this, but tenacity can hugely improve the odds of success in the longer term.'

This presents a problem, because, for most of us, the idea of randomness being a substantive element of success or failure runs counter to our intuition. There is a wealth of research supporting the idea that our minds do not readily grasp the nature of probability or randomness. We have a tendency to look for explanations to attribute to happenings that are in reality far more random. As Taleb puts it in *Fooled by Randomness*, 'Lucky fools do not bear the slightest suspicion that they are lucky fools.'[23]

To an extent the flipside is also true. Our minds start to weave a story to make sense of each rejection or setback, even though it may be down to chance factors outside of our control. We have a tendency to make each rejection mean more than it does.

Nicholas tells the story of an architectural practice that invited him in to help with the presentation of their competitive pitches. He was told that their existing clients loved their great creative work; they came back for more, and enthusiastically recommended them to others, but when it came to competitive pitches they were abject failures, and they wanted to know what they were doing wrong. Nicholas worked with them on presentation skills, messages, personal impact and so forth, but what was really interesting was getting them to question their story that they never win pitches. When they analysed the facts, their success ratio was not far outside what you would expect. They had experienced a fruitless sequence, but not one outside of the normal range. When they could identify clear explanations for decisions around specific pitches, these were largely outside of their control. Two weeks later, Nicholas received an excited phone call to say that they had just won the tender for the refurbishment of a major public building.

Look at the statistics, or simply bear in mind the chances of you getting a job or winning a pitch; in other words, taking an objective view of the balance of probabilities will help you to be objective and realistic about a rejection. It will also help you to put it into context.

## Summary

○ We tend to apply our own logic to happenings that are, in reality, pretty random
○ Tenacity in the face of rejection is a major predictor of success
○ Bulletproof people don't make a rejection mean more than it does – they maintain their objectivity

# Specific case or universal truth? Making assumptions is dangerous

Let's return to our ancestor, the cave dweller. In a simple but more life-threatening environment, it is safer and more efficient to formulate rules about the way things are: rocks hide nasty animals, water can drown, and so forth. If people at one settlement tried to rob this ancestor, it increases the odds of his survival to carry that assumption when passing the next settlement.

We tend to apply the same sort of rule formulation today. If we met a Martian and she was three foot tall, we would assume that all Martians are short. If somebody cheats us, we are likely to add a rule to our repertoire along the lines of 'people cheat'. When Bob – the salesman we mentioned earlier who had lost his confidence – found himself in conflict with a number of colleagues at work, he took the view that 'the workplace is hostile'. But for Bob, unlike our ancestor, the calculus has changed; the potential gain from setting aside the assumption is greater than the survival benefits of sticking with it.

A similar process of universalising applies along the dimension of time. We often make the mistake of mixing up the temporary with the permanent. If we are going through a stressful patch at work, we are inclined to make it mean that work is stressful.

If you are going through a tough time, the chances are it is being exacerbated by another form of thinking disorder. Our minds tend to look for patterns and, having made assumptions about patterns, these then shape the way we feel. If we are going through a difficult time, our reserves are usually being drained far more than necessary by the thought that this is the way things are going to be from now on.

If your assumptions tend to incorporate the notions of 'everyone', 'no one', 'always' or 'never', you are probably universalising. When something undesirable happens – perhaps a prospective client slams the door in your face – the pessimistic person tends to make the assumption that this is a foretaste of an ongoing pattern. His mind says, 'Well, that shows that that's the way it's going to be. Clients slam doors in faces. It's time to get out of this game.' The optimist, however, is more likely to attribute the incident to the particulars of a given situation. 'Perhaps the timing wasn't right for that client. Perhaps that client had just had her budgets cut.'

Optimists tend to be more successful. It is not just an intuitive hunch on our part: the evidence bears this out. Research among sales forces repeatedly shows that people with an optimistic outlook sell consistently more. One study among an insurance sales force estimated that those with measurably optimistic outlooks sell 35 per cent more than the norm for the population as a whole.[24]

You can also apply the temporary-versus-permanence test. You can ask, 'Is this really the way things are going to be, or can I expect things to change before too long?' If you are still unsure, examine the evidence. Death and divorce are pretty permanent; what you are going through now probably isn't. Keep reminding yourself of this.

A useful way to think of optimism is in terms of the three attributions. When something happens, is it:

a)  Universal or particular to the situation?
b)  As a result of a permanent situation or a temporary situation?
c)  Down to me or down to factors outside my control?

Become aware of how you are seeing things. What underlying assumptions do you tend to make, which affect the way you see things? (Of course, just because they are assumptions does not mean that they are necessarily wrong, but they are nonetheless just assumptions.) Ask yourself what evidence there is for and against your assumptions. What alternative explanations could there be? To what extent are you carrying your experiences from one situation into another?

It does happen, but it does not *always* happen. This is the situation now, but it is not the situation *always*.

### Case Study 5.4

Lucas was quietly confident about winning the big contract from National Consolidated – after all, it was surely time he had some luck. When he got the message asking him to return the buyer's call at National Consolidated, he felt optimistic, but the buyer calmly told him that they wouldn't be going ahead with him.

What thoughts typically go through Lucas's mind: maybe my firm's products just aren't good enough; maybe nobody's buying; the market's in unstoppable decline; maybe I am not cut out for this job after all?

Bulletproof Lucas sees the situation as temporary. It happened now, but that does not mean that it will keep happening. It is specific. It does not mean that it is part of a pattern. And maybe it was not down to Lucas at all. National Consolidated might have just had their budgets cut.

### Summary

- ○ Remember to check your underlying assumptions
- ○ We often mistake the temporary for the permanent – which is it?
- ○ We often universalise: 'everyone'; 'no one'; 'always'; 'never'. Is our statement actually true?
- ○ Optimists tend to be more successful than pessimists
- ○ Bulletproof people choose the most helpful ways to see situations
- ○ Bulletproof people regularly train their minds to habitually think in these more helpful ways

## Apply the 'down-to-*me*' versus '*not*-down-to-me' test

People who are more inclined to attribute the outcome that they get to factors about themselves are what psychologists term 'internal'. And, of course, the flipside is that people who tend to attribute things to factors in the external word are 'external'.

You may think that people who are internal are more likely to be proactive, and when they get setbacks they do something about it – hence, they are more successful. This is true, but only up to a point.

Pessimists are likely to attribute lack of success to elements about themselves that are not likely to change – and, of course, pessimists tend to fare less well during tough times.

Indeed, because most of us have a fairly self-centred view of the world, we are likely to over-attribute the outcomes that we get to things that we said or did. If a prospective customer says no, or we are rejected at an interview, we are inclined to assume that we got things wrong.

Because pessimists attribute setbacks to things that are 'stable' – in other words not likely to change soon – they are less resilient. Factors that are 'stable' and 'down-to-me', for example, might be: 'I am not a very good salesman'; 'I don't come over well in interviews'; 'My communication skills aren't up to the mark.'

What about people who attribute their successes to themselves, but then attribute their failures to external factors outside of their sphere of influence? And indeed there are many individuals who demonstrate this tendency. Surely these deluded, self-justifying characters will get their comeuppance.

Not so; in fact, it is almost the contrary. Research that tracked the relative success of medical students found that the most successful did precisely that. It seems that when it comes to performance, being optimistic about your own talents and rejecting pessimistic scenarios about your failures really does trump an honest assessment. It may be a case of 'to thine own self be true – but only up to a point'.

But, of course, that misses crucial factors: whether the internal factors are stable or not; and whether you can influence them. If you didn't make the sale because you did not research the client enough, or you didn't get the job because you didn't get a good night's sleep before the interview, these are things that you can do something about.

Apply the 'down-to-me' versus 'not-down-to-me' test when you next experience a setback. If you are attributing the setback to yourself, question this assumption. What other explanations could exist? What evidence is there for these alternative explanations?

For the aspects that are down to you, decide what specific steps you can most readily take to improve the probability of success.

## Summary

○ Bulletproof people ask the 'down-to-me' versus 'not-down-to-me' question when they experience a setback in order to help them understand what has really happened

○ Bulletproof people focus on elements that are changeable and that they can improve

# You can want something without needing it desperately

Think about when you *need* something. You need that sale to come in. You need to win that assignment. You need to be selected at that interview. How do you feel? Relaxed? Comfortable? In a position of power? Probably not, and you probably don't come across to others in this way either. When we *need* something, our mind is focused on the gap or the deficit: the cost of failure. Bulletproof people use techniques to train their minds to reduce the extent to which they need something, but sustain the extent to which they want it.

Here's a thought experiment: a star soccer player is about to step up and take a penalty to win his country the World Cup. As he steps back to take the run-up, a voice whispers in his ear: 'Miss this and, for the rest of your life, this is all you will be remembered for. It is all that your name will be associated with. Your children's name, even ... everyone watching at home and everyone in the stadium will hate your guts because you will have robbed them of that moment of exquisite joy that they are so longing for.'

No shortage of motivation here, then. But has the voice increased the probability of success or diminished it? What coach would think that such a message would enhance performance? At this point, our soccer player is dominated by 'fear-of-loss motivation': the unthinkable will happen if I don't succeed. Many of us load this sort of motivation on ourselves throughout our lives. Fear-of-loss motivation increases anxiety, which increases thought distortion. There is a saying: a desperate salesman is a dead salesman.

Fear of loss takes over because loss-aversion is a far greater driver in humans than the potential joy of gain. Indeed, psychologists and economists estimate that the emotional impact of losing something is twice as great as that of gaining something. I am sure that you can sense the inner cave dweller at work here. It could be that in our ancestor's more hostile environment placing the priority on avoiding loss was a better survival strategy, but we do not need to be hidebound by our inner cave dweller's rules.

Of course, you can't tell your mind not to think about something, but there are several useful things you can do instead. For example, a useful technique here would be for our penalty-taker to focus his attention on striking the perfect penalty, as opposed to the benefits that will flow to him if the penalty is successful.

Sports psychologists recognise that athletes who appear to be more motivated by getting their technique right because of the inner sense of satisfaction ('intrinsic motivation') tend to be more resilient than athletes who are chiefly motivated by rewards that flow from the outside world such as cups, money and recognition ('extrinsic motivation'). The former tend to bounce back better.

Dr Costas Karageorghis is a Reader in Sports Psychology and Deputy Head for Research at Brunel University and co-author of *Inside Sport Psychology* (Human Kinetics, 2011) He draws attention to the difference between intrinsic motivation and extrinsic motivation as a factor that influences the extent to which athletes demonstrate resilience by bouncing back. Extrinsic motivation comes from external factors: the stick or the carrot; the rewards of punishments that come from the outside world, whereas intrinsic motivation comes from within and relates more to our sense of meaning, self-worth, satisfaction and the extent to which goals fit with our personal values.

'Athletes or business people who only have extrinsic motivators struggle to cope with failures or losses, while athletes with largely intrinsic motivation tend to be more resilient. (The highest performers combine intrinsic motivation with extrinsic motivation.)', says Dr Karageorghis.

People who are driven primarily by a need or wish to win respect from others, or approval from parents, or to get their hands on the new BMW, or to wear designer brands, or all of the above (and, let's face it, we all are to some degree), tend to be less resilient in the face of setbacks.

Extrinsic motivation is not a bad thing per se, but when it roams unrestrained in your mind it is likely to raise the stakes for you in terms of fear of loss. The athletes who carry the weight of expectation on their shoulders are more likely to 'choke' and find it harder to recover when they do.

If we are working with an account team, for example, who are going into a major sales pitch, we advise them to remind themselves that they do not really *need* to win this piece of business. Nobody will starve if they don't. They remain unattached to the outcome. Here is the key, however: their motivation comes from delivering the best possible sales pitch.

If you are going for a job interview, remind yourself that you do not really *need* to be offered the job, but set yourself the goal of giving the best possible job interview.

These are sometimes called 'process' goals, or 'learning' goals, as opposed to 'outcome' goals. Process or learning goals mean that you are less likely to be hamstrung by fear-of-loss motivation; therefore we feel calmer and more in control. People who focus on learning or process goals are more resilient.[25]

## Summary

○ When we need something, our minds tend to focus on the cost of failure

○ The emotional impact of losing something is twice as great as that of gaining something

○ Bulletproof people train their minds to reduce the amount they *need* something, but sustain the extent to which they *want* it
○ Focus on 'learning' or 'process' goals rather than the outcome

## Imagine starting again from rock bottom

'Failure meant a stripping away of the inessential,' J.K. Rowling has written.[26] 'I stopped pretending to myself that I was anything other than what I was, and began to direct all my energy into finishing the only work that mattered to me … And so rock bottom became the solid foundation on which I rebuilt my life.

'You might never fail on the scale I did, but some failure in life is inevitable. It is impossible to live without failing at something, unless you live so cautiously that you might as well not have lived at all – in which case, you fail by default. Failure gave me an inner security that I had never attained by passing examinations. Failure taught me things about myself that I could have learnt no other way.'

Rowling was rejected by nine publishers, her mother died after a long battle with multiple sclerosis and her marriage failed, leaving her a single mother with a daughter to provide for. Rowling is right: we may never 'fail' on the scale that she did, but we can take her point. The point is not that Rowling showed super-human powers – she would be the last to suggest this – but that from the eventual position of achievement she has the wisdom to recognise that, for most people who ultimately succeed, failure is a fairly weighty chapter in their story.

We cannot achieve anything without being prepared to withstand rejection. Success comes from having the courage to propose our ideas, our products, or – most sensitive of all – ourselves to others.

We're taught the virtues of persistence from an early age. Rejection is damaging because it exhausts the reserves that we need to persist. Our minds form stories to make sense of our experiences. If we are talented performers, if we are great salesmen, if we have a great product or a great business idea, this is incongruent with the experience of being rejected. And because our minds don't readily live with incongruence for long, they accept the story that we are *not* great or talented, or that our product, idea or business plan is not worth the effort after all. As anyone who has been in this position knows, being told to 'stick at it' really doesn't help.

Once Rowling had hit rock-bottom, she had eliminated the type of fear-of-loss motivation that drains us and increases our anxiety. The prize may have seemed a very long way off, but the good news is that she was left solely with joy-of-gain motivation.

To help people to emerge from the cave and ultimately through to success, we use a branch of cognitive behavioural theory called 'solutions focus'. This is being used increasingly in a clinical setting when the need is to move somebody forward from a particularly low ebb. It is proving remarkably effective in a workplace setting. The essence is to focus on signs of success, no matter how tiny, and to focus on the first steps, no matter how small. There are the only steps forward from this position.

Anita Roddick, founder of The Body Shop, was the daughter of immigrant parents who entered Britain with virtually nothing. From an early age, she became interested in the way that immigrants who faced harsh odds would often rise to become very successful. When the obstacles seemed too great and success seemed too far off, she would put herself in the shoes of an immigrant. 'Think like an immigrant' became a private mantra.

Rowling's point is remarkably true: sometimes rock bottom can be the best foundation on which to rebuild. We're not suggesting that you aim for rock bottom in order to try this out, but there is a simple and very effective thought experiment related to this that you can do.

There is a time when every entrepreneur has no customers, no business on the books, no goodwill and brand or reputation, but it tends to be precisely the time when she has the greatest energy, focus and optimism. It is a place that all of us can go back to any time we choose. The ability to generate a sense of renewal, no matter where you are on the journey, gives you a useful source of optimistic energy to tap into.

Try this thought experiment: imagine starting again from zero, or square one. Like Anita Roddick's immigrant, you have nothing, or, in other words, nothing to lose. You *do* have energy, imagination, optimism and determination. You can combine this with the 'advocate-for-your-success' exercise.

### The 'too-late' thinking distortion

We often hear people argue that it would be too late for them to start anything anew. The sentiment runs along the lines of: '*If I were going to do [abc], I would already have done [xyz] by now.*' You have probably said it to yourself at some point. But this is simply another thinking distortion to be challenged.

The name 'Colonel Sanders' (the face of KFC) probably evokes an image of a folksy-looking elderly gentleman beaming out from a multi-billion-dollar fast-food franchise. The story of the real Colonel Sanders is a useful one to remember when you want to challenge the 'too-late' thinking distortion. For much of his career, Harland Sanders cooked for passing motorist trade at his service station at Corbin, Kentucky. It was steady business, success-ful but unspectacular. But around the age when most of us would like to retire, 65, Sanders found himself virtually bankrupt, with nothing more than a social security cheque for US$105. The opening of a nearby interstate highway had drained off both his customers and his livelihood. Sanders was left with nothing but his recipe for fried chicken. With this, he decided that his best option was to try franchising. He set about looking for potential franchisees. KFC is one of the world's best-known food brands and, through the foundation he established, Sanders was able to donate more than a million dollars a year to aid charities and scholarships. A world obsessed by youth strengthens the too-late thinking distortion – in reality many people achieve remarkable success later in life.

### Summary

○ Think like someone who is starting from zero – everything to gain, and nothing to lose

○ If you were starting from zero, what personal attributes or strengths would you point to that indicate you should succeed?

○ Bulletproof people are able to generate a sense of renewal and can therefore tap into its source of optimistic energy
○ Reject the 'too-late' thinking distortion

## Visualisations can help

All things being equal, we will experience a series of rejections, and then a success. It's useful to imagine this inevitability as being a staircase: each success is waiting for us on a landing; the rejections are the steps in between the landings. There is no reason why the successes should equal the number of rejections; simple probability tells us that there will be far more steps than landings (as most competitive situations involve a number of agents going for one prize). In fact, we only need a relatively small number of successes to achieve overall success in any given field. There is no reason why the number of steps between landings should be evenly distributed. They are not. They are random. Sometimes you will stumble over one landing after another, and other times you will find yourself on an unusually long unbroken flight of stairs.

People don't need to be told that they should keep going through the setbacks – they know that. The metaphor of the staircase gives them something that they can visualise in an active way. The key also is to think of the staircase without judging. You do not know when the next landing is coming up; all you can do is keep taking the steps up. You only need a small number of landings to succeed.

Visualisations play a crucial role in refocusing attention. In a neurological sense, to visualise yourself doing something is pretty much the same as physically doing it. If you want to refocus your attention away from less helpful thoughts and towards more helpful ones, visualising the more positive outcome really helps.

By the way, don't make the mistake of attempting to visualise the bad thing disappearing. This simply means that you are devoting important neural resources to something that is *bad* news. Kristi Richards was a world-champion freestyle skier and looked set for a medal at the 2010 Winter Games; the Canadian team even employed a squad of 'Fourteen Mental Preparation' consultants. Richards was advised to write down all of her negative thoughts on toilet paper, which would then be flushed down the lavatory. As a result she spent a good few hours pondering about the negative thoughts she could bring to mind. She finished last.

If you're on a journey on which you need extra resilience to deal with rejection and knock-backs, choose a visualisation that works for you. It may be the staircase or it may be something that is more personal to you. When you receive a knock-back or a rejection, picture yourself taking the next step up the staircase. You know that there is always a landing with a prize on it ahead of you – you do not know how many steps ahead it lies but you do know that it's there.

And, of course, you can visualise any worthwhile prize at the end of it. Holocaust survivor, Viktor Frankl, managed to help himself to survive the unimaginable by visualising himself lecturing about the experience to packed lecture halls, as he devoted the rest of his life to enlightening future generations. He focused on giving meaning to his goal.

And don't waste time with fear-of-loss motivation either. Instead, give yourself an alternative image to re-focus your mind. Visualisations are cognitively more powerful than simple thoughts, as they require more neurons to fire up together. Remember British athlete Dame Kelly Holmes, and the two-year-long spell of injury in the nineties that almost finished her career? During this period she consistently visualised the gold medal being placed around her neck and she then went on to become a double Olympic gold medal winner.

Visualisations work.

## Summary
- Visualise your success as waiting for you on a landing with your rejections being the steps between now and the future
- Visualisations are crucial in refocusing your attention on the positive things

○ Visualising yourself doing something is much like physically doing it

○ Bulletproof people refocus attention from unhelpful thoughts towards more supportive ones

○ On a journey where you need extra resilience to deal with rejection, visualise a worthwhile prize at the end

## What's your story?

Can writing things down help us, especially when we face challenges and setbacks? The evidence from psychologists suggests that it can. The process of writing about events can help us to see our lives as a narrative, or a story, as it's better known. After all, we're all familiar with stories. Humans need stories. We learn about the world through stories – and about ourselves. They can help make us bulletproof by putting things into context and framing knock-backs and problems.

'The stories we construct to make sense of our lives are fundamentally about our struggle to reconcile who we imagine we were, are and might be in our heads and bodies, with who we might be in the social contexts of family, community, the workplace, ethnicity, religion, gender, social class and culture writ large,' says Professor Dan McAdams, Department Chair of Clinical Psychology and Personality Psychology at Northwestern University. 'The self comes to terms with society through narrative identity.' Put simply, stories exist to help us make sense of ourselves and the world around us.

Writing your story is an effective way to handle any knock-back but it can be especially effective with rejection; how and when is up to you.

Thinking in terms of the story of your journey helps you to sustain optimism and focus during difficult times, thus helping you to overcome adversity. Because the essence of great stories is often about overcoming adversity, positioning a journey of change as a story allows you to be completely honest and frank about the nature of current adversity, while focusing on a realistic but positive outcome.

Creating a narrative is a powerful psychological tool. To help someone triumph through adverse experiences or circumstances, psychologists will often ask people to place such adversities within a story – a chapter, if you like – of their life. Such a narrative enables people to describe the journey, allowing a processing of the difficult reality, and thus helping to lead them towards a positive outcome. What will not help is glossing over or denying a difficult reality, or even forcing a person towards positive thinking without allowing them to ground their story in reality; this type of approach will confuse them and no doubt make their experience of the adversity worse. In order to sustain optimism and focus during difficult times it is important to focus on a positive outcome, but the journey through the adversity must be acknowledged.

If you are going through a tough patch and want to boost your resilience, start thinking about your story – where are you now and where will the story take you? What is the best, most credibly optimistic outcome for your story? If it helps, write it down.

Stories work because, in most of the stories that capture our imagination, the hero or protagonist, with whom one identifies, invariably goes through a period of adversity during which his or her resolve is seriously tested. The best stories set up a big question to be answered, a problem to be solved or a challenge to be overcome. How our protagonist deals with this reveals his or her most profound values, and gives us the moral or take-out of the novel or movie. The protagonist inevitably spends time at the heart of the story in his or her cave or wilderness.

As well as writing about what *has* happened, you can write about what *might* happen. This is your story so you can write your own ending. Obviously, it won't be helpful to make it a tragedy where you suffer horribly – but neither will constructing an amazingly wonderful, fairy-tale-like conclusion help much either. The trick is to be 'credibly optimistic'. This means describing a resolution that is possible and believable but also positive and optimistic. You could write, for instance, about how you overcame this problem, learnt from it and used those lessons in later life. Or you could describe how you eventually achieved your goal – or even a more modest version of it. Make it believable and possible but, at the same time, motivating and optimistic.

## Summary

○ Stories capture our imagination, providing coherence and sense-making

○ The power of story helps bulletproof people get through tough periods

○ Bulletproof people are able to write down a credibly optimistic outcome for their personal story – clarity increases the likelihood of success

# It's putting it into words that counts

When psychologists investigate the impact of various types of trauma on health and well-being, they find something very interesting. The type of trauma is less important in predicting mental and physiological recovery than the actions that individuals took following the trauma. It seems that those who open up and talk about their experiences recover better and quicker than those who don't. The former group – we could hypothesise – may well have been feeling the benefits of sense-making and coherence as a result of starting to piece together their story.

Psychologist Jamie Pennebaker sought to discover whether people's well-being could be improved by writing about something distressing that had happened to them in their lives.[27] Participants in the experiment were given blank journals and asked to write for roughly fifteen minutes a day, for roughly four days. The results were remarkable. Participants showed measurable and significant health benefits for several months after the experiment, compared to the control group.

It gets more interesting. Pennebaker then sought to discover whether any sort of expression would work in a similar way: the methodology was repeated to test whether a range of different modes of expressiveness, dancing, painting, sculpting and so forth would work in a similar way. And guess what? They didn't. Or, to put it more scientifically, there was no measurable difference for these versus the control. It is the process of putting it into words that counts. (So if you've ever sat in a workshop at work and a team of management consultants come in and encourage you to throw paint at a canvas to express your vision, or if your friend advises you to go dance away the pain of your divorce at that alternative therapy group, it is worth bearing this piece of research in mind.)

Psychologist Jonathan Haidt argues that this is not a case of that old folk wisdom 'letting off steam', or 'getting it all out'. Indeed, one of the great myths about emotions is that they are better once we get them 'out'. As Haidt points out, expressing anger makes us angrier. It is the act of sense-making that works for people.

### Summary

- Those who open up and put their traumas into sense-making words recover better than those who don't
- Putting things into words connects us with the cognitive – words make us think things through

## Be honest when you write

You may be the hero of your story; however, it is important that you do not make yourself perfect. Any author will tell you how a purely bad character with no redeeming features is as boring as a purely good character that does nothing wrong. Also, it's just not realistic. In the most interesting, absorbing stories, as in life itself, the best heroes are fallible people with whom others can identify.

You will only get the true benefit of writing your story if you are honest. Could you have acted rashly or unreasonably in the confrontation you're describing? Your unreasonable boss might have had a good point or, thinking about it, you might be able to understand why he or she acts the way they do. It might not be the easiest thing to write but it's important because it's honest.

Some of these things will stand out when you come to read your words later. 'Why was I so cross about that?', you might find yourself thinking, or 'How funny that I thought that was the case. Now I know it's actually very different.' Being mindful and self-aware is important when writing your storyline.

Similarly it's important to differentiate between facts on the one hand and perceptions, emotions and interpretations on the other. Did something definitely happen or was it just your perception or feeling? For example, it's a fact that the meeting started at 3pm instead of 2.30pm but it's your interpretation, your perception, that your boss was keeping you waiting because he doesn't value you. Now, if it really seemed as if your boss was snubbing you or not respecting you, then write that down. But note that it's how you felt, not what definitely happened. Feelings are important. Include them in your story, but be clear when you are describing a feeling or interpretation as opposed to a fact.

'Writing about your life and your experiences can show you an alternative storyline,' says Professor Femi Oyebode. 'A storyline offers a lens through which to view life. It offers freedom and flexibility – you're in charge.' So, he suggests, why not rewrite a 'scene' or an event with new perspective. For example, imagine your boss gave you some feedback (that's a fact, by the way), which was negative (could be a fact or could be your perception), and which was very undeserved (even more likely to be a view or personal impression than an objective fact). Having written about what happened to you and how you felt, try writing it from your boss's perspective. Put yourself in his or her shoes. What had your boss been doing just before you met? If the feedback was by email or phone, where was he or she when they wrote or said it? What else do you know is going on in their work or home life?

It might be tough initially to put yourself in the shoes of someone you'd like to punch in the face, but it can be an interesting – and very enlightening – experience.

'Writing offers freedom and flexibility, but you need to reinstall reality,' says Professor Oyebode. Let someone else read what you've written. Counterbalance it. 'Fiction is about looking at different characters and standing in their shoes. That's what writers do and you're free to do it too in your narrative. It's part of the therapy and it means that you can find a better perspective.'

## Summary
○ When writing your story, be honest
○ Look at the situation from the point of view of the other participants – even those you feel are attacking you

# It's okay to be in the cave

We've been talking about the cave dweller, but here's another manifestation of the cave: you can use it in your story to become more bulletproof.

Christopher Vogler is an expert on story structure and myth, and the author of *The Hero's Journey*, which analyses classic story structure in films and books. As well as lecturing around the world, he runs a script and literary consultancy called Storytech. Vogler is interested in the idea of 'reversal of fortune', when 'the action turns in the opposite direction'. This could be a dramatic improvement in a character's circumstances but, more often, it's associated with tragedy. This idea is every bit as relevant in modern film scripts and novels as it was in ancient Greek myths and legends. Vogler describes this reversal of fortune, the low point in the Hero's Journey, as time spent 'in the cave' – sometimes quite literally.

'Going into the cave,' he says, 'is often featured in storylines because it parallels these setbacks in life.' Even if characters in a plot don't physically enter a cave, the term is used as a metaphor for being in a bad place during one's journey. Caves are isolating; the deeper you go, the lonelier it gets. That's how it feels for a character at this point in a story. This is also how things might feel for you in real life. That is why we use the metaphor. Just like the hero of a story, you will ulti-mately come through the experience stronger and wiser.

As they think about things, our hero finds out more about them-selves. To take one slightly absurd example – but which, thereby, proves the rule – in *The Simpsons Movie* Homer undergoes a bizarre and terri-fying ordeal with a mythical Native American Indian woman after Marge leaves him to return to Springfield. However, having come through this experience, Homer learns more about himself and how he relates to the world. He is purified and reinvigorated as, suddenly shorn of everything comfortable and familiar, and alone and fright-ened, he is forced to focus on the essentials of his life. As with other characters that enter the cave, either real or figurative, this time is about basic survival and what's really important. Four-fingered yellow cartoon characters aside, if you think of almost any movie you've seen, from an all-action adventure to the fluffiest romantic comedy, there will be a moment similar to this.

Vogler tells us that it can be viewed as a form of death and rebirth: part of the character is dying, and the old part that necessarily didn't work is going. The character needs to embrace that, and this acknowl-edgement releases something, meaning the character emerges from the cave even more determined to continue with the quest. They don't just reset or reboot themselves – they've actually changed, and they now have a different perspective on life.

The fact that the hero or protagonist spends some time in the cave or the wilderness is what makes a story interesting. Almost all high achievers, in virtually all fields, have spent time in the cave before achieving success. This is simply part of their story. If you find yourself in the cave, remind yourself that most successful people have been in this situation at some time. It is simply part of your story. Time in the cave is a transient part of your journey.

## Summary

○ It's okay to be in the cave. You're not the only one to have been here ... and to have escaped

○ Being in the cave is temporary. Looking at the situation this way reminds you that it is temporary and not permanent

○ If it fits your situation, then write about it honestly, remembering that, like others, you'll escape from it, more bulletproof than ever

## Stand in the future to see things clearly

Remember how Peter Nicholas wrong-footed a class of aspiring drama students on their first day by telling them to 'write a letter to yourself now from the you of ten years hence'? He suggests that doing this after a disappointment or a knock-back will give you a sense of perspective. You might want to say something to yourself like, 'I know you thought that you'd never recover but actually in the long run it worked out.'

It seems that our minds are much better at thinking imaginatively and creatively if we are in the future, looking back, rather than standing in the present trying to imagine a way forward.[28]

Here is an interesting example: a class of Canadian undergraduates were asked to focus their attention on a colleague in the room, and they were then told that the colleague would be taking a long vacation to Europe that year, and were asked what they imagined she would be doing. Suggestions were stuttered out slowly and awkwardly, but the overall impression was fairly blank. They were then asked to imagine that they were in the future, that it was the fall, and that the colleague had just returned from her European vacation. They were asked what they imagined she did. The ideas flowed.

To recap, imagine your story. Imagine you are in the cave … in the wilderness … hit by the perfect storm. Now imagine you are in your future and things have worked out successfully. Tell your story, the story of the journey.

And if you do not have a pen and paper to hand, Nicholas suggests another technique that you can do any time:

- Again, stand in the future
- Imagine you are being interviewed. The interviewer wants to understand the story of your success, but prefaces the question by pointing out that she understands that it hasn't all been plain sailing, but far from it
- Now tell your story. And remember the tougher the time in the cave or the wilderness, the greater the story of your journey

### The I-choose Game

Imagine that in the future you eavesdrop on someone who is discussing the reasons for your success. Imagine what you hear. But, and here's the key, each attribute listed must be a behaviour you have control over. God-given, innate gifts, such as wit, intelligence or physical beauty, are banished. Instead the attribute must be a matter of your choice. For example, you have 100 per cent control over the level of enthusiasm that you display about a given mission or task, so this could be an attribute being listed.

Here is the list that one of our colleagues came up with: I choose to be contagiously enthusiastic about my work, to get interested in people and care about them, to be persistent and to pay attention to details.

Once you start your list you will find the ideas begin to flow and you will be surprised by how many of the attributes that predict success are simply a matter of behavioural choice.

### Summary

- Our minds are better at thinking imaginatively if we're in the future looking back as opposed to standing in the present and trying to imagine a way forward
- Bulletproof people are able to tell a great story of their journey by imagining themselves in the future when things have worked out successfully

# CHAPTER 6
## DECONTAMINATING TOXIC FEEDBACK
## AND OTHER ASSAULTS

Certain events can knock us off our feet and lead to us feeling depressed and confused, such as a verbal attack that comes from nowhere, being on the receiving end of harsh, critical feedback or being cruelly rejected. But, even here, being mindful, and quieting that inner cave dweller, can make you bulletproof.

### Case Study 6.1

When Mike's client asked him to present the tactical Christmas campaign to his board (at a major retailer), Mike took the request in his stride. Mike had just been introduced to Didier, his new contact at the retail client.

'I worked late about five or six nights on the trot plus a weekend,' said the 29-year-old senior marketing executive. 'I even had to ask my wife if we could postpone her birthday dinner – I just wanted to make sure that I had every detail and every fact right, as well as being able to show some great ideas.'

He persuaded his team and the agency's design department to work late, too. The ideas that Mike and his team had been developing were polished up and turned into eye-catching slides for the presentation.

'One of the guys in the design team said that it was the best work they'd ever done,' said Mike. 'I sent it over to Jonathan, my boss, who was in Hong Kong, and he emailed back, "Excellent work. Go get 'em."'

So, two days later, Mike drove down to the client's headquarters, an hour's drive outside London. He arrived early, set up his laptop, checked through the presentation for the umpteenth time, and then he and his assistant put out some toys and gimmicks around the table for the board members.

'They really liked them – in fact, I thought we'd never get around to doing some work,' said Mike, laughing. 'Yeah, I actually enjoy presentations. Once I get going and the nerves subside, I really get into it. It's even better if you believe that you've got something really special to tell the client.'

As Mike went through the agency's plans for their client during the all-important run up to Christmas, the board members looked suitably impressed. They even began to discuss the practicalities of implementing the new marketing strategy.

'Heads were nodding, they laughed at my jokes – one of them even said "great idea" about one of our suggestions,' said Mike. 'I still don't know what went wrong.'

Didier's call the next morning hit Mike like a punch in the stomach.

'I actually had the whole team with me for a review meeting when I saw Didier's number come up,' Mike told us. 'I put the call on speaker phone at first because I thought it would be great for everyone to hear the positive feedback we'd got, but then something told me to pick up the receiver.'

Didier started by asking Mike how he thought the presentation went.

'That didn't feel right. I wasn't quite sure how to answer, as surely the point was for Didier to give his opinion. I sensed an ambush and, boy, was it lurking around the corner,' said Mike.

Didier told an astonished Mike that the presentation had been a car crash and that it was going to take a lot of work to turn the situation around. Didier told Mike that the board felt his presentation made little sense and that his message lacked structure.

In fact, they felt that Mike was a poor communicator, that he had been ill-prepared, and that the whole experience was pretty embarrassing, Didier reported.

'I just felt sick,' said Mike, sighing deeply. 'I kept thinking, had they really been at the same meeting as me? It didn't make sense. I couldn't understand how I'd worked so hard leading a great team and somehow we'd apparently got it so wrong.'

## Decontaminate criticism

Critical feedback is essential to performance. Most people are not highly competent when giving feedback and, therefore, incur a high emotional cost. When listening to critical feedback, our minds sense a potential assault. Cortisol, the 'stress hormone' which is secreted during the body's 'fight or flight' response to stress, increases and automatically our minds prepare to keep us feeling safe, through defence, denial or counter-attack. How do we manage the feedback paradox? If we accept it as 100 per cent true and justified, our performance ultimately suffers through lower confidence, esteem and energy. If we reject it, accusations of not listening or being defensive become justified.

So, how can we allow useful information to be received while allowing the poor-quality, harmful feedback to embed harmlessly in the metaphorical bulletproof vest? An important way to quell what we see as an attack is by staying in what we call 'enquiry mode'.

Feedback is essential to performance. Indeed, if we look at phenomena from the natural world, any dynamic system depends on feedback to be able to grow and survive. If you look at systems such as the human body, negative feedback is far more prevalent than positive feedback. Negative feedback in essence says, 'Stop. Enough. Reverse direction. Another action is needed.' Positive feedback says, 'This is good. More of this.' Positive feedback systems are rare in the human body, the most obvious of which is sex ... but back to the workplace.

The problem with negative feedback is that we need it to perform, but the emotional cost of receiving it (and the ensuing psychological and physiological responses) often impedes our ability to perform. Some leadership gurus argue that we should abandon negative feedback altogether. The reasoning goes like this: when we receive negative feedback our minds perceive an attack and, therefore, go into defence mode and prepare for fight or flight. This, of course, brings about a temporary shutdown in creativity and our ability to learn. In our view, this is a bit like arguing against procreation because kids are tiring and stressful.

This line of reasoning then goes on to argue that the best way to improve someone's performance is not to deliver feedback that can be upsetting but 'to allow the other person to have a moment of insight'. The problem with this is that we know that we have a tendency to use self-deception strategies, particularly to support our self-esteem, when things are not going well. Our minds tend to cling to the version of reality that gives us the greatest comfort at the time.[29]

To perform at our best we need to find ways to learn from feedback but minimise the emotional cost of receiving feedback. When researching this topic, we came across an article in the *Harvard Business Review* entitled 'Finding the gold in toxic feedback'[30]. Excitedly, we looked it up to discover how the authors had unearthed the holy grail of feedback.

The article identifies a new, presumably super-human breed of managers in business which it calls the 'alchemists'. Alchemists, we are told, deploy the wise strategy of simply taking what is useful out of feedback. They focus solely on what is accurate, suspend judgement and manage their emotions, whereas those old-school human beings become defensive and emotional.

This is sound advice; or at least it would be if most of us were largely governed day-to-day by the composed, clear-thinking frontal cortex. The problem with advice of this nature is that it tells us what we *should* do as opposed to *how* to do it. And, of course, most of us don't struggle with knowing what we should do. The problem is that, in reality – in the intensity of the moment – we end up doing something quite different.

Returning to the case of Mike, conventional advice would encourage Mike to see it in a more adult way, to view the feedback as a gift, to see it as a learning opportunity. To use our metaphor, this type of advice speaks to the guide when we should be learning how to train the inner cave dweller. When Mike received the feedback from Didier, his physiological response was that of a person experiencing an attack. The slump in self-esteem, confidence and energy that ensued shortly afterwards was his limbic system telling him to withdraw from the fray and go and hide. At the same time, the part of Mike's mind that seeks coherence is scanning Mike's life-story to connect this incident with similar ones and pull them all together in a consistent story.

However, anger and denial sometimes have a place. There are people – you've probably met them – who tend to dismiss critical feedback as being unconnected with *their* behaviour but entirely, in some form or other, down to the *deliverer* of the feedback. This view of the world is known as 'defensive externalism'. Annoying though it might be for those who work with them, this strategy does, in fact, seem to work well for people up to a point. Research shows that people who deploy this tactic do tend to be more successful than the rest of us. Perhaps we can learn from them. It seems to be a more successful strategy than holding ourselves entirely accountable for any critical feedback that we may have brought upon ourselves.[31]

As an emotion, anger gets bad press. The assumption seems to be that anger inevitably increases the likelihood of ever-more-undesirable outcomes. But why do we feel anger after receiving some critical feedback? Thinking of the physiological changes that were going on with Mike might explain why anger has a useful adaptive role to play. Anger is associated with increased testosterone, the hormone which in turn is associated with increased aggression and competitiveness. We could hypothesise that Mike is unconsciously harnessing the resources to get back out there and compete.[32]

So what can Mike do to react in a positive way to this feedback and learn from it? It won't surprise you to hear that CBT and mindfulness help.

We can learn from our mistakes when we are able to set aside the emotional fallout and view them without judging. Ask yourself: 'Why am I feeling like this?' This will lead you to considering your thoughts objectively. For example, in Mike's case these thoughts could be 'Didier thinks I'm rubbish', or 'I'm going to lose my job'. Mike might be right, in which case it makes sense that he would be experiencing those feelings. But it might well be that this is not the case and he needs to check these thoughts and see whether they're just part of the automatic chain of reactions that happen for him during such a situation. Mike could challenge these thoughts cognitively. Has he done good work before for Didier or his boss Jonathan or others, for instance? What do Jonathan and others say about Mike's previous work? Thinking about the situation more dispassionately and putting it into context will help here.

As well as that, here is a technique that you can try to increase your mindfulness when you feel that you have been ambushed by a verbal assault, and negative, destructive thoughts and feelings are preying on your mind. Peter Nicholas asked Mike to relax and to become aware of what thoughts drifted into his mind. If the thought of the incident with Didier drifted into his mind, Mike was asked just to let it drift.

Practise this yourself if there is something on your mind such as some unduly critical feedback or a verbal assault:

> Imagine that it is something that you can see … a shape … it doesn't matter what shape … maybe the shape is changing … become aware of how it's drifting … imagine you could see how you *feel* about the incident. Let the feeling drift into your mind … See it. Don't judge it … accept it … let it drift.

You can practise this. Become aware of emotions as they drift into your mind. Don't try to usher them straight out again. Just let them be there. Become aware of how they feel … you might feel the emotion in a particular part of your body. It might seem to be a particular colour. Notice how you let the emotion sit there and still be okay.

Mike was now comfortable letting the thought and the feeling drift in and out of his mind. With no need to suppress it, he ceased to strengthen it. By 'seeing' the emotion, as opposed to simply feeling it, Mike was, in part, starting to place it outside of the automatic emotional processing part of his mind. He was starting the steps of what psychologists refer to as 'dissociation'.

Dissociation was traditionally seen in psychology as something less than healthy. It is normal for our memories, opinions, feelings, thoughts and automatic emotional and physiological responses, most of the time, to be seamlessly integrated and wired up together. Dissociation intentionally puts a bit of distance between them. This means that you can become aware of how an emotion feels – like anger, disgust, fear, panic – without responding to it physiologically.

## Summary

- ◯ Learning from feedback – even negative feedback – is essential to our personal development
- ◯ To perform best we must learn from feedback while minimising the emotional cost of receiving it
- ◯ Bulletproof people increase their mindfulness if they feel they've been ambushed by a verbal assault
- ◯ Bulletproof people know how to become more aware of their thoughts – they don't suppress their negative emotions and therefore don't strengthen them
- ◯ Bulletproof people can 'see' their emotion, as opposed to simply feeling it – in this way they're able to dissociate

# Evaluate the feedback objectively

Feedback is sometimes analogised with medicine: we don't like it; it tastes nasty; but if we are to get better, we need to swallow it and move on. This is true up to a point, but there is a key difference. Medicine is tested rigorously in clinical trials before being put on the market and it is fair to assume that the person prescribing or administering it has attained a high level of professional training. Not so with feedback. Feedback in the workplace is of varying quality. Some of it will be useful and helpful, some of it will be harmless junk and some of it will be toxic junk. Other than in some very rare cases, to be willing to accept it all unquestioningly or to reject it outright are both thinking errors.

The first exercise is to think through what we can control and what we cannot control in our quest to get back on our feet. This is an important characteristic of feedback. You do not control the feedback you receive. The deliverer of the feedback is entirely responsible for that. But you *do* exercise control over the extent to which you categorise feedback into 'helpful' and 'unhelpful' (this does not necessarily prevent you from feeling hurt by it, but you are entirely free to choose how you evaluate it, what is kept and what is discarded).

We encouraged Mike to write down his evaluation of the feedback that he received, using a two-by-two grid. The axes were: (i) helpful versus unhelpful; and (ii) content as opposed to style. The process of writing down the feedback put Mike in control and allayed his instinct to defend. What happened to Didier's feedback was now Mike's choice.

|  | **Style** | **Content** |
| --- | --- | --- |
| Helpful | That it happened at all. At least I know that there is some strength of feeling out there. | Should have used slides in the meeting (these guys just like slides). |
|  |  | Should have phoned ahead to check out the style and tone of the meeting with someone who knows better. |
|  |  | Be careful with humour, especially early on. |
|  |  | Rehearsal would have been a good idea (these guys value preparedness over relaxed spontaneity). |

|  | Style | Content |
|---|---|---|
| Unhelpful | (I felt) hijacked, would have preferred clear warning up front to set the context that this was going to be pretty tough feedback. | (In my opinion) very vague. Phrases like 'embarrassing', 'didn't make sense', 'all over the place'. 'Disaster' (in my opinion), vague, imprecise, overly subjective and emotive. |
|  | No balance, (felt to me like) 100 per cent assault. | Lack of clarity over what 'good' would have looked like. Lack of specific examples. Lack of specific clear requests for improvement. |
|  | Choice of words that were (in my opinion) subjective, emotive and vague (see content). |  |

If you do this exercise, you may find that there is plenty of overlap between 'content' and 'style'. Sometimes they are not easily separated. That is okay; don't worry too much about the categories. You will notice also that we encouraged Mike to put his opinions or interpretations in brackets. Some things will only make sense if you acknowledge that they require the context of your interpretation. That Didier used words that were hostile is not a fact. That Didier's words came across to Mike as being hostile is another matter. It is okay to be subjective, provided that you are clear you are being subjective.

Sitting looking at the words on the matrix, Mike felt his blood pressure lower. The incident no longer seemed so threatening. Mike had put himself in charge of what is kept and what is discarded. He was the judge of what was valid and what was junk in Didier's feedback.

When you receive some feedback remind yourself that you do not control the feedback that you receive but you are 100 per cent in charge of the evaluation process: assessing what is useful and what is not; deciding what to keep and what to discard. Writing it down helps you to feel more objective and dispassionate. In the evaluation of the feedback, it is solely your judgement that counts and your interests that matter.

## Summary

○ Feedback – some is useful, some is harmless and some is downright toxic

○ You can't control the feedback you get, but *can* control what you categorise as 'helpful' and 'unhelpful'

○ Bulletproof people put themselves in charge of what they keep and what they discard

○ By putting themselves in charge, bulletproof people are able to maximise the learning they gain from personal feedback

# View the situation from a different perspective

The next stage was to encourage Mike to take a mental walk around the incident, and to view it not just from where he was standing but to use his imagination to view it from different perspectives. If the feedback was unexpectedly antagonistic, why had Didier behaved like that?

The object of this exercise is not necessarily to forgive the person who gave you feedback, but to become as effective as possible following that feedback. It is important to note here that this is also not an exercise in attempting to mind read or to psychoanalyse people. Those strategies are doomed to exacerbate the problem. Equally it is important to keep reminding ourselves that we never *know* what another person's intentions or motivations are in a situation. At best we can take a view on what they appeared to be under a set of circumstances, but always acknowledge the large scope for error.

We asked Mike to ask a simple but useful question of himself: 'How am I feeling when I behave like Didier behaved?'

We were prepared for the inevitable, initial response: 'I never act like that a***hole.'

We persisted. Mike acknowledged that maybe he has – albeit rarely – been overly critical, harsh, aggressive, or let someone have it with both barrels. And building on this, we moved on to the next question: 'What else might have been going on for Didier, when he made that phone call?'

Gradually, Mike's tone changed. 'Didier may have been under a fair bit of pressure,' Mike acknowledged. 'Thinking back, I recall that he did say that he had tried to communicate the big ideas of our strategy to his board, but he had been through quite a tough time when he was talking to them. I guess maybe he had been beaten up and felt a bit bruised …' The conversation continued. The point is not that Mike now read Didier's mind; he didn't. The point is not that Mike forgave Didier. The point is that Didier was just another fallible human under pressure. Didier no longer cast a gloomy shadow of mythic proportions over Mike's day-to-day mood.

Understanding the person who's giving you harsh feedback will help you handle the situation – even if you can't bring yourself to love them. Understanding a more complete picture of what was happening for Didier did not make his behaviour more excusable, but it did make it a little more understandable – and, therefore, more manageable for Mike.

### Summary

- ○ We never *know* another person's intentions in a situation
- ○ You can take a view on what a person's motivations might have been, but always acknowledge the large scope for error
- ○ Remember, other people are fallible under pressure – just like us

## Learn to re-focus your mind

Mike told us that, for some time in the aftermath of the feedback, he had a knot in his stomach and a feeling of impending doom … a feeling that either he was just about to be told off or someone somewhere was already telling him off. This is a common feeling: our inner cave dweller, putting safety first, is looking out for a common story, preparing us for the eventuality that this is now a regular occurrence and that we should be prepared for an ambush around every corner.

That feeling in the pit of your stomach is created by an important neural function. The brain is sending a signal that something is amiss, so either watch out or take preventative action. Generally the moment passes and we feel that nice sense of relief. But the greater the impact of the initial blow or assault on the mind, the more that sense of doom becomes locked into the mind. It does not readily pass, even though the moment has passed.

The nature of feedback, particularly harsh feedback, is that we want to dwell on it, and our minds 're-make' the memory every time we think of it. Dwelling on it strengthens the extent to which it becomes locked into the mind. The conventional advice is to take what you can learn from it, move on and forget about it. Of course, the problem with this advice is that the mind is incapable of responding to the command to forget something. Trying to forget simply strengthens the association.[33]

We, therefore, needed to help Mike to re-focus his attention. We cannot choose what *not* to think about but we can choose where we focus our attention. Mike had a deeply rutted pathway in his mind that linked meeting with clients to the bitter experience with Didier; because it is deeply rutted, it is the pathway down which his thoughts readily travel. The key was to help Mike build an alternative, more helpful pathway, which over time would become more used than the existing one.

Mike picked an alternative incident on which to focus. He was asked to play another short movie in his mind, before any important meeting with a client: some other incident from his life, the thought of which would give him strength. On each occasion he was encouraged to allow his mind to focus on any aspect of this movie, no matter how small, to become aware and focus, or re-focus, attention. This movie appeals to all of the senses so we can smell things and feel their texture. We can turn up the contrast, volume, colour or brightness any time we choose. And crucially, if the incident with Didier drifts into

Mike's mind, that is absolutely fine; Mike was encouraged to do just that, let it drift.

Mike told us about the alternative incident he chose as his movie: 'It was the first time I won a creative pitch and brought in a big new client for the agency. I was young to be leading a pitch. All of the stars felt lined up that day. I was nervous, but focused before the meeting started, and as soon as I entered that room I felt something kick in: a feeling that this was going to be our day and nothing would get in the way. I just naturally found the right words ... the right answers to questions ... When I play it over in my mind, I just let my mind focus on whatever aspect of the movie it chooses: the feel of a handshake, the smell of the coffee, the clink of the coffee cups, the grain in the walnut of the table, the clear blue sky out of the picture window on a sunny winter morning.'

We all have 'ten moments' sitting in our personal autobiographical bank account for us to draw on. They are the times when everything comes together. Often people will not be able to think of them when they are experiencing a slump, but feel free to pick the really small ones – these are just as powerful as the big ones.

Don't beat yourself up over how you should or shouldn't feel. We can sometimes get impatient about getting over the incident. The mind does not respond well to being told to get over it. It is up to you to help your mind by choosing where you actively focus your attention.

Feedback is essential to performance improvement but any toxic elements in the feedback can contaminate future performance by affecting your confidence. You can't tell your mind not to think about it, but you can choose to focus your mind on a success or achievement. Call to mind an incident, no matter how seemingly small, of positive feedback. Enjoy dwelling on the details that spring to mind.

## Summary

○ When we get a knock-back, the feeling in our stomach is created by an important neural function – 'Something is amiss. Better watch out!'

○ We can't easily choose what *not* to think about, but we *can* choose where to focus our attention

○ Bulletproof people focus on positive life incidents – even small ones – to give them inner strength in tough times

○ Bulletproof people can turn up the contrast, volume, colour or brightness on their positive personal 'movies'

○ Bulletproof people don't beat themselves up over how they should or shouldn't feel

## Don't vent anger – identify the benefits of a situation

If someone commits a transgression against us at work – derides our work, ignores us or speaks to us in a disrespectful manner – our stress increases. People often tell us that they intend to deal with the situation by going to the gym and beating the living daylights out of a punch bag (or something similar if neither the gym nor the punch bag is available).

In the movie *Analyze This*, Billy Crystal, playing the psychoanalyst opposite Robert DeNiro's mobster boss, invites the DeNiro character to release his anger by punching a pillow (the pay-off is when the DeNiro character pulls out his revolver and shoots it). Notwithstanding the quality of the gag, it seems that the idea that we best deal with anger by expressing it has an unshakeable grip, but it's wrong. Study after study shows that expressing anger increases anger. Just as our bodies respond to what our minds are thinking, our minds constantly take readings from our physicality, and (because our minds like congruence) adjust accordingly. If you act angry, you are more likely to feel angry. Your body will generate higher levels of adrenaline and testosterone, the aggression hormone. Screaming and yelling – whether it's at your dog, at your colleague or in the privacy of your car with the windows closed – does not let off steam.[34]

Whether it's harsh verbal criticism, rejection, alienation or ostracism by colleagues, the result is that we feel social pain. The incident feels like an assault and when we feel assaulted we are not functioning at our best. The key is to enable the emotions associated with feeling assaulted to subside so that we can restore clear thinking and make the best choices. And a powerful way to achieve this is a technique that psychologists call 'benefit finding'. It's another strand of positive psychology.

Benefit finding can be done in just a few minutes but its effects are remarkable. It works like this. Michael McCullough and colleagues from the University of Miami conducted an experiment across three different groups of people each comprising a sample size of roughly 100 people[35]. All participants were asked to think about, and then describe, an occasion when they had suffered one of these non-physical assaults ... when someone's actions had been exceptionally hurtful. Then one group was asked to write in greater depth about their feelings of hurt. Another group was asked to think hard and write about any benefits that directly or indirectly arose out of the incident. These may be greater insight and awareness, greater emotional intelligence, new opportunities that arose out of rejection, benefits to focus or motivation, or any other form of silver lining that could be identified. To provide a control, participants in a third group were simply asked to describe their plans for the next day.

Attitudes towards the person who caused the upset were then measured via a questionnaire. The evidence was overwhelming. Feelings of anger, resentment and desire for revenge had subsided dramatically among the group who were focused on benefit finding.

## Summary

- 'Benefit finding' is the bulletproof person's silver lining, which brings insight, new opportunities, etc., following a non-physical assault
- When you are going through a tough time, practise 'benefit finding': imagine you are standing in the future, then imagine you are listing the benefits that arose from the situation – perhaps new insight and learning, increased confidence as you learnt to cope or perhaps the incident caused you to do something that you would not otherwise have done, which opened up a new opportunity

# CHAPTER 7
## TURNING AROUND FAILURES AND SETBACKS

Mistakes and setbacks are the snakes in the game of Snakes and Ladders of working life. Here again, the initial temptation might be to let our instincts run riot, but taking some time and being mindful is a much more effective way to start climbing up those ladders again.

### Case Study 7.1

Malcolm was the first person in his family to go to university and he was proud of his degree in accountancy, as was his family. 'My mum must have about 98 photos of me in my cap and gown with my degree,' he said, laughing, as we sat on the balcony of the flat which he shared with his partner and their daughter.

Malcolm, 38, had risen to become one of the heads of finance in a large engineering and infrastructure company. He was well respected and well liked throughout the organisation, and his bosses clearly had him marked out for promotion. Then, one day, it all changed.

'We were all in the annual budget meeting – the other heads of finance and the CFO,' he told us. 'I'd been promoted just over a year earlier and so I now had to take charge of a much bigger chunk of the budget than ever before – in fact the largest part of the whole of the firm's expenditure.'

It was a daunting prospect but Malcolm felt that he was up to it. He'd worked hard with his team over the previous few weeks to check the numbers, to make sure that every column added up and that every element of income and expenditure had been taken into account.

But suddenly in the meeting with the other senior finance people those numbers didn't make sense. Sitting around the table with coffee cups and a mass of papers in front of them, his colleagues were working their way through the spreadsheets that Malcolm had given them – and they were beginning to look increasingly confused.

'The CFO asked about some figures that he said didn't look right at all. Then a colleague sitting next to me, who I've always regarded as a bit of a rival, asked, "Aren't some of these figures last year's?" Suddenly the whole thing made sense, and I thought I was going to be sick.'

His laptop had crashed a few weeks earlier, taking with it figures he'd been working on. As a result, he'd had to upload a whole raft of figures again. Highly meticulous as always, he'd spent a frustrating day checking various files and spreadsheets and replacing some with newer versions while simply copying others from the server and deleting more.

'I thought that I'd got everything back up to date,' he said. 'The problem is that my team was all new and so they'd never have known which figures dated from last year and which were current.'

The upshot? Vital funds on which the forecasts had been planned and future budgets set simply weren't there.

'It was a complete and utter disaster for the whole of the organisation,' said Malcolm. 'As I drove home that night, I kept replaying the meeting over and over in my head and telling myself that thousands of people were going to suffer because of my cock-up.'

He was convinced that he'd be sacked. He'd never get a job in finance again. The voice in Malcolm's head was familiar to many of us. It kept telling him that he'd let all of his colleagues down badly. What's more, he'd been found out. The boy who'd got to university against all the odds had ideas above his station. He was an impostor; he wasn't actually as good at his job as he'd pretended to be and now he'd been discovered.

## Decontaminate your mistakes

We have discussed ways in which you can bulletproof yourself against the setbacks and assaults of the workplace, but what about when our undoing is of our own making? When that voice in our heads tells us we don't deserve to be bulletproof, this time the assault is not from the outside in: it's the gremlin in our personality that will 'always' expose us for the untrustworthy impostor that we are.

The issue is not that we fail to learn from mistakes and failure, it's that, nestled deep in our brains, we have a ruthless teacher to remind ourselves. The problem is that it is a teacher that lacks compassion, subtlety and flexibility. These are attributes that we need to learn for ourselves.

Mistakes, like defeats, result in a drop in testosterone and an increase in cortisol. There is a sound adaptive explanation for this physiology. After a mistake, it makes sense to withdraw from the fray. Observe a sports star who makes an unforced error. In the following moments, the sense of hapless nervousness and uncertainty is almost palpable. A crucial difference between us and sports stars is that, for the sports star, the effect is typically temporary. Through sports psychology, they learn to realign their mindset. For many of us in the workplace, we are not so lucky. The mistake can be the start of a domino effect.[36]

Mistakes and setbacks are contagious. Once one happens, it tends to contaminate the next thing you do. Top-performing sports stars learn to decontaminate mistakes and setbacks.

Dr Tim Rees, from Exeter University, has researched into and published widely in the area of recoverability from failure. Tim recognises that an athlete who has suffered a setback will be prone to the same type of thinking errors that tend to affect all of us when things go wrong. Tim encourages athletes to 'be their own sports psychologists'. Taking time to be aware of your thinking is the first step in retraining your thoughts so that they work better for you.

'Very negative thinking can emerge,' Dr Rees explains. 'We suffer a performance failure and then start thinking, "It's all out of my control, it will happen again, it *always* happens to me."' Rees recognises that the first step in reversing the cycle is simple awareness: 'Stop and ask yourself, "Why am I having these thoughts?"' Once we are aware, we can start to challenge our thinking distortions and replace them with thoughts that are more helpful.'

Top performers decontaminate failure and stop it spreading by separating the *facts* of what happened in a clear, non-emotive way from the *story* or interpretation of what happened. It is a habit that anyone who wants to be bulletproof can pick up and learn.

Because our minds like consistency and they naturally want to form things into coherent stories, when we make a mistake and suffer the consequences we start to see it as the part of a pattern or 'story'. We often feel so devastated after a mistake because somehow the mistake feels like a part of our life-story. And, of course, we fear that story determines our future. 'You see,' our minds are telling us, 'things always work out this way for me.'

When we make a mistake, particularly a big one, we are inclined to see it as being in some way about us – in some way attributable to characteristics about ourselves. And when we view mistakes in this way, we are far less inclined to make a speedy recovery from them.

As script consultant Christopher Vogler describes it, you're now in the cave, a low point in the 'script' of your life (see page 128). Either way, as we know, you will get out of it and you will benefit from it as a result.

So, writing down what happened, being aware of what is emotion and personal impression on the one hand, and what is hard fact on the other, will help. It's a useful next step to follow the factual description with: 'As a result, I am feeling ...' Then give a name to your emotion or blend of emotions. In addition, of course, build in those useful, realistic modifying phrases such as, 'At this time ...', or 'Right now ...', because this is a temporary state of affairs.

## Summary

- Reframe and describe the incident, taking the toxic, negative emotions out of it
- Note your emotions alongside the facts
- Be honest and don't try to exculpate yourself or shirk your responsibility

## De-catastrophise

Let's return to Jane from chapter two. Sitting at her desk on Monday morning, she switched on her computer and discovered an email from a client rejecting her proposal. Now imagine, Jane starts to dwell on things. After all, thinks Jane, this won't be the last proposal to be rejected, and it will no doubt happen again. In fact, it will probably happen to *all* her proposals. Soon her employer will need to take action and let her go. Then who will take her on, knowing she was let go from her previous job? With her new-found penury, her family life will break up. Friends will desert her, she concludes, as they don't want to be associated with such a failure. Unable to make the mortgage payments, she fears that she will be out on the streets … and so it goes on.

We have exaggerated Jane's scenario a little, but we know that this thinking trap, known as catastrophising, is a common one. Remember our inner cave dweller is innately anxious and pessimistic. In our ancestor's world it made sense to plan for the worst. Our minds weigh up the potential negative consequences of the situation; this presents a new negative scenario. What would be the potential negative consequences of this more negative scenario…?, and so our thinking spirals into ever greater potential catastrophe. The tendency to catastrophise is another reason why incidents often hurt us far more than they should.

Bulletproof Jane recognises this catastrophising for what it is. She is capable of stepping back from these thoughts. Sure, the worst-case scenario is not impossible, thinks Jane, but what realistically is the probability? What is the most likely case scenario based on the evidence? Recognising that dwelling on how bad things could get is really not helpful, Jane chooses to focus her attention on the things that she can directly influence to make the best-case scenario more probable.

By looking objectively at his situation with some external help, Malcolm can see that he's catastrophising. In other words, suffering as he is from shock, self-doubt and even anger that he's betrayed his own very high standards, he can begin to see that he's making the situation sound worse than it really is. Malcolm should ask himself, 'Have I just set unrelentingly high standards for myself?'

Here is a useful grading technique to use when in this situation: ask yourself, 'On a scale of zero to 100, how bad is it?' The answer will often be something like: '90 per cent bad.' Then put other people's mistakes in there. Inevitably this '90 per cent' will need to be revised downwards as you make comparisons. It might end up at just 40 per cent.

Standing back and looking at the *facts*, rather than his feelings about them, Malcolm began to realise that an error on the budgets was bad news, but it wasn't a disaster. He also understood that neither were his predictions of the disastrous knock-on effects of his mistake. These were the worst-case scenario and, therefore, not impossible, he realised, but what realistically was the probability of them happening?

'It was horrible at the time,' he said, 'but looking back I also became more self-aware. I realised that I'd actually often set myself unrealistically high standards. Why did I think that I was the one person in the world who would never make a mistake, for instance? It also dawned on me how much I've been doing to make my mum and my family proud. I should be thinking about how *I* feel, not them. Deep down, on some level, I felt like I'd let my mum down and that she'd be disappointed.'

Humans have a tendency to catastrophise: to become fixated on the worst-case scenario. Become aware of this unhelpful line of thinking. Abandon your crystal ball; far better to simply let the future unfold. It will almost certainly not be as bad as you fear and you will almost certainly be able to cope. And the good news is that these are not just idle platitudes, but are backed up by hard research. Daniel Gilbert, Harvard Professor of Psychology, has discovered that people tend to significantly underestimate their ability to cope with, or tolerate, changes in circumstances that they fear. The old adage, 'Cheer up, it can't be that bad,' has some scientific backing.[37]

## Summary

O Catastrophising is a common thinking trap that makes incidents hurt us more than they should

○ Bulletproof people step back from catastrophising, objectively weigh their scenarios and identify what is credibly optimistic

## From 'all-or-nothing' to 'both-and' thinking

### Case Study 7.2

Javier finally won a place on the graduate fast-track programme of a major corporation. Determined to make the most of the opportunity, he vowed to himself that he would be an exemplary leader and manager in the organisation. At the start of this new opportunity, he wrote down his goals and his commitments to himself, and made a point of revisiting these lists at the end of each day, and challenging himself as to whether he had lived up to them. This worked for Javier. He proved himself to be competent and focused. He was respected by the team he managed, and increasingly caught the eye of senior leadership.

One morning, Javier slept through his alarm. He arrived late for his team meeting – not disastrously late, but nonetheless, in Javier's view, *too* late. High-calibre managers don't act like this, he told himself. Javier felt that he had let himself down. He angrily ripped up his list of goals and commitments, and asked himself whom he was kidding.

A small incident had knocked Javier off track because of his all-or-nothing thinking: if it's true of me this morning, over this incident, it's true of me as a person across my career. Your New Year's resolution is to go to the gym every evening, or to always eat healthily; you miss an evening, or eat a doughnut, and you abandon your goals altogether. Successful people do not make mistakes, so when you make a mistake you conclude that you are unlikely to be successful.

Bulletproof Javier will be frank with himself. It's still not acceptable to be late for a team meeting, and this is not the standard that he requires of himself, but he will reason that even the best make the occasional slip-up. It is possible to be both great at what you do and sometimes make a mistake. His negative feelings will subside and he will be re-focused again.

'Both-and' thinking is the converse of 'all-or-nothing' thinking. Become aware of where you may be applying 'both-and' thinking. Where are you extrapolating a rule from one incident to cover something universal? What are you making this incident or event mean about you, your future or the world? When you sense that you may be slipping into 'all-or-nothing' thinking, apply 'both-and' thinking. Ask yourself is it possible for both $x$ and $y$ to be true at the same time? What evidence would you cite in favour of the idea that the 'both-and' explanation may be valid?

### Summary

O Bulletproof people know when they are applying 'all-or-nothing' thinking – and review their approach

O Bulletproof people don't extrapolate rules from one incident to cover all situations

O Bulletproof people ask themselves, 'Can *both* this *and* that be true at the same time?'

# Describe in factual and neutral terms

Something happens to you and it is preying on your mind. It may be something that you have done. You don't want to let it bother you so much, but you can't seem to shake it.

Imagine the 'wiser-you' could describe the incident that is on your mind, in terms that are as factual and neutral as possible. We call this an FaN description. Factual, as in just the elements that could be indisputably verified, and neutral, as in what a dispassionate observer would see.

The FaN description is a remarkably useful exercise. You may not find it always immediately easy to put things into entirely factual and neutral terms; the key is to avoid any adjectives or descriptors that suggest you are making any sort of judgement on the issue.

To give an example, perhaps we could make a small digression. Psychologist Elizabeth Loftus undertook a now-famous experiment in the 1970s, which illustrated how the words used about an incident can alter the reality that we observe. Participants in the experiment were asked to observe footage of two cars colliding. They were then asked to estimate the speed of one of the cars. Here's the twist: participants in one group were asked to estimate the speed of car A when it 'smashed into' car B; participants in the control group were simply asked to estimate the speed when it 'collided with'. The outcome? Those in the group where the phrase 'smashed into' was used estimated the speed at roughly 30% higher than the estimate for the control. 'Smashed' carries a judgement.

Become aware of how you describe incidents to yourself. If you are using terms like I *messed* up or I *screwed* up, or he *humiliated* me, or she *ignored* me, you are building your own interpretation of what happened into the incident.

For example, something happens. The way you think about what happened governs your feelings and the way you feel physically for some time afterwards: *I messed up again and totally failed to upload the right figures. Now I'm responsible for screwing up the whole project. The committee really ripped into me about it and everyone thinks I'm useless.*

The 'wiser-you' would ask you to describe accurately what happened but simply focus on the facts, taking emotion and interpretation out of it: *In error, I uploaded some incorrect figures. This error is likely to cause a delay in the project. The committee expressed some strong feeling about this.* This is true and accurate, but the heat and toxicity have been removed. Looking at it this way, your thinking is clearer and you are better placed to plan something constructive to do about the situation.

Stepping back from a situation and re-describing it in a factual and neutral way is something that bulletproof people make a habit of doing. Using the idea of the 'wiser-you', who is able to see things more clearly, free from the feelings that arise in the heat of the moment, is a good way to do this. Next time an incident happens that really plays on your mind, try the FaN description. Feel your thinking become calmer and clearer.

Many of us, without realising it, live our lives at the whim of our thoughts and their ensuing emotions. We act accordingly. People who take a moment to reflect on their thoughts and emotions make better choices. They recover from setbacks quicker and better. And they exercise greater control over their lives.

Again, putting your mistake into context by thinking of it as part of your story and writing it down is useful. Keep the description as factual and dispassionate as possible. Stick to what happened. (By the way, avoid using the passive tense, such as 'a collision took place'. People use this sort of language when they try to exculpate themselves. Simply stick to the facts.[38]

## Summary

- ○ Learn to imagine the objective 'wiser-you'
- ○ Work with the 'wiser-you' to remove the heat and toxicity from difficult situations
- ○ Describe what happened in purely factual and neutral terms

# Name the emotion. This is what happened. This is how I feel about it

Our emotions drive our behaviour. If they didn't we wouldn't function. People who have undergone brain damage that inhibits the emotional function of the brain do not suddenly turn into clinical, highly rational calculating machines in the mode of *Star Trek*'s Mr Spock. In fact, neurologists who treat such patients notice something quite different. They become incapable of making straightforward decisions. They might, for example, find it very difficult simply to choose a time for their next appointment. They lack the facility for a shortcut to give them a ready sense of the best option.[39]

It may seem like an advantage to be unencumbered by emotion. However, evidence clearly shows that people who have limited emotional functioning make worse decisions, not better ones. After all, aren't global corporations forever stating that they want their leaders to be 'visionary'? What is 'vision' if not a product of the emotions?

Emotions guide and propel us. Greater awareness of our emotions allows us to steward them to our advantage. But lack of awareness of our emotions leaves us at their mercy. Many people spend their lives as if they are tied to a wild and capricious horse, and in many ways the metaphorical horse is invisible to them. They suffer its jolts and vicissitudes without being aware of it. Continuing with the metaphor, the first step is to 'know' the horse, become aware of it, starting by simply observing it, and being interested in it. Mindfulness teaches us to do this with our emotions.

The legacy of being human is to have a rich repertoire of emotions. Most of the time we do what feels right. Our emotions drive us. When an event that is important to you happens, it gives rise to a thought, and then a feeling. And it is the feeling that is keeping it in your mind.

Here is the key: describe the feeling without judging; imagine you could put it on the table in front of you; focus on the accuracy of the description, as if it were being experienced by someone else; focus on accurate language, not heated or loaded terms. This is not about feeling it or amplifying.

A good way to take some of the heat out of your description, but keep the accuracy, is to add in phrases that place a little distance between you and the feeling. A good one is: *I notice myself feeling...* or *I noticed I started to feel...* Then put it together with your FaN description. For example, let's put ourselves is the shoes of Gloria. Imagine that she recently did an important client presentation, and that she has just taken a call from her colleague Jose with some news that has taken her aback.

So, *X* happened – *e.g. Jose telephoned to say that the client team had said that they were very unhappy with the presentation that I gave this morning* – and Gloria then names the emotion: *I notice myself feeling ...*

Once you have named the emotion, we suggest that you add in a couple of modifying statements which will reduce any thinking distortions and provide more accurate perspective on the situation. The first one is to remind yourself that the feeling is transient. You are feeling it right now, but not for ever. So add in the modifier 'right now', or similar. The second one is to remind yourself that the feeling is particular to the incident and not universal, so qualify the statement with 'about this situation', or similar. Phrases like 'relatively' will also remind you to keep it in perspective.

And finally, the icing on the cake of all modifying statements: finish with the phrase, '*but I am okay*' (because realistically, you know that you are).

Gloria had taken the call from Jose. Right afterwards she felt and acted like someone who had been hit by a metaphorical freight train and her mind had gone into 'under-attack' mode. Her self-talk centred on phrases like 'humiliated', 'nightmare' and 'shattered'.

By reframing, using the methods that we talk about in this section, Gloria took the heat (but not the weight) out of the way she was feeling: 'I feel relatively despondent and crestfallen about this situation right now, but I am okay.'

## Summary

○ Bulletproof people can influence their thoughts and feelings by being actively aware of them
○ Bulletproof people know how to train their cave dweller by putting their emotions into words
○ Bulletproof people can describe what they feel in a clear, accurate and balanced way

# Learn from your mistakes

### Case Study 7.3

'I'll be known for ever as the guy who lost the big one. That was all I could think of while I was watching my colleagues clear their desks.' For years,

Robin had looked forward to becoming a partner at the very traditional engineering and construction firm at which he worked.

'I had big plans,' he went on, staring at his shoes as he talked. 'I was going to make some big changes, bring us up-to-the-minute ... consolidate what we've got and then target some sexy new contracts.'

The prospect of losing the company's bread-and-butter maintenance contract had not even crossed his mind until the unusually cold and stilted telephone call came through to inform him that his company had been unsuccessful in its tender. The client in question had been the organisation's first major maintenance contract. It had formed the basis of the firm's gradual and cautious growth. Its renewal had been taken for granted.

'After the phone call, I called the whole team together and gave a stirring speech about how we were going to bounce back stronger and better than before,' Robin continued. 'It seemed to go down pretty well. But when I drew up to the car park each morning, I literally couldn't get out of my car. I just sat and stared, kind of paralysed. I felt like a fraud. I was the guy who was all talk, but couldn't hold it together when the moment came. I felt myself starting to blame everybody in my mind: colleagues, bosses, and even my family.'

Evidence from the field of sports psychology suggests that those who forensically seek to understand why they failed tend to bounce back better from failure. This seems to be at odds with the evidence from the field of medicine that suggested that those who perform best were those who deploy the 'defensive externalism' when things go wrong. Defensive externalism is the process of attributing successes to what you do, and yet attributing your failures to factors that are entirely outside of your control. In other words, the view that 'When I do well, it's down to me; when I don't, it is down to other things or other people.' People who do this tend to be more successful than average.

How can both findings be true? Well, to understand we need to look at what both the successful sports people and the successful medical graduates are *not* doing. They both use strategies to protect themselves from viewing failure as something that is due to inherent factors over which they have little influence. If something cannot be readily changed its effect is likely to be repeated. This is why many of us go on to unwittingly encompass failure in the life-story that we tell ourselves.

We suggest that successful sports people take things a step further than defensive externalism. Defensive externalism protects us from destructive thoughts, but it's less effective at creating momentum to reverse a situation of failure.

The challenge to top performers is how to think about failures enough to take steps to reverse them, but without the toxic thoughts. This is why sports psychologists understand the principle of waiting to give feedback when the emotions are stable.

Trophy-winning soccer coach, Carlo Ancelotti, understood this. Working with sports psychologist Bruno Demichelis, they together created the idea of the MilanLab at AC Milan, and imported a similar idea to Chelsea. The principle is to find a space that is so conducive to a relaxed state of mind that a player can view previous performances, and understand errors and steps required to improve them, but in a way that removes the rawness of feeling so there is no element of self-judgement. It is the ability to view self-improvement simply as a project with a series of requisite steps that marks out winners.[40]

Athletes in this relaxed state of mind match the same patterns as those who are in a state of mindfulness. This brings us back to one of the main theses in this book: mindfulness enables us to think clearly and reduce emotional distortions to our thinking, which in turn allows us to improve.[41]

Is this a mistake, failure or setback that you can learn from? If I lose a major contract or lose at a game of tennis, there is a fair chance that I can learn from the incident. If it is a one-off unusual error, like Malcolm's, the chances of learning will be less (but the likelihood of repeating it will be smaller). If you want to learn from your mistakes, mindfulness helps. Relax and become aware of the emotion that you associate with the mistake. Imagine you can see that mistake in front of you, like a cloud drifting across the sky. Don't judge it or react to it: just be comfortable letting it drift. Imagine now that you are switching on a small black and white TV set. Imagine that you are watching solely to learn. Enjoy the process of learning from your mistake and praise yourself for any useful insights that you garner. If you feel the emotion returning, that's okay. Remember to let it drift like a cloud.

## Summary
- Bulletproof people set aside the emotional story that seems to want to accompany any failure or setback
- They view bouncing back as a project, and simply identify the things that they can improve upon. They then set about planning those improvements, one step at a time

# Focus on what you can change

People who most readily bounce back from failure are those who focus on things that they can change: things that are within their direct sphere of control, about which they can start making systematic changes, no matter how small. Think of a tennis player who has just suffered a humiliating defeat on the tennis court. It may seem that the most obvious goal to set oneself to recover is to trounce one's next opponent (better still if it's the opponent who has just handed out the humiliating defeat). This, however, may be counterproductive. Sure it may be a worthwhile goal, but it is an external or result-based goal. There are too many elements that are outside of our tennis player's direct control. Our tennis player gets little rewarding sense of progress until the next match. Even at the next match he has no control over how his opponent plays, so much of whether he achieves this goal or not is outside of his control. It would be far better for him to focus on perfecting his backhand or serve, or another relevant aspect of his game.

Sports psychologists would encourage the tennis player to focus on 'process goals'. These are goals that are not result areas, but which lead towards results, in a way that can readily be identified and measured and most crucially over which our tennis player has complete control.

For example, if our tennis player recognises that it was his serve or his backhand that let him down, he may set goals around improving the speed or accuracy of his backhand or serve.

Julie Douglas is a top sports psychologist and ex-international swimmer from Loughborough University. She explains how she works with a swimmer who has just suffered a real slump in performance: 'It's really important to highlight the importance of focusing on their own personal improvement. We encourage athletes to focus on their own goals – process goals – and this gives them something to work on that they can control.'

Bulletproof people work hard at improvement but they are also clear about what they can control. When Robin first heard that his team had failed to retain the bread-and-butter account, he may have felt that the biggest and boldest way to bounce back would have been to win the next big tender. It would certainly be stretching and focus the mind, but this is what we call an 'outcome goal' rather than a 'process goal'. Robin would be overestimating the extent to which he controlled the outcome. The goal may fail due to reasons out of his control or because the stretch was too great. The result: another punch in the solar plexus and an increased risk of failure contamination.

Bulletproof people recognise that some things will always be outside their control. Broadly speaking, effort leads to improvement, but the actual results cannot be guaranteed. Bulletproof people focus on 'process goals'. Set yourself goals related to the effort and input that you can control, praise yourself for achieving these goals, and give yourself plenty of small rewards along the way. It would be more effective for Robin to focus, for example, on delivering the perfect sales presentation, or writing the perfect project proposal. These are process goals; they are entirely within his control.

Misha Botting, a sports psychologist working with Sportscotland Institute of Sport, also finds that the best way to help an athlete to recover from setbacks is to focus on process goals. 'After a competition,' he says, 'we specifically review the performance in relation to process goals. We break down the processes to identify the things that are in the athlete's control to work on and improve. That way we can control their focus, moving from dwelling on the sense of setback or failure to thinking about what can be controlled and what can be improved.'

To recover from setback and failure, focus on the process goals – the goals you influence directly – and make them challenging, but go for one small step at a time and take pleasure in noticing your improvements. Enjoy improving simply for the pleasure of improving. Identify an aspect of performance in your role, no matter how seemingly small, over which you have control, and take pleasure in working on improvement. Set yourself the goal of becoming as good as possible.

## Have a recovery plan

### Case Study 7.4

As a medical man, Louis recognised the signs of panic in his own body. As he looked down at the invoice, his sight and vision seemed to go fuzzy as his heart palpitated. The invoice showed that (while tired and overworked) he had over-prescribed a powerful drug by a factor of ten. Louis had worked hard to qualify as a pharmacist and he knew this could be the end of the road. He telephoned the retirement community where the elderly patient resided to find out how much trouble he was in, and he discovered that he was unlucky. The patient had been rushed to hospital in the night and died – the overdose was almost certainly a major contributing factor. Some weeks later, Louis was contacted by the local police. They wanted to interview him in connection with a possible manslaughter charge. Louis faced a possible custodial sentence. What was significant is what Louis did between identifying the mistake and the call from the police: he did nothing.

Just as many of us find after making a big mistake, Louis was caught in a stasis between debilitating fear and delusional hope that it would somehow go away. Had he taken decisive action and informed his employer (and received legal and medical council), Louis would not have saved the gentleman, he may not even have saved his career in pharmacy, but he would have avoided criminal charges, recovered his self-esteem and lived to fight another day.

You *will* make mistakes. When you do so, you need a recovery plan. You need to ask yourself: Are you avoiding the issue? Are you somehow hoping that it will go away? Because it won't! Instead, when you make a mistake, follow the three 'C's of control, challenge and commitment:

1. In fixing the situation or improving it as much as possible, what elements are within your **control**?
2. How can you frame the process of fixing or improving the session in terms of a **challenge**?
3. Once you have defined the elements that you can control and set the challenge, go about it with the greatest **commitment**.

## Summary

○ Differentiate realistically between what you can affect and what you can't when it comes to achieving success
○ Set yourself process goals – goals related to the effort and input that you can control – rather than outcome goals – results which you can't
○ Praise yourself for achieving these goals, and give yourself plenty of small rewards along the way

# Achieve something small in order to achieve something big

If you take some relatively small steps, focusing on things that are within your control, and you achieve some small successes, you will increase your sense of personal effectiveness and subsequently your confidence and energy. Initially termed by the eminent psychologist Albert Bandura, this is what psychologists now call 'learnt self-efficacy'. The idea is a vital one for anyone looking to bounce back from a slump in confidence and performance.

Bandura set about helping people to overcome phobias, such as a phobia of snakes, which can often be debilitating: even for people who live where snakes don't exist, the mere thought of them can take over their lives. By working closely with the subject on a one-to-one basis and encouraging the client to push himself further step by step, exposing himself to the source of his phobia, Bandura could enable subjects, who had previously been incapacitated by the mere thought of a snake, to comfortably handle live snakes within a few hours.[42]

But the story did not end there. Follow-up research with the same patients discovered that many of the subjects had experienced a sharp increase in other achievements in their lives. It seems that the confidence boost from handling the snake had convinced the subject that he could readily achieve other goals in other aspects of life. Bandura captured the psychological process that appeared to be happening in the term 'learnt self-efficacy'. Once we start to experience success in one aspect of our lives, however modest, the mind harnesses the confidence that we gain, and uses it as a template to achieve other goals. If you want to give your bulletproofing a boost, give your self-efficacy a boost.

Dr Karen Reivich, co-author of *The Resilience Factor*[43] and one of the world's leading researchers into resilience, came to the same conclusion: she identified 'self-efficacy' as one of the key pillars of resilience. Self-efficacy is confidence in your ability to solve problems. This is partly about knowing what your strengths and weaknesses are and relying on your strengths to cope. Reivich stresses that this is different to self-esteem. In other words, it is not just about feeling good about yourself; it is about knowing that you can master the skills that will be needed to cope in a situation.

Think about somebody you know who is a high achiever. The chances are that this person will be a high achiever in more than one aspect of life (infuriating, isn't it?). Our minds like congruence and consistency. Achieving in one aspect of life activates a template in our minds that we then tend to take forward into the next situation.

Set yourself some near-term goals that are challenging, but readily achievable through factors within your control. When you achieve them, make a point of letting your mind dwell on the success – how it came about, how it felt and what it says about you. Go and achieve something small but stretching, and then a slightly larger stretch goal, and keep repeating the process, making each goal slightly more stretching than the last. (And of course, you should fail at least some of these goals because, if you don't, you are not setting goals that are stretching enough.)[44]

## Summary

- O The best way to achieve a big success is to get in the 'success habit' by achieving some smaller successes first
- O First set yourself some more modest and readily achievable goals
- O Dwell in the feeling and enjoy the success, and then set yourself some relatively more stretching goals

# CHAPTER 8
## WINNING IN THE FACE OF POLITICS AND OSTRACISM

Humans are naturally sociable animals. We prefer to live and work in groups. Whether it's day-to-day politics, or getting the cold shoulder from colleagues, being ostracised or rejected by a group, however subtle it might be, triggers our sense of unease. Either extremes of dealing with office and politics and being ostracised by completely ignoring the problem, or, conversely, dealing with it using a forceful approach are not helpful; this chapter will look at how to win in the face of politics and ostracism.

### Case Study 8.1

Jack had been relaxed about the merger. After all, at the age of 51, having worked in IT for nearly 30 years, he had seen it all before. His division had been de-merged several years ago. Now the pendulum was swinging the other way and it was all about integrating various different units to get greater synergy.

'Or something like that,' said Jack, rolling his eyes. But this time it was different. 'It began to dawn on me pretty soon that the rest of the people I worked with had either jumped ship or had new roles as leaders in this new, larger division.'

As we walked through his local park kicking leaves and enjoying the pale autumn sunshine, Jack went on.

'Then I started to hear rumours on the grapevine that I was being talked of as a troublemaker, some sort of Luddite who wanted to cling to the past and resist change.'

Jack was told his performance was not up to scratch. A working group was set up, which appeared to be duplicating exactly what Jack's team had specialised in. Consultation with Jack on the matter was cursory and perfunctory. He felt that he had gone from a senior and admired stakeholder in the company to a dead man walking.

'Suddenly everyone seemed to have new titles except me, and then this new guy was brought in – he was still in short trousers, for goodness' sake – and everyone else was running around trying to please him,' said Jack. 'I watched people of my age who I've worked with for years suddenly spouting this trendy management speak. It was awful – I just couldn't stand the politics.'

## Case Study 8.2

Claire was surprised to be appointed head of HR. She had been one of a team of HR business partners, and she, like the others, had assumed that the vacancy for their boss's position would be filled with an appointment from outside. She was, nonetheless, delighted. She would now head up the team of HR business partners, all of whom she knew well.

However, Claire noticed that things were amiss. Her colleagues seemed uninterested, surly and recalcitrant at team meetings. They seemed to be actively enjoying expressing their lack of enthusiasm at any suggestion put forward by Claire. Simple tasks that she requested would remain undone, met with lame excuses. The team would talk little in her presence but animatedly by the coffee machine – conversations that seemed to Claire to be conspiratorial and exclusive.

She felt her status as team-leader was under attack and she responded by using more overtly high-status behaviour and attempts to demonstrate her authority. Word soon reached Claire that team members had been disparaging the rest of the team to internal clients, claiming it was divided and leaderless.

'I'd always assumed that the head of department role would go to some-one from outside the company and I only went along to the interview because I thought it would be good to keep my interview skills polished,' admitted the 38-year-old mother of two. 'But when I got it, so many people inside the company and outside told me that I deserved it. I remember that my husband looked surprised when I said that I couldn't believe that they'd offered me the job. He sat me down in the living room and said, "You've worked so hard over the years – you deserve this." The kids made me cards to say "Well done, Mummy".

'Things started well but after just a few weeks I began to feel that my colleagues were no longer committed in the way I was,' she said. 'I assumed that perhaps they were just getting used to the new situation – after all, some of them had been on the same level as me just a few weeks earlier and one or two had even been technically senior to me, whereas I was now the boss.'

Claire found that people arrived late for her departmental meetings and that they either sat in silence or put up objections to her ideas. They seemed to be enjoying expressing their lack of enthusiasm at any suggestion she put forward. Simple tasks that she requested would remain undone, despite her repeated reminders. Her new ideas never seemed to see the light of day and even regular activities were overlooked.

'I'd walk out into the open-plan office where I used to sit and suddenly the chat and laughter would stop. A few times I went into the kitchen area and the other people there fell silent – I was sure that they'd been talking about me. I can understand that some people were jealous about my promotion but I'd been given the job fairly and squarely and that was it.'

Claire's attempts to organise a drink after work fell flat and she soon began to feel seriously low, especially when the company's CEO started to notice that the HR department was falling behind.

## If you put three people in a room, you've got politics

When you're caught on the wrong side of office politics, it isn't pretty. Everyone (or almost everyone) claims to dislike politics, yet virtually everyone says that they witness it, in some form or other, in their place of work. The apparent contradiction is explained by the fact that we only see a situation as politics when we are caught on the wrong side of it. Otherwise, it is just the way people are.

There is a saying that if you put three people in a room, you've got politics. And why wouldn't you? If politics is about power, influence and relationships, then these phenomena are at the heart of our modern species.

Collaboration is an essential part of being human, and the primary means by which we have survived so long. The idea that evolution leads us to become more selfish is wrong. Evidence shows that we have actually evolved to become more and more cooperative. It is likely that those in the past who were disinclined to cooperate would have been unlikely to survive. This is because, in the field of human endeavour and organisation, win-win situations are more common than zero-sum-gain situations.[45]

Central to human survival and growth is the idea of 'Non-Zero-Sum-Gain': the idea that if we cooperate together, we are both better off. To do this, we need language to cooperate and then we need emotions that facilitate interaction with others, for example, sympathy, empathy, trust, a sense of justice and ethics.

Here's an optimistic note! Not only does conflict arise out of our evolutionary past, but so does conflict resolution. Naturally, in survival terms it is better not to fight; resolution saves the cost of fighting. Conflict resolution is central to being human – though if you are caught in the cut and thrust of politics right now, it probably doesn't feel that way.

Our cave-dwelling ancestor needed to be very quick in forming judgements. This also helps to explain a phenomenon that psychologists refer to as 'Negativity Bias'. In short, our ancestors were particularly fine-tuned to threat or danger and quick to see the negative. For them, mistaking a potential friend for an enemy was a wasted opportunity, but mistaking an enemy for a friend was likely to be fatal. This means that today we are also sometimes inclined to judge too quickly, to be too steadfast in our initial opinion and to overemphasise threat and hostility. Our minds too readily polarise situations into friend or foe.

## Summary

○ Politics is about power, influence and relationships

○ We only see a situation as politics when we're caught on the wrong side of it

○ Although conflict arises out of our evolutionary past, so too does conflict resolution

○ *But* we often judge too fast, overemphasise threats and too readily polarise situations as friend or foe. Standing back from the situation, trying to avoid seeing everything as black and white or good and bad, will help create a more accurate, useful picture on which we can act

# Engaging in office politics is a survival technique – recognise this and don't get emotional about it

Humans collaborate because of the principle of Non-Zero-Sum-Gain. If we band together to hunt the woolly mammoth, we get a share of a much bigger kill, and so we get to eat better than if we hunted individually. If, as the accounts department, the sales execs and the IT people, for instance, we all work together on a project, we all benefit far more than if we tried to do the whole thing ourselves.

Where there is clear alignment between the individuals' needs and those of the larger team, there is harmony. As this team increases in size, its overall goals become more complex, as do the fears and motivations of the people in it. The fields of both psychology and economics tell us that the fear of loss is a greater motivator than the joy of gain. We suggest, therefore, that most politics are defensive. Far from scheming world domination, when most people indulge in politics it's because they are seeking to defend themselves.

And, by the way, individual interests come first for all of us, and so they should. Collaborating to achieve collective goals is the means by which to meet individual interests. If our ancestor had simply allowed individual interests to be subordinated to collective goals, this would have been an unwise survival strategy and we would probably not be here today.

On the other hand, in our view corporations often put implicit pressure on people to take part in a masquerade whereby participants are required to pretend that individual needs either do not exist or are somehow unmentionable and not legitimate. Politics arises where people feel the need to disguise individual interests, needs and concerns. Instead, these manifest themselves via implicit and unseen relationships and alliances.

Politics comes down to the needs of the individual that remain unspoken. We can openly discuss our motivation to perform, achieve team goals, beat the competition and make money for our employer. We somehow feel the need to pretend that we do not have other obvious needs, such as: the need to protect our own personal livelihood and security, should these come under threat; the need to put ourselves in line for the next scarce promotion opportunity; the need for a sense of belonging, inclusion, status and respect among the group.

As we know, a useful way to reduce unhelpful feelings and to restore clear thinking is to write things down. When he did this, Jack was careful to recognise that he, too, has material and psychological needs with regard to the potential to gain and risk of loss that comes from working with a group of people. It is also important to keep reminding yourself not to make a judgement about the legitimacy of other people's interests. Don't expect the way in which other people respond to their interests to be entirely rational and reasonable, either – they're fallible human beings like you.

Put yourself in the shoes of colleagues who are also involved in the situation. What might be their material or psychological needs that they feel are currently under threat? Note that this is not slipping into the mind-reading trap; it is simply attempting to imagine the situation from other people's points of view. You must remain conscious that you do not know for certain what they are thinking.

For example, if a colleague on a project seems to be keeping you in the dark and preventing you from receiving information, it may well be because they feel insecure. When under pressure, it might feel that knowledge is power and that keeping this knowledge to themselves is useful in shoring up their position. Perhaps they're just feeling out of their depth generally.

The first step in dealing with politics is to restore your clear thinking in order to allow your unhelpful feelings to subside. This involves seeing the politics for what it is. You might still feel unhappy with the way that you see certain colleagues behave, but nothing is as conspiratorial, pernicious or insidious at it might feel in the heat of the moment. People are just looking to protect themselves, as you are. To be human is to feel insecure.[46]

## Summary

○ Humans collaborate using the principle of Non-Zero-Sum-Gain – it's better to work together
○ But we still have our individual needs, and politics occur as we try to pretend that they don't exist
○ Bulletproof people deal with politics by maintaining clear thinking and calming any unhelpful feelings

# Learn how to cut through bullshit

Bullshit is a close relative of politics, and the two of them can often be seen together. Like politics, bullshit arises when people feel the need to enter a shared pretence. The pretence is that we do not have individual needs and priorities.

In his essay 'On Bullshit', the philosopher Harry Frankfurt draws an important distinction between lying and bullshit. Lying, Frankfurt argues, requires an active awareness of the truth and then a planned deception. Bullshit, on the other hand, is neither as clear-headed nor as intentional. Bullshit arises out of our mind's ability to create a version of reality that works for our needs and which we then manifest through our words and deeds. Some aspects we may know to be untrue; others we allow to slip into the vague twilight world between truth and our preferred reality.

For example, Steve joins Company X as head of quality from its main competitor, Y Corporation. Steve has a reputation for shaking things up, reducing waste and cutting costs. He can't wait to bring in Acme Consulting to lead a big project to do this. He can't wait to prove his value to Company X. But Jim, who's head of operations, doesn't like the idea. Why should he? If the project succeeds, it puts the spotlight on Jim for not cutting waste sooner. On the other hand, Richard, the sales director, is happy to have waste cut in operations, but feels he has a clear run at the CEO's job when the current CEO retires. If Steve turns out to be a hero because of the success of this project, it might just complicate things. Kim is head of HR. She wants to launch a big project or her own and this one may just compete for budget and resources. Nobody will say no to Steve's project. Jim welcomes the plan but points out that if they are going to do it, they must do it right. You can't rush these things, and the proper diligence and stakeholder authorisation should be sought. It will need to be ratified by various committees. Kim says that she, too, is very keen on the project, but that it would be better to wait for a working group in the company to feed back its findings, just so that everything is aligned, you understand. Richard is very enthusiastic, but it would be far better not to do it as the busy Christmas sales period is approaching. Eventually Steve leaves the company, frustrated. That's bullshit.

Steve's project was in Company X's interest, but Steve failed to identify and work with the interests of Richard, Jim or Kate, or at least to allay their fears.

However, straight-talking conversations, if picked wisely and thoughtfully, can cut through bullshit in a refreshing and helpful way. Two people might see things differently, but nobody has superior intentions or a superior perspective. It is tempting to use the corporate 'we' to sound as though you speak from greater authority. Equally, it is tempting to position your message as *this is what everyone thinks,* or *this is what people have said.* You have integrity and credibility when you speak for yourself.

If you're working within one of the many organisations where bull-shit is spoken fluently, try this for a setting-out-the-stall statement in a peer-to-peer conversation: 'The way I see it is that we both want ABC. From my point of view, XYZ is important, and I suppose 123 is very important to you. Have I got that right?'

Steve could have said to Jim, 'I am very keen to bring in Acme Consulting because I know they're good. If I put myself in your shoes, I know I'd be really keen that operations are seen to have ownership of this and that your guys get due credit for any savings that come out of the project. How can we do this so it works for both of us?'

This is the *we-want-I-want-you-want* opening, and remember it is always followed by a statement along the lines of 'Have I got that right?', or 'Would that be fair to say?'

The first part draws attention to the common interest. The second part establishes your authenticity by putting your cards on the table. And the third part acknowledges that the other person has perspectives and priorities, which, while legitimate, may not be identical to your own. The question at the end acknowledges that you are not making assumptions and that you value the other person's point of view.

One of the best books on the subject is Professor Samuel Culbert's *Beyond BullSh*t.* Professor Culbert stipulates the conditions for 'straight-talk', which he explains requires a relationship, not good honesty in a single conversation. He makes the point that 'I-speak', where a person owns his or her views, allows people to speak their views with candour because it leaves room semantically for the other conversant to give a different view. This is in contrast with the 'King's we', which implies objectivity that no one really has, suggesting that 'this is the way everyone sees it or should think'. Culbert says, 'The way you see it is the way you see it; there's no need to posture as if you are speaking a universal truth.'

In addition to the 'King's we', we encourage people to avoid 'you-speak'. 'You-speak' is the antithesis of 'I-speak'. It implies that the culpability for the situation lies with the person to whom you are talking. Watch out for 'you-speak', for example:

- *You* do this …
- *You* cause this to happen …
- *You* make people feel …

Instead, try 'I-speak', for example:

- It seems to *me* …
- *I* see this happening …
- *I* feel concerned that …
- *I* get the impression that …
- *I* sense that …

Building on the principle of 'I-speak', 'This is the way I see it' is a great phrase that you will hear among people who make a habit of straight-talking. It's important, of course, that you give equal weight to the second part: 'How do *you* see it?'

Now, people sometimes ask: 'Shouldn't you start by asking the other person for his or her point of view?'

There is certainly a time and place for asking open questions and seeking to understand. However, our suggestion is that, in a straight-talking conversation, if you have a clear opinion about something, your integrity and credibility will increase if you are open about it from the outset. It does not, in any way, lessen the importance of listening to others.

The next point is to use 'interest-driven' not 'position-driven' language. When we take up a position, we encourage others to take up a position, too. When we argue from the point of view of our position, we cause others to defend their position.

We are at our most effective when we free ourselves up from *positions* and focus on *interests*: 'This is my interest in this situation. Let me understand yours, so that we can work out a way forward that works for both of us.'

During times of pressure or conflict, there is always a risk that we use position-driven language, as opposed to interest-driven language.

Interest-driven language encourages others to be more open and less defensive:

- Help me to understand
- What's important to you?
- I can understand that this is really important to you
- Tell me how you see the situation
- How can we work through this together?

Position-driven language encourages others to defend their position:

- The spotlight's on everyone. No one can stand still, or the grass grows under our feet
- And surely you must appreciate that
- I need you to show a more positive attitude
- Can't you see the bigger picture?

### Case Study 8.3

Kate was head of intermediary business at a big insurance firm. She aimed to launch a training programme about sophisticated 'partnership selling' for all senior executives. Kate felt that she had worked collaboratively to get the buy-in of all the senior stakeholders in the company, and she looked forward to launching the programme. It was a bit of a punch to the solar plexus when she received a frosty email from Sergio, the head of training, saying that he intended to veto the programme. He claimed that he had not been consulted and involved and that, therefore, Kate had not followed due process. Kate felt sure that she had done so. She referred back to notes which showed that a meeting had taken place at which agreement had been sought and apparently reached.

Kate's cave dweller started to steel herself for the fight. Determined to win this round, she gathered her evidence. But Bulletproof Kate knows that this would simply leave Sergio determined to block her, or at least win the next round.

Bulletproof Kate sat down with Sergio and said, 'I think it is really important that you are fully consulted and engaged with this programme. The way I saw it was that we had achieved this together in the meeting on ... but I now understand that you see it differently. I know people are waiting for this programme, and I think it would be great if we could show that we are collaborating together on it. What do you see as the best solution that would work for both of us?'

Try out a straight-talking conversation. Become aware of how it works for you. As always, become aware of your thoughts, the assumptions that you are taking in with you, and visualise yourself leaving them at the door. Give yourself permission to be straight-talking and at the same time recognise that you have shared interests and, simultaneously, your own personal interests.

You may well find that, step by step, you find yourself enlisting straight-talking allies across the organisation.

## Summary

- Like office politics, bullshit arises when people create a pretence that we don't have individual needs
- Bulletproof people use straight-talking conversations wisely to cut through bullshit
- Bulletproof people use 'I-speak', not 'you-speak', in their straight-talking conversations
- Bulletproof people use 'interest-driven', not 'position-driven', language

## Avoid being a martyr to politics

Think back to Jack, the 51-year-old, whose IT department went through a merger, the politics of which led him to feel like he had gone from a senior and admired stakeholder in the company to a dead man walking.

Until he started to take action by writing things down and looking more objectively at his situation, Jack had been made stressed and unhappy by what was happening. It hovered over him, even when he was outside of work. Jack was in danger of making himself a martyr to the politics. Distortions easily enter our thinking, particularly at a time of conflict. The process probably served two purposes for our ancestor. One is the process of increasing our personal feelings of righteous indignation, helping us to summon the resources for a potential fight. The second is that making our potential adversaries unambiguously in the wrong reduces any potential moment's doubt that could have been fatal to our ancestor if a physical fight ensued.

As Jack felt under increasing pressure, his mind was beginning to polarise: martyrdom or victory. Jack needed to learn how to avoid being a victim or a martyr to politics, how to quieten the inner child who angers at life not being fair, how to survive politics with your integrity intact, and how to see politics for no more than it is and create situations where you play to your strengths in spite of the politics.

If you are reading this at a time when you feel that you are on the wrong end of the politics, then you are understandably likely to feel hurt, tense or stressed. There are a number of things that you can do.

It's important to consider how you are defining success in this situation. Your instinct will be to seek outright victory over your political opponents. We would suggest that you can only effectively define success as the achievement of your higher goals, regardless of the politics. This seems eminently reasonable and it is a plan that will appeal to your frontal cortex. This part of your brain likes to assess the situation, weigh things up in a practical way and have a plan.

But remember, to your inner cave dweller fairness is extremely important, and the adversarial principle is deeply rooted. Again, succeeding in the face of politics means allowing your frontal cortex to run things, while your inner cave dweller takes a vacation.

We start our working lives expecting life to be fair and, in particular, hoping that large corporations run by adults will be fair. Of course, they are not. They are a complex set of interdependent relationships and competing interests. No two people have exactly the same perspectives and priorities. Humans collaborate together to meet both their collective and their individual interests.

One of the earliest coherent thoughts that we are capable of articulating as humans is the concept of 'it's not fair'. One of the most common sources of anger is the feeling that this innate sense of fairness has been transgressed. We are capable of articulating to children the idea that life cannot be expected to be fair, but this crying infant inside us never seems to altogether go away. To be effective, we need to quieten the toddler inside us.

As Dr Amy Silver advises, by identifying his thoughts Jack was able to try out more 'functional' ways of looking at things. Jack became aware that he was carrying a very strong sense of '*should*' in his mind: 'They should admit that they have been out of line'; 'They should acknowledge my experience and contribution to the company'; 'They should admit that they have been petty and vindictive.'

These were Jack's rules about the way that people *should* behave. Of course, as Jack always recognised, his '*shoulds*' would never be met, but they were still difficult to let go. Jack reframed his rigid rules into a flexible preference:

- I prefer to feel that colleagues are …
- I prefer things at work to be [this way] …
- … but, if that's not likely to be the case, I am okay

Note that Jack modified the statement to 'I prefer to *feel* that colleagues are' as opposed to 'I prefer colleagues to *be*'. This acknowledges that Jack observes things in his colleagues and feels a certain way. The phrase does not pass judgement on his colleagues, as if his judgement were an objective fact.

Jack needed to calm his inner cave dweller who railed against things not being fair. This was not to say that Jack suddenly became free of any emotional processing (nor would that be healthy or realistic). The key was to put a little space between Jack and his instinctive emotional responses. He pictured his inner cave dweller as a hot-headed little brother. If feelings of unfairness welled up, Jack would calmly remind him that he could live with it, and the important thing was to stay focused on his higher aims. Jack told us, 'It was as if he [Jack's inner cave dweller] soon started to say, "Okay, I know what you're going to say. I'll simmer down."'

If you're going through a tough time, how are you seeing yourself? If you feel badly or unfairly treated, is there a risk of slipping into martyr-syndrome? Are you still hoping that things will be fair?

The feeling of being on the outside also causes 'social pain'. We need to challenge our inner cave man. Being on the outside and lacking a sense of status creates visceral fear and anger, because we still feel that not having a seat around the campfire will mean that we don't get to eat or mate so well. We need to remind ourselves that we don't need to react like our inner cave dweller. This bout of politics won't hurt us.

Jack was encouraged to think about his thoughts to understand how these were governing his behaviour.

Our minds look for meaning in what happened. The meaning that we give things can soon become conflated with the facts. It is always worth asking ourselves: 'When X did this, what did I make it mean about myself? What actually happened and how much is it my interpretation of what happened? What other interpretations could there be and how do they work for me? When I have thought "Y" (for example, "These people are plotting to get me"), how did I act and how did that work for me? When I have thought "Z" (for example, "These people are probably okay with me and have their own priorities"), how did I act and how did that work for me? What if I could choose?'

Now go through this exercise: How are you defining a successful outcome in the situation? Does it involve triumphing over the colleagues with whom you are at loggerheads? If so, redefine it. Then think: Is my definition broad enough and flexible enough?

## Summary

❍ Corporations might be run by adults, but they aren't always fair
❍ Bulletproof people avoid being a victim or a martyr to politics

○ Bulletproof people reframe any rigid personal rules into flexible preferences
○ Bulletproof people define success as achieving their higher goals, regardless of politics

## You don't need to be in with the in-crowd

There will always be an in-group and an out-group. In the same way that group collaboration and bonding occur spontaneously, so too do group fragmentation and polarisation. And no matter how frequently you get people together at conferences to sing the company song, *them and us* becomes an issue in all organisations. We once worked with a small market research agency. All of the company was on the same floor, but as the company expanded and took on more floor space, some staff were relocated to the other side of a linoleum walkway that ran down the middle. Pretty soon people started talking about 'them, on *that* side of the office'. Again, this tendency is part of an ingrained human habit. In experiments, psychologists have discovered that they can readily cause a group to split and polarise simply by assigning group members one of two different colours. Experiments show that hostility between groups can be created on the flip of a coin.[47]

There are many books promising to tell you how to win at politics. Many contain some good advice, but if playing the politics game is not naturally your thing, we would suggest that attempting to carry ever more complex strategies around in your head will prove exhausting and distract your focus. Our goal with Jack was to help him to function effectively, given the inevitable backdrop of company politics; part of that involved helping Jack to realise that it is okay not to be in with the in-crowd all of the time.

In his book, *Who Really Matters: The Core Group Theory of Power, Privilege and Success*, Art Kleiner argues that typically both large and small organisations tend to evolve into a larger group of outsiders and a smaller group of insiders: an 'in-group' and an 'out-group'. Kleiner refers to this in-group as the 'Core Group'. You've probably seen this in an organisation that you've worked for – people who seem to have the CEO's ear, who seem to know more than you about what's going or who always seem to be given the best assignments.

Essentially, the Core Group appears to be the group of individuals for whose benefit the organisation seems to work. They become the locus of power and influence, often formally, by virtue of their positions in the company, but their real power and influence is implicit and informal. It is implicitly understood that they have special privilege and influence. As Kleiner puts it, the organisation seems to simply 'have fallen in love with' this group.

Naturally we do not carry a gene that organises us into Core Groups and outsiders, although it is quite conceivable that something in our neural circuitry, which relates to social organising, means that these distinctions are likely to occur.

The existence of the Core Group can lead to feelings of marginalisation, envy, politics, Machiavellianism and a range of other organisational neuroses. The strength of the Core Group comes from their power of patronage. In other words, because others seek to enter the Core Group, this is a favour that they can grant or withhold at will. And because of this source of power, entry to the Core Group will never be given away lightly. Demand to enter must always outstrip supply. (Of course, Core Group members do not sit around thinking of how to withhold or bestow patronage, nor would they be likely to acknowledge its existence, at a formal level. However, most organisations intuitively follow this dynamic.)

The tragedy is that many of us spend much of our valuable working lives either trying to manipulate our way into the Core Group or resenting those who are in it. People resent the political manoeuvrings of others. People try political manoeuvres of their own. People cry into their beer and complain about brown-nosers or schmoozers … and the fact that they could run the company better. All of these responses are, of course, wasteful, disempowering and counterproductive.

Politics often comes down to the idea of the in-crowd and the out-crowd. We want to be part of the in-crowd, primarily because we fear the risk of being in the out-crowd, with those who are ostracised, who have no or few alliances, little profile and whose name simply doesn't seem to surface when it comes to possibilities of advancement, perks or promotions. Most of us do not consciously decide to get actively involved with politics (with a few exceptions); most of us are drawn into politics out of fear. We wish that we did not have to play the politics but we feel that we have no choice. We feel that we should because if others are doing so they'll get ahead of us and we'll be the nice-guy losers.

The first strategy to deal with the in-crowd is precisely as we advise people about dealing with bosses. In this case, view the Core Group as simply another customer group. The advice here is always to remember that you have skills, expertise or knowledge of value. Working with the Core Group as your customers means that the value you create soon becomes clear and, assuming that they want to sustain this sort of value, they will need to ensure that you are rewarded for it. You can be respected and valued by the Core Group without ever having to develop strategies to enter it. The alternative is to create your own Core Group. People who have the drive and initiative to strike out independently are rewarded with their own Core Group. People show entrepreneurial spirit, setting up their own ventures.

There will always be an in-crowd. The power of the in-crowd is contingent on people wanting to join it. If we are relaxed about whether we are in or out of a clique, it fails to exert any emotional power over us. Not only can we get on with our jobs and with doing what we came into the organisation to do, but we'll feel a whole lot happier.

Just as we encourage people to view a toxic boss as a high-maintenance customer, view the Core Group as people with whom you are required to interact in order to deliver a service with the expertise that only you can offer. It would be nice to feel invited into the Core Group, but you don't *need* to. Imagine you were doing your job as an expert consultant, working very closely with this organisation. It would be great to make some friends here, but you don't *need* to. It would be really nice if everyone were always civil, but how other people act doesn't say anything about your expertise or competence.

We only gain power when we stop wanting organisations to be fair and start expecting them to be human, and when we recognise politics for what it is: the unspoken (and often 'undiscussable') emotional needs of the people involved.

## Summary

○ Organisations typically evolve into a small group of insiders and a larger group of outsiders

○ Bulletproof people treat the Core Group just like a boss, i.e. simply as another customer

○ You can be respected and valued by the Core Group without ever trying to enter it

# Challenge your assumptions

Let's return to Claire, the HR manager, who felt ostracised by her team. She was feeling isolated from a group in a very different context; her group was the very group she had been appointed to lead.

One of the most common requests that we receive is to work with a dysfunctional leadership team. We point out that teams are like families: being dysfunctional is their normal state. No two people in a team can ever be expected to have identical perspectives and priorities. Moreover, the individual, unspoken emotional needs are every bit as powerful as any shared team goal. As trust is eroded, team members feel a greater wariness about honesty and openness, and a greater desire to disguise their needs and wants. And, of course, trust is then further eroded. In a team where individuals feel 'unsafe', implicit alliances are formed. Far from making the individual feel safer, the cycle continues.

There is a further phenomenon that exacerbates the situation among teams. Evidence shows that, in a group, attitudes and feelings tend to be amplified. Individuals who feel isolated in teams will tend to find that their colleagues exacerbate the divisions. They look for evidence to support their judgement about isolated team members. Attitudes that have taken root among a team are much harder to shift than attitudes held by an individual. Most managers reach for the traditional cures of either team-building activities or social events, or both. At best, these are fruitless; at worst, they provide a magnifying glass for the dysfunctions.

When we met Claire, she was clearly feeling tired and emotional about the situation. She listed the unhelpful behaviours that she had witnessed from the team. She also listed all of the attempts that she had made to improve the situation – and the ungracious responses with which they had been met. Her message was clear: Look, I've been reasonable and this is how they repay me. Claire was clearly looking for evidence that would reassure her that she was right.

First Claire had to answer the question: 'How might I have been contributing to the problem?' And when it came to the team's behaviour: 'How am I feeling when I behave like this?' By answering the second question, Claire came to gain insight into the first. Team members begrudged the feeling of being subordinated and, therefore, tried out ways implicitly to challenge Claire's authority. Claire had responded by seeking to reassert her authority and, therefore, invited more surly non-compliance back from the team. They were caught in a cycle.

Claire recognised that she had been in a cycle of thought-feeling-behaviour. The behaviour that she observed from the team would trigger the unhelpful thoughts described above, from which she would feel under attack, insecure, threatened and frustrated. As she felt her status as team leader was under attack, she would respond by more overtly high-status behaviour and attempts to demonstrate her author-ity. She would micro-manage in order to keep control of the team. This just made them more resentful, and the cycle continued.

Claire needed to separate the behaviour that she witnessed from her team from what it caused her to feel about herself: her 'if ... then ... assumptions'. She feared that her team didn't respect her authority. 'If ... then I am not fit to be a leader. I *always* get found out, so I will *never* make a success of my career.' By becoming aware of this unhelpful line of reasoning and challenging these assumptions, Claire was able to approach the situation that the behaviour of her team members came down to their feelings. It did not mean anything about Claire. And what's more, Claire needed to remind herself not to feel the need to indulge in mind-reading exercises with the team.

Being able to let go of mind reading and to challenge and question her 'if … then … assumptions', being able to identify her 'story' and separate it from the facts, did not solve the entire situation for Claire, but it was the first stage in taking the intensity out of those feelings that were leading to behaviour that, in turn, was pushing the whole boat further and further off course.

If you are caught in a situation that is giving rise to some toxic feelings, it may well be that your 'if … then … assumptions' are at play. Did a team member really snub you in the corridor? Or were they simply distracted by something? Is that person who seems so unhelpful and stand-offish actually having problems at home?

Don't assume, for instance, that you're necessarily the focus of and cause of other people's behaviour. Were Claire's team getting at Claire personally? After all, they knew her so well because they'd worked with her for years. She began to realise that the team felt as if the company was ignoring them; Claire's promotion was really just a catalyst for these negative feelings.

Abandoning her 'if … then … assumptions' and seeing potential distortions in her thinking helped Claire to see the situation more clearly and she started to feel more calm and centred. She felt her confidence start to recover.

## Summary

- ○ Negative feelings get amplified in groups – and group feelings are harder to shift than individual attitudes
- ○ We become more wary about being honest and open in a team that's lacking trust
- ○ Bulletproof people can separate team behaviour from what it causes them to feel about themselves

# How to deal with being ostracised

Human beings are naturally social animals, and so being ostracised is unpleasant for us at a very basic level. We often feel devalued and inferior to those who are ostracising us. Sadly, some people will resort to using techniques such as ostracism or ignoring and cutting people out of social groups to meet their needs. This can be the obvious 'silent treatment' or it could be more subtle, such as not inviting people to meetings and social events or failing to reply to their emails. With today's hi-tech, instant-response culture of emails and mobile phones, we expect replies to be faster than ever before; if they're not immediate, we can easily feel ignored or snubbed.

Ostracism in the office environment has many of the detrimental effects of its more common social relation, says Professor Kip Williams, of Purdue University, who has studied ostracism. He adds that there is evidence that ostracism of office workers lowers their perceptions of their own work-related competency (even though this really isn't a logical conclusion); they feel the pain that is signalled by and the distress that is associated with lower feelings of belonging, self-esteem, control and meaningful existence. In the office environment, unlike many other situations, it's senior people, such as team leaders, who can be ostracised, or at least feel ostracised, as much as – if not sometimes more than – those of lower status. Professor Williams believes that ostracism – or the silent treatment – can sometimes be the great equaliser. He argues that lower-status people, people less effective at arguing, or those who are unjustifiably angry, can use ostracism without getting into trouble (or, at least, making it more difficult to get into trouble). Unlike calling someone names or punching them, it is easier to ostracise without proof or accountability. Think of phrases such as 'I don't know what you're talking about; you must be paranoid.'

So, how do you make yourself bulletproof against ostracism by colleagues, whatever their level of seniority in relation to you? As we've seen so often, trying to tough it out probably won't work. It seems that challenging the behaviour and trying to make it stop can also be counterproductive in this instance. If the perpetrator's aim is to cause hurt, you will only be providing more evidence that their approach is working, which is likely to further fuel the fire and inspire them to continue.

Professor Williams believes that we intuitively know that ostracism hurts for a couple of reasons: partly because we've also probably had experience of it ourselves; and partly because it may be an adaptive hard-wired behaviour.

He advises us to ignore the ignoring, as it may be adding fuel to the fire: the more those who are purposefully ostracising us know it is affecting us negatively, the more they may be attracted to continuing to use it as a weapon. He feels that ignoring the fact that you're apparently being ignored by acting in a cheerful way usually, oddly enough, overcomes ostracism more effectively than a simple plea to stop.

Ostracism is tough and can even lead to depression, but Professor Williams believes there are solutions. He advises people to actively engage in maintaining old friendships or starting new ones, focusing on one or two close relationships rather than 'friending' a vast number of people on Facebook. What works in your social and family life also works in the office. It seems that, when it coincides with overcoming ostracism, developing and maintaining a few good friends is the answer.

The natural inclination is to blame and dislike those who are ostracising us, but stepping back, being mindful and self-aware can help here, most easily by putting yourself in their shoes. Claire realised, for instance, that her team were understandably jealous of her. 'Thinking about it I realised that in HR we'd been ignored by management for ages,' she says. 'We'd had no new resources, no additional staff and very little training. Then suddenly I was offered something that the rest of my colleagues would have loved. I imagined how I'd have felt if Bev, who used to sit opposite me, had suddenly been given a promotion. I'm not surprised that they felt jealous and underappreciated.' She also realised that her attempt to exert authority over her team had been unhelpful.

Working to remove some of the understandably negative emotion from your feelings, and looking at the situation in a more objective way with a long perspective, can help. Everyone is ostracised in varying degrees at some point in their lives. It won't last for ever. Once you've come through it successfully, you'll have learnt valuable new people-management skills and have improved your resilience.

## Summary
- Ignore the ignoring – act like the person you want to be treated as
- Remember ostracism is temporary
- Choose a few key relationships and go for quality rather than quantity

# Have the confidence to be vulnerable

It is worth saying a word about team dynamics here. If you intend to change the attitudes of a team, it is very unwise to make serious attempts at this when the team are all together – at least at the early stages. Teams are prone to 'group think' and, because collective attitudes are amplified when like-minded people get together, they tend to be more entrenched in their attitude.

Claire tried behavioural experiments. We encouraged her to think about what would be possible for her if she had supreme confidence in her natural and effortless authority as leader. One of the things that she said was, intriguingly, that she would have the confidence to admit to not knowing everything and asking for help. We felt that this insight might be a real gem for Claire. Her behavioural experiment was to act as if she had the 'confidence to admit to vulnerability'.

It may seem counter-intuitive, but vulnerability is an immensely powerful tactic in the repertoire of the bulletproof mind. Vulnerability is disarming.

Remember, if we are at loggerheads with a colleague or group of colleagues, it is unlikely that they simply chose us randomly as an adversary. Recall, also, that most people tend to be more motivated to fend off threats than to pursue gain, hence there is a fair chance that we have invoked feelings of threat, insecurity or envy. Vulnerability suggests openness and honesty. We do not demonstrate vulnerability to those we perceive as a threat; hence, if people see that we are prepared to show vulnerability to them, it gives them a clear sense that we do not view them as a threat and they are free to lower their shield – at least a little – but that is the all-important first step.

People are rarely motivated by the desire to plot our downfall. Others tend to be primarily concerned about their own world view, which, like all of ours, is highly self-centred. That is not to say that people do not act unreasonably, judge you unfairly or aim to enlist others to their point of view. We just don't loom large enough on their radar that we have to take them on in a moral duel. If you find yourself in an adversarial situation with colleagues, the best place to operate from is underneath their defensive radar.

Now try this experiment: With whom are you feeling in an adversarial situation right now? Go to that person and ask for some advice, information or knowledge. It is something that is really important to you but you know that this guy knows more about it than you do – or, at least, you somehow got the impression that he did. It's the way he talks knowledgeably about other things. Our expectation is that people would never show a weakness to a potential adversary.

As ever, test out how it feels to you. You have nothing to lose. And either way, there is a vital psychological principle that is borne out by a wealth of research: we like those people whom we help. So, even if it is only the tiniest step, you will have moved things forward on the popularity front. You might feel that you're losing face or looking weak. Just remember: it actually takes confidence and strength to do this. Watch how high-status individuals who have nothing to prove can often admit that they don't know something or can listen attentively to others who are lower down the pecking order.

A final thought from Matthieu Ricard, the scientist-turned-Buddhist teacher and writer: 'The idea that a powerful ego is necessary to succeed in life undoubtedly stems from the confusion between attachment to our own image and the resolve to achieve our deepest aspirations. The fact is, the less influenced we are by the sense of our self's importance, the easier it is to acquire lasting inner strength. The reason for this is simple: self-importance is a target open to all sorts of mental projectiles – jealousy, fear, greed, repulsion – that perpetually destabilise it.'

Put simply, the less attached you are to your ego or self-image, the less readily you can be destabilised by the actions of others.

Let it go.

## Summary

○ Trying to change team attitudes? Avoid getting the whole team together to do it – collectively, attitudes get amplified and become more entrenched

○ Vulnerability is disarming – to express it requires strength and confidence

○ Bulletproof people always remember to ask an adversary for help and advice

# Divide and influence – it's better to focus on individuals than the group

When we find ourselves on the outside, when others seem to be massing against us, or cliques seem to be forming, we tend to see our adversaries as a single entity opposing us. When we're under pressure, our language reinforces our belief.

When Claire sought to confront the attitudes she saw as undesirable, she would challenge the group with phrases like:

● 'You lot are always ...'
● 'I'm trying to get you lot to see things from my point of view ...'
● 'It seems to me that you all tend to ...'

It might be tempting to challenge the group, particularly when you're at a low ebb and feeling irritated by others' attitudes, but this is the last thing you really want to do: reinforce the sense of common group identity among those you see as your adversaries. It is equally counterproductive to draw attention to the fact that you are isolated versus the group. We know that attitudes and opinions become more vehement and entrenched when people group together with others of a similar mind.

Political researchers have identified this in focus groups. If they put voters with a similarly socially conservative attitude to law and order together, they tend to come out of the focus group advocating today's equivalent of hanging for the theft of a sheep.

Want to turbocharge the sense of righteousness and evidence gathering among those with whom you find yourself at loggerheads? Then treat them as one homogenous mass. The key to influencing a group is to break it down to relationships with individuals.

It may seem counter-intuitive to focus on points of conflict and disagreement among the team, but we believe that constructive conflict and diversity of opinion are helpful.

After we talked to Claire about how she should handle the group, she learnt to withhold her view and be seen to listen. She began to ask questions such as: 'Thanks for that. Now I'd like to hear from somebody with a different point of view'; or, simply, 'Thanks for that ... now who feels differently?' She encouraged team members to debate respectfully but passionately with each other. She learnt to encourage diversity of opinion by praising it when she saw it happen. 'It's great that we have so many different opinions around the table.'

Claire also learnt that it is far more effective to focus on individual group members for one-to-one conversations. In these conversations she was far better able to use rapport skills and could make a point of asking for advice or views on business matters.

Asking advice builds relationships in two ways. First, it flatters the other person as it suggests that we value their expertise. Second, as we've already seen, when someone does us a favour or gives us something they tend to like us more.[48]

## The third-party technique

Jack had similar success in building one-to-one relationships following the changes in his company which had left him feeling isolated and unwanted. One of the techniques he found most helpful was the 'third-party technique'.

It works like this: we tend to like people who like us – it's almost impossible not to. We like people who compliment us … who show they admire us. These people make us feel better about ourselves. However, we are often suspicious of people who pay us compliments, assuming they may be attempting to 'play' us in some way. During times of heightened politics, people tend to have their bullshit detectors switched to 'red alert'. This explains why attempts to build bridges are often misunderstood and counterproductive. There is a smart way to circumvent this and make sure your compliment lands effectively and pulls the desired strings. Say something complimentary about the person concerned to a friend or colleague who knows you both. It will almost certainly get back to the desired individual. And because you appear to have no vested interest, its authenticity will appear all the greater.

Compliments like 'Jane's great' or 'I really like Tom' are too vague and generic to make much difference to anyone. Compliments that really work – just like criticisms that really hurt – relate to something the individual considers important about himself. In psychologists' jargon, it fits with his 'self-concept'. In other words, show you have given the person some thought, for example: 'I notice Jane has a brilliant head for figures. She can very rapidly grasp what's important in a set of numbers, ahead of anyone else'; or 'I love Tom's dry sense of humour. I've noticed how it really helps break the ice.' This approach works better than a general compliment about something which could apply to anyone.

## Summary

O It's far more effective to focus on individual group members for one-to-one conversations

○ Bulletproof people avoid reinforcing common group identity in adversarial situations
○ Pay compliments via a third party to win over your adversaries
○ Make compliments specific and relevant to the individual
○ Ask advice from your adversaries
○ Reciprocity and compliments work

## Focus on what's working ... not on what's bust

Claire felt that she was being isolated by the team she had been appointed to lead. Frequently a new CEO or department head can feel out on a limb. Their instinct will be to go for the *You-lot-have-gotta-change-or-die* speech. The temptation is to break the cycle or change the mindset by holding up a mirror to show how bad things are. The assumption is that recognising the desperate nature of a situation will prompt people to leave the petty politics to one side. A little understanding of group psychology will help you avoid this tactical error.

The more unsettled, hostile or messier the environment, the more that group hostility towards outsiders increases. Researchers have discovered that as the conditions of a given environment are manipulated – for example, when the evidence of litter, mess and anti-social behaviour is increased – the subjects within that environment are more likely to express suspicion of, or even hostility to, different socio-ethnic groups. Conversely, the more benign the environment, the more benevolent the attitude towards outsiders.[49]

Claire's team viewed her as outsider. We were initially invited to facilitate a gloves-off 'clear the air' session. We advised a different approach. We encouraged her to ask the team the following important question: 'What would be possible for this team if it were functioning excellently – as effectively as it could?' Responses were slow and stilted at first. It was clear the team's reflex response was to return to talking about problems. When problem talk emerged – as it inevitably did – Claire acknowledged that there were plenty of raw feelings. She appreciated that several team members saw many fault lines, but she encouraged people to put them to one side. We reassured the team that they would have the opportunity to talk about anything they wished in due course. Eventually people got into their stride, generating rich descriptions about what the team could achieve. We encouraged everyone to describe in specific, observable terms what would happen under these scenarios. Vague generalities were banned.

We then encouraged people to identify specific examples of where the team was currently functioning at its best. This met with the expected reaction: 'Haven't you been listening? That is the whole problem! We hardly ever perform at our best.' We countered this with the challenge that 'hardly ever' isn't 'never'.

We suggested that Claire pointed out that the examples might be brief, fleeting and seemingly insignificant. No matter how bad things seem, sometimes we are better than others, so what can we learn from these times? Here, the 'why-not-a-zero' question proved useful. If the state of excellence the team had described were rated at 10, how would people rate its current state? Unsurprisingly they rated it a two or three. We then asked them to brainstorm, in as much specific detail as possible, all the reasons they did not rate themselves at zero.

We then said we would move on to giving feedback. 'Ah, now this is what I was expecting,' people seemed to be thinking. 'Time for the tears and tissues.' By this point Claire was leading the facilitation. She asked group members to give feedback to colleagues in the room, but with a specific twist. Bearing in mind all of the answers to the 'why-not-a-zero' question, members of her team were asked to give feedback to each of their colleagues about the specific personal attributes and qualities that they see that have helped them to achieve the things that they listed in the 'why-not-a-zero' stage – and which, of course, they looked forward to seeing more of, if the team were to move towards the 10. Bit by bit, Claire felt the levels of positive energy creep up, like mercury in a steadily warming thermometer. And then the inevitable started to happen: one by one, team members started drifting over to Claire and involving her in the feedback. The session ended with an agreement that the next immediate and readily achievable action – specific and observable, of course – that both individuals and the team would carry out before the next meeting was to move up just one notch.

Claire announced that the next dozen meetings would start with the question, 'What's better since last time?' and each team member would answer in specific, tangible terms. And each meeting would end with a specific commitment to the up-one-notch action.

So, whether you're handling a team or just thinking about a particular situation yourself, focus on the positive, ask why it's not a zero and look at what is going well and what has improved, so that you can develop and expand these elements.

### Summary
- Focus on the positives and not the negatives
- Think about what works and learn from it rather than what doesn't work
- Use the 'why-not-a-zero' technique

## Borrow some perspective ... and get *elevated*

Research shows that certain positive character traits, such as gratitude, hope, kindness, leadership and teamwork, increased in Americans following 9/11. In addition, other work has shown that having had a serious physical illness can result in increased levels of bravery, curiosity, fairness, humour and an appreciation of beauty.[50]

Most of us are familiar with the concept of post-traumatic stress disorder. We know that people who undergo exceptionally traumatic or adverse effects are likely to suffer psychologically for some time after. But this is not the entire story; the reality is more complex. Indeed, far from causing us long-term damage, it appears that the view 'What doesn't kill me makes me stronger' is gathering scientific support. This is pretty good news for humankind and something from which we can all learn. There is evidence, for instance, that those who suffer difficult childhoods build up reserves of strength for later life.

Psychologists have increasingly been researching the idea of 'post-traumatic growth': that people who have suffered great adversity in their lives are better than the rest of us at coping with whatever life throws at them. And this is not just a case of 'look on the bright side'; the evidence is robust: surviving tough times makes us more resilient and better equipped to survive in the future.

Why should this be? There are several hypotheses. One is that the adverse event changes our self-concept. Because we have survived, we are more inclined to see ourselves as a survivor. The governing thought that these individuals carry into future situations is 'I can survive' or 'I will be okay'.

In addition, we become more aware of the full range of resources at our disposal. We have drawn on our deepest reserves of energy, optimism, wisdom, emotional resilience and intelligence. We are confident they are there and that we have the wherewithal to tap into them.

One of the most crucial resources these survivors have learnt to draw upon is, of course, other people. Many survivors of adversity come to understand the importance of investing in relationships and report real improvements in them. As these survivors understand the importance of kindness and helping others, they are more likely to act accordingly and therefore reap the emotional benefits.

Survivors of traumatic life events have a further advantage over the rest of us: they have perspective. In the heat of the moment, our toxic boss, bullying client or passive-aggressive co-workers become the most important issue in the universe. In reality, situations at work are not a matter of life or death. The salesman on a losing streak will not die if one more client says no. Perspective allows us to lower the stakes. And when we lower the stakes, we act with confidence and think more clearly.

### Case Study 8.4

Harry worked for an oil multinational. Every Monday morning he was one of several presenters who had to present figures to a senior finance committee. The slightest discrepancy or inconsistency would have the presenter hauled over the coals. When a younger colleague asked how he coped with nerves, Harry answered, 'I used to be a pilot. I have done an emergency landing on a swamp, in a storm, with one poorly functioning engine and not lost a single passenger. I just remind myself that no one else in the room has ever done that.'

So do we have to undergo life-threatening adversity to feel like survivors, value the important things in life, have better relationships and gain perspective? Imagine if we could train our minds to harness the emotional and cognitive benefits without risking our lives, so that we could *act* like we had. Acting involves thinking as if you've had the experience of someone else's life. Imagine if those life experiences had the ability to make us stronger; employing the methods actors use would subsequently serve to benefit us in our own lives.

We talked to a personal assistant who was diagnosed with claustrophobia. When we asked how she managed to travel on the crowded London Underground, with its long delays on crowded trains several hundred feet underground, she told us of a novel way: 'I imagine I'm a refugee escaping from a Nazi-occupied part of Europe. The train I'm on is my lifeline. I managed to get on it by the skin of my teeth. I only have to sit and wait and I'll escape with my life for ever.'

Psychologist Jonathan Haidt has been pioneering research into the concept of 'elevation'. We know that hearing of morally repugnant acts causes us to feel disgust, and this feeling has a physiological manifestation. Well, 'elevation' is the flip side. Common sense tells us that when we hear stories of people doing great, kind and morally courageous things we feel better. We may even feel inspired. But there is increasing evidence that when we hear stories of people doing great things, the emotional and physiological effects are considerable. Stories of people doing great things, particularly acts of courageous kindness, give us inspiration and strength in literal and measurable ways. There is still more to be done, but researchers believe that elevating stories affect the vagus nerve. This is associated with regulating the heart's activity – hence the association between love and the heart – and with the body's release of the bonding hormone, oxytocin. Oxytocin is believed to help with clear thinking, learning and possibly with the body's immune system.

### Case Study 8.5

Mark is CEO of a medium-sized packaged foods company. When he was seventeen, he went travelling around Europe. It was his first time away from home without his mother and father. Mark received a message that his mother had suddenly become seriously ill. He immediately made arrange-ments to fly home first thing the following morning. But as he prepared to leave for the airport, Mark got the message that his mother had not made it through the night.

In a daze, Mark found himself telephoning his sister from a payphone kiosk at the airport. He simply felt that he needed someone to whom he could express his pain. As he hung up the phone, he felt a hand rest gently on his shoulder. As he turned around, he saw a man in late middle age, who said, 'I couldn't help overhearing you … is there anything you need? Is there anything I can do for you? Are you okay for money? Maybe a cup of coffee?'

It was a tiny gesture but it was just when Mark needed it. And Mark was aware that for so many of us it is so easy to walk on by. Mark told us, 'When I need to remind myself to do the right thing. I think of that stranger. I'm quite sure that I don't always live up to it, but I am equally sure that it helps.'

Elevation increases health and well-being, both mentally and physio-logically. It costs nothing and is available when you need it. Seek it out. Identify stories of moral courage and remind yourself of people doing great – and the right – things. These could be inspirational stories, which appear regularly in the media (alongside the doom and gloom!), autobiographies, or even stories of people within your organisation or sector who went that bit further to help someone.

Elevation is very powerful in a group setting when you want to manage group climate. Ask each person to share a morally inspiring story in which he or she may have participated. [51]

## Summary

○ When we hear stories of people doing great, kind and morally courageous things, we feel better

○ Bring these to mind when you want to be bulletproof and see how you can learn from them

○ Who or what you are going to remind yourself of, when you want to get a sense of proportion or do the right thing?

# CHAPTER 9
## DELIVERING FEEDBACK IN A WAY THAT WORKS

**Case Study 9.1**

As they both went home to their families, Joe couldn't help thinking about how Francis would be feeling that evening. They had joined the bank at the same time. They had been friends since the first day of that year's graduate intake. Francis was outgoing, charming and gregarious. He had been a great support to Joe in those early days. It was almost embarrassing for Joe, some years later, when Francis ended up reporting to him as part of the task force that Joe was heading to implement a major new IT system. It soon became clear that Francis was not delivering. He was talking a great story but his practical progress on the assignment was way behind that of his colleagues. Suggestions started to circulate that Joe had let the situation drift; that he lacked the leadership skills to deal with it. When Joe finally delivered his message – that the situation was unacceptable and that he would not tolerate its continuing – he couldn't help but notice that Francis seemed even more wounded than Joe had expected.

So far we have discussed techniques to bulletproof yourself against the setbacks and assaults of the workplace. But what about the occasions when it seems like you are the one that has to deliver the bullets?

As a leader, you are paid to communicate your feedback to others. In the workplace, negative or critical feedback is as important as praise, but it can leave you feeling deeply uncomfortable. The evidence shows that most of us are not good at giving feedback and will avoid it if possible. We like to be liked and we like to be in rapport with people. Our belief that giving criticism will make us unpopular is not altogether unfounded: the mind's typical reflex response when receiving critical feedback is to defend and it has no qualms about shooting the messenger.

Feedback is inherent in any system of progress and improvement. If you have had any sort of coaching in sports or any other endeavour, you will recognise that to improve you need feedback. In nature, evolution operates on the basis of random variations in an organism and then feedback from the external environment. If the variation is better for survival (positive feedback), it will likely be inherited by future generations; if it is detrimental to survival, it will likely disappear (negative feedback).

The terms 'negative' and 'positive' feedback carry connotations in day-to-day language. Would you rather be described as a negative person or a positive person? But we should not make the mistake of allowing these connotations to colour our understanding of the way that feedback works as a driver of improvement.

Negative feedback (that says 'stop – something different needed – change direction') is essential to performance improvement. If you are an athlete, a musician, an actor or any other performer, you want to know about any aspect of your performance that is not up to scratch. Recent research[52] indicates that top performers or virtuosos in any field are more likely to seek out and benefit from negative feedback, whereas praise is more beneficial for novices.

Most biological mechanisms in the body, the functioning of the livers, kidneys, pituitary gland, work on the principle of negative feedback. One of the most common examples of a negative-feedback mechanism is a room thermostat. It senses that the temperature in the room has dropped below the optimum and applies a little more heat. If it senses that the increased heat has gone above the optimum, it ceases heating and starts cooling, and so on.

So, if feedback is so essential to performance, why are we so lousy at it? Put it this way: the thermostat has no need to preserve self-esteem and rapport. The information does not cause hurt to feelings or awkward and uncomfortable moments. The problem with humans is that they come with a fully integrated complex repertoire of emotions. These help us to navigate social situations but they also bring a range of complications.

As Harry Levinson argues in his classic *Harvard Business Review* article, 'Management by Whose Objectives?', people simply do not like to evaluate another human being like a piece of machinery. But the underpinning assumption of most organisations is that they readily do so.

Most corporations assume that line managers 'performance-manage' their people. By this we mean an active process of communicating with their people to help to draw out the best performance. We sought to test the extent to which this is genuinely happening by asking for the perceptions of employees.

Threshold researchers asked the views of a representative random sample of 1,000 employees across the United Kingdom, all of whom work in corporations and have a line manager[53] (while we focused on the UK, we hypothesise that the findings would be broadly similar in other developed countries; after all, we are dealing with human universals here).

The results expose the myth that performance management is happening. Consider this:

- Less than half of employees (44%) feel that they receive helpful feedback from their line manager frequently enough
- Scarcely more than half (51%) feel that their line manager is good at giving straight, honest feedback
- Considerably less than half (41%) feel that their line manger gives performance feedback that is detailed and specific enough
- And again, considerably less than half (44%) feel that they receive regular enough feedback from their line manager that helps them to do their job better
- It also appears that most employees do not feel that underperformance is effectively tackled in their organisation. Only 30% of employees agree with the statement: Where I work, underperformance is discussed openly and honestly

- It would appear that there is a lack of 'straight-talk' at work. When asked whether, in their workplace, managers are good at giving straight-talking feedback, scarcely one third agreed (31%)

The findings may be eye-opening for all of those corporations who assume that their line managers actively manage performance, but a crucial question is, of course, whether or not these findings really matter to the bottom line. The short answer is yes.

If given honest feedback, are employees more likely to commit additional discretionary effort to their work? The research shows that there is a clear correlation between the parameters above and discretionary effort. We define the 'high-discretionary-effort group' as those who answer 'strongly agree' to the question: Do you feel motivated to put exceptional effort into your job, and do more than what's asked of you?

In contrast to the population as a whole, the high-discretionary-effort group are considerably more likely to receive frequent, honest, straight-talking feedback from their boss. In short, straight-talking feedback makes a difference to performance. If you are going to be a leader, you will need to give feedback.

## Give yourself permission to be straight and direct

Most managers are ineffective at giving feedback, but the problem is compounded by another factor: most people tend to overrate how effective they are at it. If you are like most of us, then maybe you're being rather too generous when judging how brave, clear and honest you are when you need to deliver feedback.

When Threshold asks managers to rate the general effectiveness of honest performance conversations in their organisations as a whole, most rate this as below average. On the other hand, most managers rate themselves as above average at delivering honest performance conversations. We have repeated these questions with literally thousands of managers, in every continent in the world, and the pattern is consistent. The simple fact is that most of us tend to overrate how good we are at honest performance conversations.

Have you ever avoided an awkward conversation? Have you let something go, which you know you really should have challenged? Have you indicated that you thought something was just fine when really it wasn't? If you have, you are like the majority of us. As the research bears out, most of us shy away from straight-talking feedback. The more you can make yourself bulletproof, the more readily you can tackle the sort of straight-talking conversations from which most people shy away.

To understand why humans are not great at giving honest feedback, we need to go back to two fundamental psychological imperatives that – it won't surprise you to hear – were very important to our cave-dwelling ancestor: *'esteem'* and *'rapport'*. Both of these are exceptionally important to humans and we will invest considerable effort to sustain them.

Esteem is important because it is associated both with our personal standing among a social group and with the inner reserves of confidence and resilience that we need in order to perform. Rapport is also vitally important to a social species like humans, because our survival requires interaction with others. Being out of rapport with those around us triggers that sense of unease; it is not a situation that we want to be in for long.

Our instincts tell us that straight-talking feedback will risk both of these. We will jeopardise rapport with the other person and we will jeopardise his or her self-esteem, and, as a result, we will become unpopular. We want to be liked. We are 'wired to please'. We humans love being in rapport with other humans; we will do anything to sustain it and we hate to break it.

Bulletproof people recognise that honest feedback does not have to put the other person's self-esteem at risk. They also recognise that a brief break in rapport is harmless – and even sometimes necessary – and that rapport can easily be re-established.

Recall what we said about rigid rules. One of the most common is, 'I must always be popular or I must always be liked.' If this rule is too rigid, you will greatly limit your ability to be flexible and effective when communicating with others.

A note of caution here: many people are tempted to free themselves from needing to be liked by going to the other extreme. Teenagers will often say things like: 'I don't care what anyone else thinks … people can just take me as I am!' (which is a little ironic as anyone who knows teenagers will know that they tend to be most acutely sensitive to what others think of them). Replacing 'I must always be liked' with something along the lines of 'I don't care if I am hated' is counterproductive. The statement is patently untrue, and therefore it is unlikely that it will work for you. That's why the emphasis is on simply reframing the rule into a preference, the essence of which is true, but which is more flexible: 'I prefer to be liked, but if once in a while I am not I can live with that.'

Similarly an alternative way of flexing a rigid rule that often works well for people is the 'permission to be' statement.

What rigid rules are you applying and where would you benefit from being more flexible? What do you give yourself permission to be? Before the next straight-talking conversation that you need to have, remind yourself what you give yourself permission to be. Say the words to yourself. It might be, 'I give myself permission to be direct.' Or maybe, 'I give myself permission to be out of rapport for a while.' We guarantee that you will be far more effective in the conversation and you will find any break in rapport or hurt to feelings will be temporary.

## Summary

- ○ Most manages are ineffective at honest-feedback conversations
- ○ Most of us overrate how honest and straight-talking we are
- ○ We avoid honest-feedback conversations with others because we dislike being out of rapport and we are hard-wired to be liked
- ○ Being flexible about our need to be liked and be in rapport makes us more effective

# Set the context clearly

The two most common and yet woefully ineffective ways to start an honest-feedback conversation are:

- The *so-how-do-you-think-it's-going* approach
- The feedback sandwich

Let's take them one at a time. So often when we work with someone who has a potentially tricky conversation coming up and we ask how the person intends to start the conversation, the answer that comes back is along the lines of, 'Oh, I'm going to start by asking, "How do you think it's going?"'

Now, we have all been on coaching courses where we have heard about the great virtue of open questions. It seems that the underpinning hope here is that the would-be recipient of your potential feedback will help things along by teeing up the conversation nicely for you or, better still, have a moment of insight about precisely the shortcomings that you want to address. Surely this person is sufficiently self-aware and honest, and must have noticed – like you – that all is not as it should be.

It won't surprise you to hear that there is flaw in this approach. People persistently overestimate the extent to which other people think like them and hold similar views. This person is unlikely to share your point of view. And the problem is compounded by the phenomenon that psychologists refer to as 'confabulation'.

Confabulation is that uniquely human ability to spontaneously fabricate a version of reality that works for us and gives us the most comfort, or makes us look good. It is the way we delude ourselves to make ourselves feel better. It is the story we tell ourselves, and we convince ourselves of its truth.

When we are under pressure, we are particularly likely to see reality in a way that protects our self-esteem. We will fabricate explanations that put us in a better light. That is why any feedback that drives improvement can't be entirely mediated from within. It requires the input of a measure or observation from the outside. And that is where you come in.

If you start a conversation by asking a question when your real aim is to communicate a point of view, you appear disingenuous. There is another snag: given that the other person is likely to give a response that does not match your own perception, you have lost control of the conversation. From that moment on, you are likely to be attempting to claw it back on to your agenda.

Now let's come on to the feedback sandwich. The concept of the sandwich is that the most effective critical feedback is delivered between two slices of praise, one to start and one to finish. The 'praise sandwich' has been a staple of many feedback courses for many years. It is very popular with the poor soul having to deliver the feedback because it gives the illusion of staying comfortable, before and after the criticism, and with any luck you can skate quickly over the nasty bit.

We have worked with tens of thousands of managers on the subject of giving feedback. We ask their preferred method of receiving feedback and we ask them for real examples of feedback that has worked for them. The 'sandwich' is ominously absent. The most commonly cited three words that these managers use to describe the way they would prefer to receive feedback are 'honest', 'direct' and 'straight'. As one manger put it, 'After you have been on the receiving end of the sandwich, you are always left waiting for the "but".'

The sandwich gives mixed messages: the praise is contaminated by the criticism and the criticism is diluted by the praise. You need to be prepared to feel uncomfortable if you have difficult feedback to deliver. Do not be tempted to soften it with praise.

Indeed the sandwich has become such a staple that people are often a little taken aback by our challenging of its supremacy. One senior executive asked, 'But surely you should always start with a positive?' Recall that one of the difficulties of delivering honest feedback is the risk to rapport. If you start with praise, you either seem disingenuous or you set a climate at the start, which is simply going to underscore a far greater rupture in rapport when you have to deliver the criticism.

We recommend you start the crucial part of the conversation by setting out the context stall clearly. A good setting-the-context statement opening does these things:

- States the context
- States your positive intent towards the other person (i.e. your commitment to listen and do what you can to help)
- States the need for change

It should be clear and brief. Be prepared to stay silent once you have set out your stall. Don't feel the need to keep talking. Get in the habit of preparing setting out your stall in advance. Hone it down. Practise it. For example:

- 'I need to talk to you about X. I'm not happy about the situation and I sense that you are not either'
- 'I want to support you in putting the situation right'
- 'I am not prepared to let things continue the way they are'

This is not to suggest that praise is not important – quite the contrary. Praise generously and authentically. If you praise authentically, the recipient will view you as someone whose views are valid. Keep the praise separate. It is too important to use as a Trojan horse to make criticism more comfortable to deliver.

## Summary
- ○ Start an honest-feedback conversation by setting out the context clearly
- ○ Praise generously and authentically, but never as a Trojan horse for criticism

# Describe the gap

Amanda came to us with her problem: she was a junior architect at a large international design and building firm, had set herself the goal of becoming a junior partner within a given timeframe, but expressed frustration that she had not received feedback on how she was progressing from the senior partner to whom she reported. We suggested that she ask for feedback.

When we next saw Amanda, she seemed like a new person, but not for the better. 'I asked for it straight,' she told us, 'but he was brutal. He ripped into everything. It really slayed my confidence.'

When we suggested that it did not sound as though the senior partner had gratuitously bashed her confidence, she replied along the lines: 'Well, what else could he do? He was only being honest.'

This is the misconception that is at the heart of the paradox about giving feedback. There is an erroneous assumption that a trade-off is necessary: we either deliver it in a sandwich surrounded by comforting fluffy slices of bread, or we are hurtful and prompt inevitable defensiveness in the recipient. Neither is necessary. We encourage people to look at feedback simply in terms of describing a gap. Looked at this way, the toxicity is taken out of a situation.

This is an incredibly simple but effective way to give feedback that you fear may be difficult, emotive, sensitive or uncomfortable. Try it out:

- State in clear, non-emotive terms what you are currently seeing versus what you would like or expect to be seeing. 'What I would like/expect to see is … , but what I am currently seeing is …'
- Think of it this way: you are taking all of the heat but none of the weight out of the situation

The senior partner's best approach would have been to state where Amanda should currently be if she were on track to reach her goal, state where he perceives her to be currently, and agree that the gap between the two is what they need to work on together.

And, of course, the gap is the *way you see it*. Remember the principle of 'I-speak'. You speak for yourself in a feedback conversation. It is your observation, and your observation is valid and important, but you don't have the monopoly on universal truth. If you suggest that you do, you are more inclined to alienate the recipient of the feedback.

So, you have clearly stated the context at the outset and you have stated the gap as you see it. Now is a good time to show that you are happy to do some listening and that this is not simply a one-sided download. The important thing is that you have put your observation out on the table. Now that you have delivered your feedback honestly, you have set the groundwork to start listening.

Once you have described the gap, ask an open question. Keep it open and broad. You do not want to lead the other person in a given direction. We once worked with a manager who gave one of his team some feedback about reports persistently being handed in late. After describing the gap, he asked his question: 'Is it because the deadlines that I give you are not realistic in the first place?'

'Sure, that's it,' replied the employee. End of conversation.

So, keep the question open and broad. Good phrases are simply: 'What do you say?' or, 'What are your thoughts?'

If Joe used this approach with Francis it would look like this: 'I want to have this conversation with you, Francis, because I am not happy with the way I see things going. I want you to know that I am committed to listening and giving you all the support I can in helping to improve the situation. By this point in the project I would expect to see … but in reality, I feel that I am only seeing … That leaves a gap and I am really concerned about. That's the gap that I would like us to work together on closing. What do you say?'

Looked at this way, there is no lack of clarity or impact in what Joe is saying, but the heat or toxicity has been taken out of it.

## Summary

○ When you give feedback, simply approach it as describing a gap
○ Point out that the gap is the thing that the two of you will work together to close

○ Ask a question to show that you are ready and willing to listen – keep it brief, broad and open

## Always preserve the other person's self-esteem

When you are describing the gap, you are solely addressing the behaviour that you observe and nothing more. That is both your right and responsibility as a leader, coach or friend. If you step beyond that, you can scarcely be surprised if you encounter defensiveness or even hostility.

Recall how our inner cave dweller likes to make rapid judgements and form them into universal rules – a safety-first survival strategy that worked for our ancestors but causes untold obstacles in communication and relationships.

Most of us like to believe that we are good judges of character, that we get a fix or a read on a person very rapidly. The simple fact that most people rate themselves as above average as a judge of character is a good indicator that this is erroneous.[54]

Research has repeatedly shown that we are likely to *over*-attribute the behaviour that we observe in others to their character or personality (what psychologists call their 'disposition'). Evidence also shows that once we have formed a judgement we fairly stubbornly convince ourselves that we are right. When people are confronted with hard evidence that this thinking error is very common, they tend to recognise it and agree – but nonetheless believe that it applies to others and, in spite of this, *their* personal judgements remain true.[55]

Even well-recognised personality profiling tools, such as the Myers-Briggs Type Indicator, measure dimensions of personality that are not in reality particularly stable at all. On immediate re-testing, a fifth of people discover that their personality type has apparently changed and, over a longer period, two-thirds of people show different results when re-tested.[56]

Whatever feedback you need to give, your mind has probably started to explain the phenomenon in terms of the other person's disposition; far better to leave this explanation where it is: in your mind.

Not only is there a fair probability that you are mistaken, remember that the recipient of the feedback is hard-wired to preserve self-esteem. If you relate the gap that you are describing to causes stemming from the other person's disposition, you only leave that person two options: defend or counter-attack. A counter-attack may be open or in the form of surly passive-aggressive behaviour. Either way, the other person is not listening and you therefore have not achieved your objective.

Now, you may accidentally stray into a 'dispositional' feedback or you may be wise enough not to, but the recipient of the feedback may react defensively or aggressively, even though your feedback has been exemplary. Remember, we all put our own interpretations on what is happening, and the recipient of your feedback is no different. If he feels under personal attack, he is not listening. You need to act. You need to step in to assure the recipient that his sense of self-esteem isn't under threat in this conversation.

The best tactic is to reassure him that the issue is not about him personally, it is about the situation as you see it and the behaviour that will be needed from him to fix the situation, for example, 'My sole concern here is that Project X, as I see it, is off-track. It's your area of accountability, so I want to work with you to fix the situation.'

Again, the law of reciprocity may help here. If you accept in some small way you may have contributed to the situation – perhaps you weren't sufficiently clear about expectations in the past – you will take some of the heat out of the situation.

Another useful tactic is to reassure the other person of your positive intentions by reaffirming your commitment to a common interest. Be prepared to do this at any time. Examples of this approach are: 'I'm having this conversation with you because I want us to have the best possible working relationship'; or, 'I'm having this conversation with you because I want your project to be as successful as it can possibly be.'

While feedback in the moment is generally best, if feelings are still heightened following an incident it is wise to wait until the intensity of the moment has passed. Sports psychologists typically recommend that coaches do not give feedback immediately after a failure or defeat.

Sports psychologist Julie Douglas, from Loughborough University, also points out that praise is important in boosting self-confidence. As Julie points out, once people have willingly accepted our praise they more readily accept our criticism. After all, the sole purpose of giving feedback is to improve performance. While the recipient of some negative feedback has digested the impact and had a moment to reflect, you might want to refer to something done well to remind the individual that he or she does have the capacity to perform and turn things around, for example, 'Look, remember that piece of work that you did on Project XYZ. That piece of analysis was really well researched. That's the sort of thing that I would like to see more of.' But, of course, never use praise purely as a precursor to criticism.

Preserving self-esteem does not mean that you can – or should – keep the other person unceasingly feeling good or happy. It is also worth pointing out that you can't prevent somebody from feeling a temporary 'low' following negative or critical feedback. This is an inevitable part of the mind and body's physiological response to negative feedback. If you are witnessing this response, it is likely that the feedback has been received. It is often wise to allow the other person to go through this cycle of emotions before moving the conversation forward to solutions. And, yes, you may have to be okay with being temporarily not liked.

## Summary

○ Do not criticise – or make assumptions about – the other person's disposition or character
○ Stick to talking about the behaviour as you see it
○ Be prepared to assure the other person at any time that he or she is not under attack
○ Remind the other person why it feels so important to you to have this conversation: the commitment to a common interest

# Be clear about what you are asking for

Astrid asked for our help with a particularly difficult conversation that she needed to have with one of her team, Thomas. When asked what the aim of conversation was, she explained that she wanted to make it clear to Thomas that she was not happy with his attitude. When asked to be more specific, Astrid continued, 'I want him to realise the effect that his behaviour has on the rest of the team, and ask him to cut it out ... come to work with a different attitude.'

You can probably figure how the conversation will go, and you can probably spot the crucial piece that is missing. And yet, when giving negative or critical feedback, we frequently put the entire focus on communicating what we are unhappy with, and give little thought to precisely what it is that we would prefer to see instead. The term we use is 'clear request'.

A clear request requires you to describe what it is that you would like to actually see happening as clearly as if you were able to sit and view it on a screen.

Frequently employees receive performance reviews that exhort them to: be more proactive; be more of a team player; show more initiative; show a more positive attitude. However, in the case that we referred to at the start of this chapter, Joe only started to make progress with Francis when he described what he would be seeing if he was confident that good progress was being made on the assignment. For example, Francis would come to him with progress updates on the project every Friday. It was a small thing but it started to paint a picture for Francis of what was in Joe's mind. It transpired that Joe ultimately created a role for Francis that played very much more to his strengths, but the honest communication between them meant that the relationship was salvaged.

Dr Tim Rees takes it further. Dr Rees is a researcher and Senior Lecturer in Sports Psychology at the University of Exeter, and he has pioneered research into helplessness and the effect that this has on performance. His persuasive thesis is that, for feedback to work, the recipient needs to feel confident that he or she is in control of the factors that are required to bring about an improvement. 'Perceptions of control,' he says, 'have a big impact on how people interpret failure. If you can find areas that you can control, if someone can help you to understand the aspects were within your control, improvement is likely to follow.'

But of course, as Dr Rees points out, the flip side is also true. 'If a coach or leader leaves you with the impression that there is no way to get better, you won't get better.'

Negative feedback is vital to performance, but in isolation it is unlikely to bring about improvement. The focus must be on both the shortcoming and also the possibility of improvement and the specific actions – within the control of the recipient – that will make a difference.[57]

In Francis's case, deep down he knew that he simply did not have the technical expertise to engage with contractors on the technical aspects of the specific assignment. Because this was not going to change, he took his solace by creating an alternative explanation of what was happening. He responded to helplessness by deluding himself. When Joe was able eventually to confront him with reality, progress was made by focusing on the factors which were under Francis's control, such as the quality of communication, the timeliness of reports and the accuracy of information.

If you have not described clearly and objectively what these would look like to you, you can hardly complain if you do not see an improvement. Your clear and specific request may not be the *right* answer. You may have to listen and develop the best solution together. But if you are giving feedback you need to have thought through 'what "good" looks like', and focus on things that are within the other person's sphere of control.

## Summary

○ Too often we leave people with the message that we want to see a change, but we fail to articulate what that change looks like

○ If you have a clear picture in your head of what 'good' looks like, be prepared to describe it to the other person

○ Think of it this way: if the two of you were looking at a screen into the future, what would you want to actually see happening on that screen

○ Focus on specific aspects of improvement that are within the other person's sphere of control or influence

# Navigate the landmines and pitfalls

Honest-feedback conversations have a nasty habit of taking you in a direction that you did not intend. Before the conversation, you have a clear sense of where you intend to reach by the end of the conversation, and a plan to get there, but nonetheless you come away from the conversation feeling, 'Now, that's not what I intended to happen.'

Preparation is vital, but you also need a toolkit of techniques to deal with the unexpected in the moment. Here are some of the common pitfalls and some of the tactics that we have found useful:

### Disappearing into the specifics

People often feel that they go in with a specific example to illustrate their point and then they end up disappearing into a rabbit-hole of detail about it. If the aim is solely to discuss a specific incident, no problem, but much of the time it isn't: it is a pattern or repeated issue that concerns you and the discussion about details misses the point about the bigger picture.

A good way to avoid getting bogged down in the detail of a specific incident is to acknowledge the incident, without dwelling on it, for example, 'Francis missed the meeting.' Point out that, to you, it seems that it is part of a pattern, and then move on to the likely effect of the pattern. The crucial thing is the effect that this is having on you and on the project as a whole.

Joe may have said to Francis, 'Francis, it's not just about what happened last Monday ... it feels to me like it's part of a pattern, but the real issue here is that this is having an effect on our relationship, the project and the team.'

## Arguing like two lawyers

In business, we are encouraged to evaluate situations as objectively as possible. Before an honest-feedback conversation, you gather your objective evidence to back up the points that you intend to make.

The problem with this approach is that you are not attempting to persuade a jury; you are attempting to engage with and convince another person. Most of us are not readily convinced by evidence alone, especially when our self-esteem may be under threat. As screenwriter Robert McKee points out, when people listen to evidence it tends to encourage them to search out evidence to counter the points that they are hearing. You may well have had the experience that you go into a conversation with a document chest full of evidence, but, rather than convince, it invites the other person to put up even more evidence to the contrary.

If evidence has not worked, it can be very effective to explain how things feel subjectively from your point of view, for example, 'When I see this happen … , I feel …' This is because no one can dispute your subjective feeling. It is okay to tell someone how you feel about a situation, as long as you acknowledge that it is your subjective feeling. And by the way, keep it to: when I see *xyz*, I feel *abc*.

Joe might, for example, say to Francis, 'When I get a call to say, "Where's Francis? He didn't show up at the meeting," I feel concerned and I find myself questioning how committed you are to the project.'

## The feedback boomerang

You intend to give somebody some honest feedback, but she seems to take the cue that it is open season on giving straight-talking feedback, and it turns out that she has some home truths for you. In fact, when you come away from the conversation, far from delivering your message effectively, you find yourself distinctly on the back foot. Sound familiar?

The feedback boomerang is a difficult one to deal with. If you listen with an open mind, you soon find yourself losing control of the agenda, and you fail to meet your objective in the conversation. If you don't, then how can you possibly ask another person to listen openly to what *you* have to say?

The solution is to agree to listen generously to the other person's feedback but make it contingent on him doing you the courtesy of listening to yours first, for example, 'Francis, I am more than happy to listen to any feedback that you have for me and I will fix up a conversation to do that, but I first need to feel confident that you have heard and understood my concerns about *xyz*. Is that fair?'

Agree to make the discussion of their feedback a separate conversation. You may meet resistance, but stick with it. Consider phrases like: 'I appreciate that your feedback to me is also important, but I would like to keep the two things separate. Right now I have asked that we talk about *XYZ*.'

## The defensive-aggressive reaction

It can sometimes seem that some people just refuse to take feedback, they stubbornly refuse to take advice on board or acknowledge that they may have a failing.

You prepare carefully; you choose your words judiciously, and deliver them tactfully. You even visualise the conversation going well in your mind – but the recipient of your feedback responds with defensive aggression. You feel as though you have made a mess of the conversation, but this is not necessarily so. Remember you alone control *what you do* in a conversation. You do not control what you get back. Your behaviour is not the sole factor that influences the other person's response. All conversations have a broader context. There will be a range of other factors at play, and your role in the conversation is only one.

Remember the importance of self-esteem and the extent to which people will go in order to preserve it. A defensive-aggressive reaction is often a temporary short-term, self-esteem-protecting measure. It is neither wrong nor dysfunctional. Pushing your message further is likely to heighten this reaction. A self-esteem-protecting reaction will be particularly likely if the individual is feeling under pressure or if things have not been going his way.

People often ask what they should say. Quite often what people ultimately do with the feedback and how they react in the heat of the moment can be two very different things. Beyond making your point and ensuring the person recognises that you are not intending to attack their self-esteem, it is often wise not to say anything, but to let the moment pass and let the message settle. Just because somebody appears to reject your message in the heat of the moment, it does not mean that the message has not landed and it does not mean that the other person will not act.

A useful technique, if you want to set the right climate at the start of a meeting, is to remember that people have an inbuilt tendency to behave in the way in which we indicate that we expect them to behave. This is sometimes known as *giving them a reputation to live up to*. If Joe says to Francis, 'Look, Francis, I know you are the sort of guy who likes people to be straight and direct with their feedback,' Francis is likely to agree. What's more, he is, therefore, more likely to display this behaviour during the conversation.

We recommend something similar at the end of a conversation, along the lines of: 'I want to say thank you for being good enough to hear me out and take it on the chin.' Regardless of how the individual has acted in reality, he is inclined to identify positively with your description of what just happened, and to behave accordingly.

## Summary

- ○ Don't get bogged down in the detail of a specific incident
- ○ Refer to the incident and then swiftly move on to the fact that you see it as a pattern and that pattern has an effect
- ○ If you are stuck arguing over evidence, subjectively state how you feel
- ○ Agree to listen to feedback in a separate conversation, provided that you feel you have been heard and understood

# CHAPTER 10
## BULLETPROOF REINFORCEMENT

## Bulletproof your mind through your body

Remember that your body has feelings, too. The stress engendered by feeling that you're under attack takes a physical, as well as psychological, toll.

We've talked in this book about how being bulletproof involves deflecting attacks, rather than meeting them head on, and about how wearing a metaphorical silk shirt that will allow you to remove the arrows works more effectively that wearing a professional suit of armour. This less confrontational approach offers physical, as well as psychological, well-being.

In one study,[58] 255 medical students were questioned to establish their level of cynical hostility. When the group was revisited 25 years later, it was discovered that the most hostile were five times more likely to have suffered heart disease and general cardiac problems than those who were less hostile.

Research by Peter Borkenau, from Bielefeld University, indicates that the way in which we physically move can have a significant effect on our state of mind, with happy people showing a tendency to move in a distinct way, characterised by a more relaxed gait, swing of the arms and more animated hand movements.

Try this out as an experiment: spend a couple of hours moving as a highly relaxed and happy person would move; become aware of how this affects your state of mind. If it works well for you, as it appears to do for most people, remember that you have the option of slipping into this mode of movement every time you want to give your happiness a top up. Who knows? You might just find yourself moving in this way as a habit.

Acting coach, Peter Nicholas, points out that we carry far more of our thoughts and feelings in our physical being than many of us realise. He encourages both actors and business people to understand the connection between their physicality and the way in which they feel and think.

Science is increasingly supporting Nicholas's view. It used to be thought that the brain was the one and only seat of our emotional and cognitive life, sending instructions out to our machine-like muscles and organs. However, fascinating new insights suggest that this relationship is far more complex and interrelated.

It seems that, to a degree, we literally think and feel with organs and muscles of our body. Our thoughts and feelings can be sensed in our organs before they can be registered in the brain. Neuroscientist Antonio Damasio has demonstrated through a series of experiments using sensors attached to the skin that our organs can respond to situations – such as anxiety about risk, fear of loss and excitement about gain – before the brain could conceivably have registered the data that were causing these feelings.

Damasio asked his subjects to take part in a simple gambling game. There are four decks of cards, two black and two red. The subject simply has to turn over one card at a time from any deck. Each card indicates that the subject has either lost or won a certain amount of money.

It is set up to look entirely random, but it isn't. Unknown to the subject, two of the decks offer greater amounts of money, but the risks of losses for these two decks are also greater (from these decks, the losses may be several times greater than the gains). The remaining two decks offer much more modest and balanced wins and losses. If the subject selects from the more modest decks he makes a profit. The higher-risk decks deliver a loss.

It takes a good fifty turns of the card before the typical subject recognises a pattern and adapts his strategy accordingly, but fascinatingly the hand recognises this before the brain. The sensors on the hand indicate higher anxiety associated with the higher-risk deck before the subject is conscious of a pattern.

The hand has the feeling before the brain. The hand feeds information to the brain. Imagine our ancestor in his or her threatening environment. When confronted with a predator, fear causes blood and oxygen to flow to the muscles to prepare for fight or flight. It now appears that her organs were already gearing up before her visual cortex had recognised the stimulus that was causing the fear.

Our muscles and organs, to some degree, give instructions to our brains. We know that we tend to feel more confident when we stand in a more confident way. Most people say that they feel better if they smile. Tense and highly strung people often appear to carry a lot of physical tension in their bodies. People with low self-esteem tend to adopt a stance that makes them appear apologetic, as if they are trying not to take up too much space.

Peter Nicholas adds that athletes and professional performers learn to pay attention to their physicality. But most people don't. If you stoop your shoulders, tense up your neck and your back, foreshorten your lungs, now become aware of how much less confident you feel.

Our thoughts and feelings become encoded into our muscles and continue to send signals to our brain for some time after the initial incident that caused the feeling. Notice how when you stretch out your muscles you feel better.

Both yoga and t'ai chi operate on the principle of combining muscle stretching with the breath, and it is no surprise that both have been around for millennia. They work; they are not simply for New Age hippies. The term 'yoga' originates from a Sanskrit word meaning to unite or make whole. The process of stretching out the muscles creates a sense of regeneration and renewal. The top-performing tennis players can be seen to combine what author and researcher Jim Loehr refers to as 'recovery rituals' into their game.[59] Those relaxing stretches between points are crucial and make the difference between top performance and mediocre performance every bit as much as what happens during live play.

To make your mind more bulletproof, pay attention to your body. Become aware of where you carry tensions and feelings. How do you physically stand or carry yourself when your confidence is either high or low? Where do you notice the difference? Practise yoga and t'ai chi; the techniques you learn will increase your awareness of the connection between your body and your thoughts and feelings. You do not have to join a club or go to classes. A couple of minutes a couple of times a week will make a difference.

Even visualising yourself stretching out your muscles will help to relax your mind. The reactions and responses created by visualising yourself doing something are – in a neurological sense – remarkably similar to the reactions and responses of physically doing it.

When physically getting up and stretching may look a little odd – say, for example, in a meeting – this technique will help you to become more centred:

1. Sit on a chair, with your feet flat on the floor a couple of feet apart
2. Take one deep, slow breath, and let your neck and shoulders physically relax
3. Then slowly take nice, easy breaths into the diaphragm and, as you do so, extend your arms directly upwards, until they are straight
4. Look up and picture your fingers reaching up to the sky
5. Then, with a nice slow exhale, allow your torso to bend gently downwards, feeling each vertebra stretch out one by one, until your head is hanging downwards loose, using its weight to stretch out all of the tension from your back
6. When you are ready, bring your torso back upwards, picturing yourself breathing into the small of your back. Picture each vertebra, one by one, moving back to its original position
7. Now repeat the process; move only your arms, but in your mind's eye picture your whole body moving
8. Now repeat the process letting your arms rest still, but as you visualise your whole body going through the movement, just raise your

hands at the wrist, and let them fall forward, just as your body would be falling forward

9. Do the slow, easy breath in time with the visualisation
10. Finally repeat, just moving your little fingers in time with the visualisation and the breath

Relaxation is as vital to performance as practice or feedback, but not all relaxation is the same. It's important to be able to differentiate between active and passive forms of relaxation. What might be called 'passive' forms of relaxation – the unholy three of alcohol, cigarettes and television (which could be extended to internet and computer games) – tend not to have the beneficial effects of 'active' relaxation: yoga, sport, taking a walk. Reading a book or going to a play or movie is more effective than passively settling in front of the TV or internet, because these activities require you to invest a little more cognitive effort and as a result you have the therapeutic benefits of distraction.

We all have our weaknesses: sweets, junk food, alcohol or cigarettes, to name but a few. When we feel stressed or anxious because we're under attack, it's very easy to obey our immediate instinct to reach for one of these familiar comfort blankets.

But just as it's better to pause, and be mindful of the effect of going with the immediate instinct to snap back at those who are attacking us or lose our tempers with the situation or descend into defeatism and self-pity, it's also better to pause and think about how we'll feel if we rely on sugar, alcohol or junk food to get us through these difficult times. Of course, it's okay to have a chocolate bar or a beer; the important thing is not to rely on these. In other cases, when our minds are distracted or our stomachs knotted with anger or fear, eating often slips off our to-do lists, but good food and a balanced diet are important for anyone looking to be bulletproof.

Remember Jim Loehr's observation about elite tennis players: recovery rituals are essential. Your body and mind simply cannot function without regular breaks. Gentle physical activity is ideal, so try going for a walk or doing gentle stretches.

## Summary

○ Be prepared for the physical strain that being under fire can have on your body
○ Keep making healthy choices about diet, exercise and relaxation when under fire
○ Take regular and frequent short breaks, ideally combined with some gentle physical activity

# Fake it until you make it

Humans express their feelings of power and confidence through open, expansive postures. The guy with his feet on the table and his elbows spread behind his head is obviously self-assured and in command. Similarly when we feel insecure or helpless, we exhibit closed, contractive body language, making ourselves seem smaller and aiming for protection with such positions as tightly folded arms.

But can this relationship between feelings and body language work the other way? In other words, can adopting confident, powerful stances actually make you *feel* more confident and powerful?

This is actually more useful than it might sound because feeling powerful does more than simply boost self-confidence, important though that is. Psychologists have, for instance, shown how it can enhance cognitive functions as well as make us feel more positive and constructive. Powerful individuals are also more likely to take action.

The level of testosterone, the hormone that helps us in competition and gives us drive, is greater when people feel powerful, while the natural level of the stress hormone cortisol is higher in people who feel that they aren't powerful. Chronically elevated levels of cortisol are connected with a variety of mental and physical problems.

A group of psychologists from the universities of Columbia and Harvard recently investigated the intriguing theory that the connection between exhibiting confident, powerful body language and actually experiencing these feelings could work both ways.[60]

Forty-two participants were positioned in either high-power poses (open body language such as leaning forward on a desk with arms spread wide across it) or low-power poses (closed, self-defensive positions, which included sitting with hands clasped in the lap).

Tests from electrocardiographs and saliva showed that high-power poses caused an increase in testosterone and a decrease in cortisol while low-power poses did the opposite. Also, high-power posers were more likely to focus on rewards, and they reported feeling significantly more 'powerful' and 'in charge'. The scientists conclude: 'The implications of these results for everyday life are substantial.'

So, resisting the temptation to close up physically when you're under attack and adopting, instead, confident poses can not only make you look more confident but can make you feel it as well. It can also improve your mind's ability to work through the situation.

If you want to feel more confident, boost your levels of testosterone, the get-out-and-compete hormone. We now know that you can do this by simply striking a powerful pose and holding it for a couple of minutes.

Here's one to try: stand purposefully behind a chair, lean forward and rest your hands on the back of the chair, with your legs relaxed and flexible. Lean forward as though you are about to talk assertively to a group of people.

## Summary

- Strike a high-power pose for a couple of seconds if you want to boost your feelings of competitiveness and confidence
- Become aware of your physical posture and the effects that it is likely to be having on your levels of testosterone or cortisol

# Distraction is preferable to rumination

### Case Study 10.1

Jon and Lola are married, and they work at the same corporation. Both knew that trading conditions were tough and the organisation was looking at cutbacks. As the spectre of redundancy loomed, the climate at work was deteriorating, which, in turn, was leading to stress for both at home.

Lola knew that the small department that Jon headed up was likely to be in the firing line, suffering the most swingeing cuts, of which Jon, personally, could be one of the casualties.

Lola wanted to talk about the situation, but every evening, stick in hand, Jon took their Labrador for a vigorous walk across the nearby common. Lola was worried that Jon was running away from the situation, an  avoiding confronting the reality. Surely, she reasoned, he needed to talk about it ... unless he got these feelings out, the pressure would become too much.

Until recently the received wisdom very much supported Lola's view – but Lola is mistaken, at least up to a point.

The word 'ruminate' comes from the Latin for chewing and it refers to the process in which cattle chew up, swallow, and then regurgitate and re-chew their feed. As humans we often do this with problems and worries.

The difference is that, unlike cows and grass, regurgitating thoughts and worries doesn't do humans any good. In fact, according to research carried out by Dr Susan Nolen-Hoeksema, a psychologist at Yale University, ruminating on a problem too much can make finding a solution *more* difficult. Worse that than, it can lead to a loss of social support as friends and family lose patience with a ruminator. It can also cause depression, according to Dr Nolen-Hoeksema's research. Ruminators, she calculated, are four times as likely as others to suffer from depression.[61]

She discovered, for instance, that following the San Francisco earthquake of 1989, ruminators exhibited more signs of depression and post-traumatic stress disorder than non-ruminators.

The temptation when we have a problem at work is to run it over and over in our minds, but, according to Nolen-Hoeksema's findings, rumination can actually impair problem solving. Even when they come up with a solution, ruminators don't have much confidence in it and are likely not to implement it. Women, according to her findings, are more likely to be ruminators than men, perhaps for cultural reasons.

One way of avoiding unhelpful rumination is to distract yourself. There is increasing evidence that distracters deal with stress better than ruminators. Actively immerse yourself in an absorbing activity; sports, reading, theatre, cinema or other hobbies, including a vigorous walk, all help.

Distracting is not running away from the problem. It simply allows your mind to take a break and come back to the issue refreshed.

Once you've controlled unhelpful, unproductive rumination, you can focus on practical solutions. Pondering a problem with a view to solving it by thinking about measures that you can take is more practical and helpful than rumination.

## Summary

- If you find that you're endlessly turning a problem over in your mind that means you're ruminating on it
- Actively distract yourself from this rumination
- Focus instead on practical solutions – and then make a conscious effort to implement them

# Become more mindful

We've looked at the wide variety of mental and psychological skills that can allow you to become bulletproof but it's worth adding another dimension: psychological well-being. This not only includes mindfulness but also its close relation, meditation.

Meditation increases the area of the brain that's linked to regulating emotion and can bring about improvements in physical well-being by increasing blood flow, reducing blood pressure and reducing the risk and severity of cardiovascular disease. Studies show that people who have learnt mindfulness experience long-lasting physical and psychological stress reduction.

Professor Mark Williams works at the Oxford Mindfulness Centre, which is a UK-based charity that is part of the Department of Psychiatry at Oxford University and that works with partners around the world to prevent depression and enhance human potential through the therapeutic use of mindfulness. He says, 'I was initially quite sceptical about mindfulness because it seemed a bit "alternative" but one of the things that convinced me was practising mindfulness myself and realising that it can help you see new elements of your life.'

He began to realise that mindfulness could affect all the mental processes that damage people's mental health. 'There is a growing interest in mindfulness among the medical community. It's now in the National Institute for Clinical Excellence guidelines for treatment.' The courses that Professor Williams and his team at the Oxford Mindfulness Centre run have been shown to approximately halve the rates of relapse among people with recurrent depression.

The Oxford Mindfulness Centre is now bringing mindfulness into the workplace, as it also has important lessons for those of us who don't suffer from depression but are experiencing temporary difficulties and challenges. Similar mindfulness programmes have already been adopted by companies such as Apple and Google.

We looked at the use of being in the moment: focusing on the sounds and sights around you as you walk to the supermarket or from the station, instead of thinking about what you've got to do in the future and what has happened earlier. That's a form of meditation. Here's a very simple exercise in meditation:

1. Sit or lie down so that you're comfortable. Make sure that if you're lying down you're not going to fall asleep, though
2. Close your eyes for a moment and then start focusing on your breath. Feel your chest and abdomen rise as you inhale, and fall again as you exhale
3. Bring your full attention to this breathing. The focus is on the breath in meditation because it's always with us, always happening, and because it's a neutral, natural activity
4. After a few moments, your attention will almost certainly wander and you'll start thinking – or worrying – about something else. That's natural and it's not something to feel annoyed about. When it happens,

note the thought, whatever it might be, and let it float through your mind as you bring you attention back to your breathing

5. Try this for 10 minutes or so to start with. With practice you'll find the time spent focusing completely on the breath and nothing else will increase. You might also want to meditate for longer periods

Another more obvious way to handle the stress that comes with being under fire is to simply plan other activities. If you like films, go to the cinema. If shopping's your thing, then do that. It's the same with reading, cooking or painting.

But this time when you take part in these familiar pastimes, make sure that you're focusing on them. Try to avoid letting your mind drift back to the conflict you're involved in, the injustice you've suffered or the attack that's been made upon you. Whenever your mind wanders, bring it back to the activity – focus on every aspect, every word and every detail of the film or play. If you're shopping or going for a country walk, really see, hear, and breathe in what's around you. Imagine you're *in* the book you're reading or really savour the touch and smell of the food you're cooking. It's great to do this anyway, but particularly when you really need to switch off.

## Summary

- ○ Meditation improves physical well-being by increasing blood flow and reducing blood pressure
- ○ Practise being in the moment, focusing only on the sounds and sights around you
- ○ Distraction is better that rumination: read a book, cook, go for a walk, go to the cinema or the theatre

# Use the power of social contact

Dr Michael Ungar is Killam Professor of Social Work at Dalhousie University, Halifax, in Canada. He is a world expert on resilience among young people. Many of those with whom he has worked have suffered severe deprivation in their lives, but the many elements that have provided them with their powers of resilience are relevant to adults working in the corporate world.

One of these is: relationships and social connections. Young people who can rely on strong networks of family and friends are far more resilient that those who don't have these networks. 'This is also important for another element of resilience – establishing your identity and finding your place,' says Dr Ungar. His research has shown that reminding yourself of your social networks helps with bringing about a sense of cohesion and belonging, which is essential for resilience.

Seeing friends and spending time with family also helps when dealing with the stress of being under fire at work, which is an experience that can be compared with bereavement in terms of the stress it causes within an individual. Psychologist Jonathan Haidt writes: 'Adversity doesn't just separate the fair-weather friends from the true; it strengthens relationships and it opens people's hearts to one another.'[62] Professor Susan Nolen-Hoeksema, an expert on bereavement at Yale University, conducted research into the effects on people of losing a loved one; many of those in the study reported a greater appreciation of other people in their lives.

'I'm really not in the mood,' or 'Sorry, I'm just no fun at the moment' might be the immediate response when friends or family ask to see you when you're feeling under attack or going through a tough time at work, but, as we've seen, that immediate response is usually not the best one in these circumstances. You don't need to be the life and soul of the party, but getting out and tapping into social and familial networks will help you to become more bulletproof. Above all, the human is a social animal; that's one of the things that makes us exceptional.

Becoming bulletproof requires a change in thinking and, like most things worth learning, it takes a little time and effort, but the good news is that the benefits from using even a few tools from the bullet-proof toolbox are obvious almost immediately. When these tools are practised, they become habitual responses to workplace 'attack' situations – those that are anticipated as well as those that are not.

When we feel psychologically bulletproof, our confidence expands, relationships improve, judgement and creativity are enhanced and our leadership qualities manifest.

## Summary

O Social contact makes us stronger

O Consciously appreciate people close to you

O Maximise your social contact even when you are not initially in the mood – you will be surprised by the effect that it can have

# CHAPTER 11
## THE BULLETPROOF TOOLKIT
## – 82 WAYS TO BE BULLETPROOF

**1. Become aware of your inner cave dweller**

○ Remember that the legacy of our evolutionary past is always with us

○ The instinctive responses that evolved because they kept our ancestors alive may have been excellent back then, but they are not always so useful today

**2. Learn to guide your cave dweller**

○ The cave dweller reminds us of the sheer power of our automatic responses to situations – listen out for him

○ Practise calming and quietening your inner cave dweller. Become aware of how you learn to make better choices even in the heat of the moment

**3. Be aware of your mind seeking patterns and stories in events**

○ The mind seeks out consistent themes and patterns because it tries to create meaning for us. As natural 'meaning-makers', we frequently make things mean more than they do. When we suffer setbacks, failures or assaults we tend to interpret these things as part of a pattern. We expect them to become repeated

○ Bulletproof people become aware of unhelpful patterns of thought and challenge them

○ They remind themselves that incidents that have happened do not determine what is likely to happen in the future

**4.  Challenge your thinking distortions**
O  How we think about things affects the way we feel
O  The way we feel drives what we do and affects the outcomes we get, and not always for the better
O  Bulletproof people develop the habit of choosing how to think about an incident or situation

**5.  Ask 'What am I making this mean?'**
O  Asking, 'What am I making this mean?' helps us to challenge our distortions and understand our thinking errors
O  Bulletproof people are able to reframe their thoughts and take out the inevitable distortions

**6.  Positive self-talk**
O  Accept that you're facing a challenge – don't deny it
O  Become aware of draining, weakening self-talk ('I can't') – and drop it
O  Find a phrase that is honest but positive, such as 'I can', and say it to yourself

**7.  Don't suppress thoughts – practise letting go**
O  Stepping 'outside yourself' and being aware of your thoughts and feelings is important in becoming bulletproof
O  Developing a calm self-awareness is an essential life skill for bulletproof people
O  Imagine the 'wiser-you', standing alongside yourself and seeing your thoughts and feelings with a bit of objective distance

**8 .  Recognise negative thoughts – let them drift, don't fight them**
O  Identify memories and thoughts as they enter your mind
O  See them for what they are: a point of view, and not some objective truth
O  Observe them dispassionately and watch them float past you

## 9. Stop mind reading

- One of the most common thinking traps is mind reading
- Even when we are convinced that we know what is in another's mind, we are often wrong
- Mind reading is not the same as putting yourself in other people's shoes
- Don't waste time and energy mind reading

## 10. Remember ... nobody noticed ...

- Bulletproof people know that when they make a mistake most people don't notice
- Bulletproof people liberate themselves from potentially embarrassing situations: 'Hey! No one is looking at me'
- Remember, even a Barry Manilow T-shirt flies under most people's radar

## 11. Modify your rigid rules into flexible preferences

- The rules we define about ourselves help us to create the sense of a consistent self, but we lose effectiveness when our personal rules become too rigid
- Bulletproof people don't maintain *must-always* and *should-always* rigid rules
- Bulletproof people develop flexible preferences: 'If that doesn't happen, I'm okay'; 'I prefer to ... but I'm okay if ...'
- Bulletproof people are like flexible trees, swaying in the harshest wind but never losing their firm rooting

## 12. Don't let your cave dweller pick your fights

- Bulletproof people pick their battles wisely
- They recognise that while their inner cave dweller has the urge to settle a score or avenge a slight, they are capable of choosing a wiser and more beneficial course of action
- Bulletproof people calm and guide their inner cave dweller in order to make the wisest choices

○ Let the small stuff go, fight only the important battles and fight them with guile, and with a calm focus

## 13. Turn criticisms around

○ Wrong-foot your opponent by not defending an attack
○ Take breath and a pause, and then move on to what you want to talk about
○ Phrases like 'I need to consider what gave you that impression' make you sound proactive but emphasise the fact that it is an impression only

## 14. Use pauses and silence to your advantage

○ Pause and breathe
○ Do not be scared to allow a moment of silence before you respond
○ Take a moment to note how you feel during a confrontational conversation
○ Identify the thoughts that are leading to these emotions
○ Remind yourself that your thoughts and emotions are not accurate dispassionate 'truths' about the situation

## 15. 'Reflect' before responding

○ Reflect back to the other person what they have said (and how they feel), without putting any spin on it
○ Develop rapport – make it clear that you understand and share their concerns
○ Make a personal reference wherever possible

## 16. Ask for the 'thought behind the question'

○ Before you answer a question, consider the thought behind it. This is the issue that the questioner is really concerned about
○ Make sure that your answer to the question addresses this thought, or else use a question in return to tease out more details

## 17. Shift the focus on to the other person's underlying interest

○ Do not take up a position
○ Enquire about the other person's underlying interest
○ Shift the focus on to the desire to meet common interests

## 18. Insist on specifics

○ Take the sting out of hostile comments by asking for specific details
○ Politely but firmly drill down to find exactly what the questioner is concerned about
○ Once you've identified these precise concerns, explain how you'll act on them
○ If someone suggests that they doubt your competence to deliver something, don't immediately defend – ask specifically what would allay their concerns

## 19. Show that you share the same values

○ Match and reflect the *emotions* of your audience
○ Show that you have the same *values* as your audience
○ Then explain what *action* you're going to take

## 20. Use stories in communication when under attack

○ Use the power of stories to take your audience on a journey with you
○ Having a problem solved, a question answered or a challenge overcome will keep them on board and help persuade them

## 21. Place an issue into a context that works for you

○ Aim to put an argument or an issue into context
○ Pan back from the issue in question to look at the whole organisation or the whole sector or even the state of the country
○ Explore the extremes – and then show why you've opted for your choice, which is the best of both worlds

## 22. Correct inaccuracies when the storm has passed

○ Don't correct an inaccuracy during the heat of the moment – wait until emotions are more stable

○ When you do correct an inaccuracy acknowledge that you in no way diminish the underlying issues and the feelings caused

## 23. Show concern for your assailant

○ Showing concern for the person who might be seen to be attacking is often more effective than counter-attack

○ Suggest that an assault on you may stem from you assailant having difficulties or being under pressure elsewhere

## 24. Outflank your opponent's point of view

○ Establish rapport by listening and reflecting concerns

○ Once you are in rapport, play back the other person's issue or concern, but make a point of overstating it

○ If your best option is to apologise, it is better to over-apologise than risk being seen to under-apologise

## 25. Use the principle of reciprocity

○ Giving ground over a small issue and accepting a point that is obviously of concern to your opponent establishes a rapport that improves communication and helps you win the bigger battle

○ Your adversary is likely to reciprocate with a larger gesture in your favour

## 26. Treat presentations like a performance

○ Remember – those nerves are there to help you, to improve your performance, and not to make life more difficult

○ Become aware of your body gearing up for a performance, and remind yourself to welcome the sensation

○ Use physical stretches and preparation to relax mind and body like any athlete would before a performance

○ Visualise the butterflies in your stomach lining up in formation, as if they mean business

## 27. Practise drawing on different levels of confidence

- ○ You have the full range of levels of confidence within you
- ○ Become aware of what you are like at each level and practise moving between them
- ○ Think of moments when you were at a 'level 10' and play the movie in your head whenever it helps
- ○ Sometimes you'll be aware of a drop in confidence. Remind yourself that that's fine
- ○ Take a breath and imagine yourself 'breathing in' a higher level of confidence

## 28. Create an ally among your audience in advance

- ○ If you have a meeting or presentation coming up with a tough group, contact one individual from that group in advance
- ○ Point out how much you respect this person's opinion
- ○ Ask his or her advice as to the best way to approach the meeting or presentation
- ○ This will flatter the individual and give him or her a perceived stake in your success

## 29. Don't let your boss's problem become your problem

- ○ Bosses aren't exceptionally virtuous or malevolent – they're actually fallible humans with all the usual insecurities
- ○ It's unlikely you loom as large on your boss's radar as you assume – it's unlikely that your boss's behaviour is intentionally directed at you
- ○ Don't waste time hoping for your boss to change – it's easier for you to change your behaviour than for you to change your boss's
- ○ Remember, you almost certainly have higher emotional intelligence than your boss, therefore you are the one who is best placed to navigate the relationship

## 30. Make your boss a customer

O Your boss is first and foremost a customer; knowing this implies a healthy distance

O Your boss is transient; you need to navigate this relationship until you can move on

O Bulletproof people put themselves in the driving seat by creating options for themselves

O Identify the extent of control and influence you have and use it to the maximum

## 31. Remember life may not be fair, but you can live with it

O People often end in a dead end by being determined to satisfy their innate desire for fairness

O A strong belief in fairness can often lead to unproductive behaviours

O When 'It's not fair', calm your inner cave dweller. Bulletproof people say, 'I'm okay and can live with it'

## 32. Deflate the drama

O Avoid drawing attention to your boss's behaviour – avoid becoming an emotionally high-maintenance employee

O In conversation with a toxic boss, take a deep, easy breath before responding

O Puncture a person's silence ploy by drawing attention to it – 'Are you still there?'

O Bulletproof people minimise any sense of drama by keeping their tone adult and businesslike

O Bulletproof people don't take on the role another person is nudging them to play – they know how to break the rapport

O If you want to change your boss's mind about something, don't suggest that her initial judgement was wrong; instead suggest that the situation has changed or new information has come to light

### 33. Create options

○ Stress at work is often accompanied by feelings of helplessness as confidence falls and our focus narrows

○ Stress comes less from job demands and more from the lack of control we have when delivering against those job demands

○ To reduce stress and become more resilient, consider how to increase your own control, freedom and latitude to make decisions – create new options for yourself

○ Create leverage with your boss's boss

○ Like any good supplier, you should always be looking out for more fruitful and productive customers

○ You do not need to use them – just having them empowers you

### 34. Use the three Cs: control, challenge and commitment

○ You have power over the way you think about and relate to your boss

○ Challenge yourself to identify any aspects, large or small, in the current situation over which you have *control* – and take action

○ Consider dealing with them to be a *challenge* and an opportunity rather than a hopeless task

○ If you are under pressure do not reduce your *commitment*. Increase your commitment to your work

○ Don't let the problems you're experiencing with them damage your relationships with others

### 35. Find a mentor

○ Bulletproof people are more resilient and have no concerns about reaching out for support when they need it

○ Having a mentor has been shown to be extremely effective, even when the mentor does not do a great deal

○ Bulletproof people externalise their thoughts by describing them to another person – even imaginary – to gain perspective and make better choices

○ Find a mentor – even an imaginary one

## 36. Teach yourself to be resilient *before* you need it

○ Resilience can be learnt – you can develop and strengthen it

○ Bulletproof people strengthen their resilience *before* they have a knock-back

○ Imagine yourself in the future: write yourself a 'worth-it' letter from *you in the future* to *you in the present*, explaining why sticking at it was worth it

## 37. Practise switching on emotions

○ Switching on positive emotions, especially after a knock-back, is not always easy but you can learn to get better and better at it with practice

○ Using certain thoughts as levers will improve your feelings of optimism and positivity

○ In your mind do an audit of everything you can be grateful for right now. Include the big stuff and the tiny stuff

○ On your list of gratitude choose an item on which to dwell

○ Become aware of your mood changing as you do so

## 38. Do a stock-take of your strengths ...

○ Bulletproof people regularly de-catastrophise by doing a stock-take of their successes

○ No success is too small to add to the stock-take

○ Alternatively, list every success, no matter how small, that you have had on the left-hand side of a piece of paper; on the right-hand side, list the personal strength or attribute that each success evidences

## 39. Use the advocate-for-your-success exercise

○ Imagine that you have hired a lawyer to work for you

○ The job of this lawyer is to seek out and present every possible shred of evidence as to why you should succeed

○ Make a list

○ Read through it

○ Become aware of your mood and energy as you read through it

## 40. Keep separating the facts from the story

○ It's natural to look for interpretation and meaning – but it isn't always helpful

○ The facts are what happened, but the story is what we make them mean

○ Bulletproof people are clear not to confuse fiction with fact

## 41. Don't make 'no' mean more than it does

○ We tend to apply our own logic to happenings that are, in reality, pretty random

○ Tenacity in the face of rejection is a major predictor of success

○ Bulletproof people don't make a rejection mean more than it does – they maintain their objectivity

## 42. Apply the specific-or-universal test

○ Optimists tend to be more successful than pessimists, and your inner cave dweller is a natural pessimist

○ Remember to check your underlying assumptions

○ We often universalise: 'everyone', 'no one', 'always' or 'never'. Is this actually true?

○ Remind yourself that a failure, rejection or setback is likely to be specific to that situation

## 43. Apply the 'down-to-*me*' versus '*not*-down-to-me' test ...

○ Bulletproof people ask the 'down-to-*me*?' versus '*not*-down-to-me?' questions when they experience a setback to understand what has really happened

○ If something was unsuccessful, was it *really* down to you? Is it *really* something about you that cannot be changed?

○ Remind yourself that the answer to at least one – and probably both – of the questions above is likely to be 'no'

## 44. Apply the temporary-versus-permanent test

○ When you are going through a tough time, it probably feels as though things will always be this way

○ Remind yourself that the tough time that you are going through is almost certainly temporary

○ Things will change

## 45. Want it – don't need it

○ When we *need* something, our mind tends to focus on the cost of failure

○ The emotional impact of losing something is twice as great as that of gaining it

○ You can want something very much – that's a healthy form of motivation – but let go of needing it. Whatever the outcome you want, you don't need it. You can still be a healthy, happy individual, even if it does not happen

○ Focus on 'learning' or 'process' goals rather than the outcome. What are the things that will contribute to achieving your goal that are entirely within your influence? Focus on perfecting these one step at a time

## 46. Imagine starting again from 'rock bottom'

○ Think like someone who is starting from zero – everything to gain, nothing to lose

○ If you were starting from zero, what personal attributes or strengths can you point to that indicate you should succeed?

○ Bulletproof people are able to generate a sense of renewal and can therefore tap into its source of optimistic energy

## 47. Use visualisations

○ Visualise your success as waiting for you on the landing of a stair-case, with your rejections being the steps between each landing

○ Use visualisations to refocus your attention away from unhelpful thoughts towards more supportive ones

○ On a journey where you need extra resilience to deal with rejection, visualise a worthwhile prize at the end

## 48. What's your story? Write it down – put it into words

- The power of story helps bulletproof people get through tough periods
- Stories capture our imagination, providing coherence and sense-making
- Bulletproof people are able to write down a credibly optimistic outcome for their personal story, and clarity increases the likelihood of success
- Those who open up and put their traumas into sense-making words recover better than those who don't
- Use the power of words to think things through

## 49. It's okay to be in the cave

- Remember, like the protagonist of any great story, it is likely that you will spend some time in 'the cave'
- The cave represents the lowest, darkest point in your journey
- Remind yourself that like others you'll come through it, more bulletproof than ever

## 50. Stand in the future to see things clearly

- Our minds are better at thinking imaginatively if we're in the future looking back as opposed to standing in the present and trying to imagine a way forward
- Bulletproof people are able to tell a great story of their journey by imagining themselves in the future when things have worked out successfully

## 51. Decontaminate criticism by evaluating it objectively

- Feedback: some is useful, some is harmless and some is downright toxic
- You can't control the feedback you get, but *can* control what you categorise as 'helpful' and 'unhelpful'
- Bulletproof people put themselves in charge of what they keep and what they discard

○ You do not have control over the feedback you receive, but remember you do have control over how you evaluate its usefulness, i.e. what to learn from and what to discard

## 52. View the situation from a different perspective
○ We never *know* another person's intentions in a situation
○ You can take a view on what a person's motivations might have been, but always acknowledge the large scope for error
○ Remember, other people are fallible under pressure – just like us

## 53. Learn to re-focus your mind
○ When we get a knock-back, the feeling in our stomach is created by an important neural function – 'Something is amiss. Better watch out!'
○ We can't easily choose what *not* to think about, but we *can* choose where to focus our attention
○ Focus on positive life incidents – even very small ones. This gives you inner strength in tough times
○ Re-run positive memories in your mind like a movie
○ Practise turning up the contrast, volume, colour or brightness

## 54. Identify the benefits of a situation
○ 'Benefit finding' is the bulletproof person's silver lining, which brings insight, new opportunities, etc., following a non-physical assault
○ If it helps, imagine yourself in the future; challenge yourself to think of every possible benefit that may have arisen out of the tough time that you are going through

## 55. Decontaminate your mistakes
○ Reframe and describe the incident, taking the toxic, negative emotions out of it
○ Note your emotions alongside the facts
○ Be honest and don't try to exculpate yourself or shirk your responsibility; describe what happened and how you feel as a result of it

## 56. De-catastrophise

O  Catastrophising is a common thinking trap that makes incidents hurt us more than they should

O  Bulletproof people step back from catastrophising, objectively weigh their scenarios and identify what is a credibly optimistic outcome from a situation (one that is both positive and believable)

## 57. Switch from 'all-or-nothing' to 'both-and' thinking

O  Bulletproof people know when they are applying 'all-or-nothing' thinking, and change their approach

O  Don't extrapolate rules from one incident to cover all situations

O  Remind yourself that if you have made a mistake it does not mean you have blown everything

O  Ask 'Can *both* this *and* that be true at the same time?'

O  You can *both* slip up *and* succeed in your goals

## 58. Describe in factual and neutral terms

O  Learn to imagine the objective 'wiser-you' alongside yourself giving a calm, dispassionate assessment of the situation

O  Work with the 'wiser-you' to remove the heat and toxicity from difficult situations

O  Describe what happened in purely factual and neutral terms

## 59. Name the emotion

O  Bulletproof people know how to train their inner cave dweller by putting their emotions into words

O  Name the emotion. Try this format: This is what happened (describing in factual and neutral terms); this is how I feel (describing the emotions)

O  Then add the three vital modifying phrases: 'About this' (because it's specific); 'right now' (because it's temporary); 'but I'm basically okay' (because you are)

O  Re-read the sentence and become aware of how you feel as you do so

## 60. Focus on what you can change

○ Set aside the emotional story that seems to want to accompany any failure or setback

○ View bouncing back as a project; simply identify the things that you can improve upon – things that are directly within your control

○ Differentiate realistically between what you can affect and what you can't when it comes to achieving success

○ Set yourself process goals, that is, goals related to the effort and input that you can control, not outcome goals (in other words, results which you can't control)

○ Praise yourself for achieving these goals, and give yourself plenty of small rewards along the way

## 61. Achieve something small in order to achieve something big

○ The best way to achieve a big success is to get in the 'success habit' by achieving some smaller successes first

○ First set yourself some more modest and readily achievable goals

○ Dwell in the feeling and enjoy the success, then set yourself some relatively more stretching goals.

## 62. Be okay with politics – recognise it for what it is

○ Politics is mostly defensive. It is about people protecting their own interests

○ We only see a situation as politics when we're caught on the wrong side of it; otherwise we say, 'It's just the way we are'

○ Nobody is plotting your downfall – you don't figure large enough on their radar

○ Beware of judging too fast, over-emphasising threats or too readily polarising situations as friend or foe. Stand back from the situation, and avoid seeing everything as black and white or good and bad

### 63. Learn to cut through bullshit

- Like office politics, bullshit arises when people create a pretence that we don't have individual needs
- Bulletproof people use straight-talking conversations wisely to cut through bullshit
- Pick straight-talking conversations wisely
- Use 'I-speak', not 'you-speak', in your straight-talking conversations
- Use 'interest-driven', not 'position-driven', language
- Be honest about your interest but focus on addressing the other person's interest

### 64. Reject the martyr syndrome

- Corporations might be run by adults, but they aren't always fair
- Bulletproof people avoid being a victim or a martyr to politics
- Define success as achieving your higher goals rather than winning at the politics

### 65. Remember: you don't need to be in with the in-crowd

- Organisations typically evolve into a small group of insiders and a larger group of outsiders
- Bulletproof people treat the core group just like a boss, i.e. simply as another customer
- You can be respected and valued by the core group without ever trying to enter it

### 66. Ignore ignoring – and focus on a few good friends

- Be objective and remind yourself that it won't last for ever
- Choose a few key relationships and go for quality rather than quantity
- Ignore the ignoring – act like the person you want to be treated as

### 67. Have the confidence to be vulnerable

- Vulnerability is disarming – to express it requires strength and confidence

○ Bulletproof people always remember to ask an adversary for help and advice

## 68. Divide and influence – it's better to focus on changing individuals rather than the whole group

○ It's far more effective to focus on individual group members for one-to-one conversations

○ Trying to change team attitudes? Avoid getting the whole team together to do it – collectively, attitudes get amplified and become more entrenched

○ Bulletproof people avoid reinforcing common group identity in adversarial situations

## 69. Disarm others with 'third-party' compliments

○ Pay compliments via a third party to win over your adversaries

○ Make compliments specific and relevant to the individual

○ Ask advice from your adversaries

○ Reciprocity and compliments work

## 70. Focus on what's working ... not on what's bust

○ Focus on the positives and not the negatives

○ Think about what works and learn from it rather than what doesn't work

○ Use the why-not-a-zero question, instead of the why-not-a-ten question. Ask others to rate how good a situation is from zero to ten, and then enquire about all of the reasons why the rating was not a zero

## 71. Borrow some perspective ... and get *elevated*

○ When we hear stories of people doing great, kind and morally courageous things, we feel better

○ Bring these to mind when you want to be bulletproof and see how you can learn from them

○ Who or what are you going to remind yourself of when you want to get a sense of proportion or do the right thing?

## 72. Give yourself permission to be straight and direct

○ We avoid honest-feedback conversations with others because we dislike being out of rapport and we are hard-wired to be liked

○ Being flexible about our need to be liked and be in rapport makes us more effective

○ Before a straight-talking conversation, remind yourself what you give yourself 'permission to be'

○ Remind yourself: I prefer to be liked, but I'm okay if sometimes I'm not liked for a bit

## 73. Set the context clearly

○ Start an honest-feedback conversation by setting out the context clearly

○ Praise generously and authentically, but never as a Trojan horse for criticism

## 74. Describe the gap

○ When you give feedback, simply approach it as describing a gap

○ Point out that the gap is the thing that the two of you will work together to close

○ Ask a question to show that you are ready and willing to listen – keep it brief, broad and open

## 75. Always preserve the other person's self-esteem

○ Do not criticise – or make assumptions about – the other person's disposition or character

○ Stick to talking about the behaviour as you see it

○ Be prepared to assure the other person at any time that he or she is not under attack

○ Remind the other person why it feels so important to you to have this conversation – the commitment to a common interest

## 76. Be clear about what you are asking for

○ If you have a clear picture in your head of what 'good' looks like, be prepared to describe it to the other person

○ Think of it this way: if the two of you were looking at a screen into the future, what would you want to see actually happening on that screen?

○ Focus on specific aspects of improvement that are within the other person's sphere of control or influence

## 77. Navigate the landmines and pitfalls when giving feedback

○ Don't get bogged down in the detail of a specific incident

○ Refer to the incident and then swiftly move on to the fact that you see it as a pattern and that the pattern has an effect

○ If you are stuck arguing over evidence, state subjectively how you feel

○ Agree to listen to feedback in a separate conversation provided that you feel you have been heard and understood

## 78. Bulletproof your mind through your body

○ Be prepared for the physical strain that being under fire can have on your body

○ Keep making healthy choices about diet, exercise and relaxation when under fire

○ Take regular and frequent short breaks, ideally combined with some gentle physical activity

## 79. Fake it until you make it

○ Strike a high-power pose for a couple of seconds if you want to boost your feelings of competitiveness and confidence

○ Become aware of your physical posture and the effects that it is likely to be having on your levels of testosterone or cortisol

## 80. Distraction is preferable to rumination

○ If you find that you're endlessly turning a problem over in your mind that means you're ruminating on it

○ Actively distract yourself from this rumination

○ Focus instead on practical solutions – and then make a conscious effort to implement them

## 81. Become more mindful

○ Meditation improves physical well-being by increasing blood flow and reducing blood pressure

○ Practise being in the moment, focusing only on the sounds and sights around you

○ Distraction is better that rumination: read a book, cook, go for a walk, go to the cinema or the theatre

## 82. Use the power of social contact

○ Social contact makes us stronger

○ Consciously appreciate people close to you

○ Maximise your social contact even when you are not initially in the mood – you will be surprised by the effect it can have

# EPILOGUE
## GAVIN'S STORY

Gavin was an IT manager in a large financial services company whom we met when he was a participant at a workshop we were running. He expressed particular interest in the ideas we were discussing, many of which we have touched on in *Be Bulletproof* – in fact, so much so that he persuaded his employer that he should develop a role for himself as an 'embedded' communications and performance coach for his colleagues. His employer was supportive and we worked together to help Gavin to develop into the role, which he took to with an intuitive insight and zest – the way people often do when they find themselves in a situation where they finally feel free to play to their strengths.

A couple of years down the line we received a call from Gavin, saying that he wanted to meet and talk. When we met near his organisation's head office, it was not the conversation that we had been expecting. Things had changed when a new boss arrived to head up Gavin's department. Gavin had been called into his new boss's office for what he'd assumed was to be a routine meeting, but he had an uneasy feeling when he realised the head of HR had also been asked to join the meeting. As soon as the boss had started to talk about restructuring the department, Gavin had known what was coming. Soon he'd only been able to see his boss's lips moving, but the actual words that his boss had used to terminate his employment had scarcely registered.

For Gavin it was out of the blue. He had been absorbed in his work and never considered being let go. In the early days, shortly after being rejected by his employer, Gavin made the mistake of trying to tell himself that he didn't give a damn, only to find that he crumpled up with despondency when the truth of the situation leaked back into his conscious mind. He felt lost and helpless for months. He oscillated between feelings of rage about the hurt and betrayal that had been inflicted upon him, and feelings of loathing towards himself for messing up again – for being found out.

Thankfully the conversation did not end there. It was the next stage on this journey that Gavin really wanted to talk about. Suppressing negative thoughts strengthens them, so Gavin learnt to become *mindful* of these painful ideas when they bubbled up. When he experienced that familiar sense of sinking, loss or emptiness, he would let it drift into his mind. He would imagine himself just standing back and taking a look at it, like a cloud, or feeling it like a chill breeze.

There is invariably a turning point when people suffer a blow like this, and Gavin recalled his. It struck him that this was simply part of his story, and that he was in his *'cave'*. The next question was, 'So what would be the most *optimistic, credible outcome* to his *story?'* His boss simply handing him his job back was neither credible nor within his control. The outcome needed to be something that was within his sphere of influence.

By asking this simple question, he allowed the next important insight to enter his mind. For it to be the *most* optimistic, credible outcome, simply answering that getting back to where he was before would not be good enough. The hardship of redundancy should take him forward in some way. With pen and paper in hand, he imagined himself in the future and set about *benefit finding*.

Like many before him, he had experienced the indifferent cruelty of redundancy, and its dislocating sense of rejection. He gave himself a simple focus: to use his coaching and communication skills to help others to reclaim their lives after redundancy. This goal energised him. Like Victor Frankl in the concentration camp, he had given the situation *meaning* beyond his own personal needs. By focusing on others, he had moved away from *all-about-me* thinking. He also drew on the principle of *elevation* – that acts of kindness and compassion to others give us greater energy and emotional resources ourselves.

Gavin acquired clients by word of mouth. As word got around, he was asked to give advice on the local commercial radio station about bouncing back from redundancy. Gavin relished helping others to focus on their strengths and restore their confidence, and to come across well in interviews.

Every small and modest step that made the situation a little better for his children increased his *self-efficacy* and spurred him on to another step. By focusing on at least one important outcome in the whole situation, one that he *could* influence, he increased his sense of *control* and minimised his sense of *helplessness*. And because the outcome concerned helping people with whom he could identify, there was no shortage of *commitment*.

The initial thinking distortions – 'The world is cruel', 'I am unde-serving', or 'I always mess up' – were rendered harmless. The actions he had taken – focusing with absolute determination and compassion on doing worthwhile work that played to his strengths – provided clear evidence that these thoughts were unfounded.

He did not vent his anger at his erstwhile employer. He did not enact his frustration. He was too focused on his primary goal. And because he didn't vent or enact these feelings, he didn't keep fanning the flames of unhealthy emotions.

He spent a lot of time with people whom he would not otherwise have met. Many became friends. Many had extraordinary, fascinating and rewarding stories. In this respect he had no difficulty in *benefit finding*.

While he was absorbed in his work, Gavin, who was not independ-ently wealthy, did not have the longer-term security that he had before. He still felt occasional anxiety or insecurity. He learnt not to deny his negative feelings, but to reframe his feelings in a modified and balanced way. He would remind himself: 'Sure, there are many aspects of this situation that are not ideal, right now, but I'm basically okay.'

By doing this he was using *I-can-cope self-talk*. Gavin even tried a variation on the '*advocate-for-your-success*' exercise. He went through an exercise of writing down all the evidence that he could think of in favour of the idea that he would be okay. It was similar to the *stock-take* of your strengths exercise. 'It felt stilted and awkward at first,' Gavin told us, 'especially as I still had plenty of raw anger, but I forced myself to do it … to write down the words … and in the end I started to feel better and stronger as the words started to flow.'

The use of the phrase 'right now' reminded him that the pain was *temporary and not permanent*. And, of course, seeing the situation as part of his story meant that he saw the situation as a chapter in his story, and not his entire story.

Gavin understood the power of *writing things down*, putting them into words to make sense of the story. He would set his alarm clock half an hour early every morning to put his story – together with thoughts and feelings – into words.

As he developed enough consultancy and coaching work to support himself, Gavin eventually started to notice something different in the way he was working. He felt more relaxed, less agitated by the niggles of office life. He noticed himself feeling less nervous before meetings with senior people, and less anxious about work. He had the ability to put work issues more into perspective. Gavin wasn't familiar with the term but we pointed out to him that it sounded like he was experiencing *post-traumatic growth*.

Eventually Gavin got to a point where he really did not have to rack his brains very hard at all to find benefits in his change in circumstances. Gavin was lucky enough to meet his future wife when he coached her in interview technique following her redundancy. But that's another story.

# ACKNOWLEDGEMENTS

*Be Bulletproof* was very much a collaborative effort. We would like to thank all of those who have generously contributed their time, insight, wisdom and humour: our colleagues at Threshold, Dr Amy Silver, Peter Nicholas, Helen Ayres and Occupational Psychologist Luckwinder Goulsbra; Diane Smith for support with copy; and, for their expertise in sport and performance psychology, Julie Douglas from Loughborough University, Dr Tim Rees, Exeter University, Misha Botting, SportScotland Institute of Sport, and Dr Costas Karageorghis, Brunel University.

We would also like to thank Femi Oyebode, Professor and Head of the Department of Psychiatry at the University of Birmingham, for his expertise on the subject or the healing effect of stories, and similarly Professor Dan McAdams, Department Chair of Clinical Psychology and Personality Psychology at Northwestern University.

Thanks, too, to Hollywood screenwriter and writing coach, Robert McKee, for his exceptional authority on the power of story, and to Christopher Vogler, particularly for his expertise in the area of the 'Hero's Journey' and being 'in the cave'. Similarly we extend our gratitude to Simon Lancaster, leading speech writer, for sharing his tips learnt from working with many leading politicians about communicating under pressure.

Finally, we thank Professor Mark Williams, of the Oxford Mindfulness Centre, University of Oxford, and Professor Kip Williams, for his groundbreaking work in the field of Ostracism and Social Pain.

# ENDNOTES

## Introduction

1   Cherniss, Cary (2000), 'Emotional intelligence: what it is and why it matters', *The Consortium on Emotional Intelligence*, Graduate School of Applied and Professional Psychology, Rutgers University

2   Britt, Thomas W. (January 2003), 'Black Hawk Down at work', *Harvard Business Review*

3   Dweck, Carol (15 November 2011), speaking on BBC Radio 4, Brain Culture

4   Gladwell, Malcolm (22 July 2002), 'The talent myth: are smart people overrated?', *New Yorker*

## Chapter 1

5   Barkow, J., Cosmides, L. & Tooby, J., (Eds.), *The Adapted Mind: Evolutionary Psychology and the Generation of Culture* (Oxford University Press, 1992); Burnham, Terry, and Phelan, Jay, *Mean Genes from Sex to Money to Food* (Perseus Publishing, Cambridge, 2000); Wright, Robert, *The Moral Animal: Evolutionary Psychology and Everyday Life* (Pantheon, New York, 1994)

## Chapter 2

6   Borton, J. L. S., & Casey, E. C. (2006), 'Suppression of self-referential negative thoughts: a field study', *Self and Identity*, 5, 230–246

7   Savitsky, Kenneth, Gilovich, Thomas & Husted Medvec, Victoria (2000), 'The spotlight effect: an egocentric bias in estimates of the salience of one's own actions and appearance', *Journal of Personality and Social Psychology*, 78 (2), 211–222

8   Camilleri, Joseph A. (8 November, 2002), 'Evolutionary forensic psychology perspectives', lecture delivered at Westfield State University, Westfield, MA

9   BBC News (16 August 2010), 'Ministry of Sound nightclub killer jailed for life'

10  Nisbett, R. E., & Cohen, D., *Culture of Honor: The Psychology of Violence in the South* (Westview Press, Boulder, CO, 1996); Shackleford, Todd K. (2005), 'An evolutionary psychological perspective on cultures of honor,' *Evolutionary Psychology*, 3, 381–391

# ENDNOTES

## Chapter 3

11  *Sunday Times* (21st August 2011), 'Glaxo enters dragons' den'

12  Drabant, E. M., Kuo, J. R., Ramel, W., Blechert, J., Edge, M. D., Cooper, J. R., Goldin, P. R., Hariri, A. R., & Gross, J. J. (1 March 2011), 'Experiential, autonomic, and neural responses during threat anticipation vary as a function of threat intensity and neuroticism', *Neuroimage*, 55 (1), 401–410. Beatty, Michael J., Behnke, Ralph R. (1991), 'Effects of public speaking trait anxiety and intensity of speaking task on heart rate during performance', *Human Communication Research*, 18 (2), 147–176

13  Liening, S. H., Josephs, R. A., & Mehta, P. A., 'HBEV: 00100 Competition', Elsevier Inc.

14  Carré, Justin M. & Putnam, Susan K. (2010), 'Watching a previous victory produces an increase in testosterone among elite hockey players', *Psychoneuroendocrinology*, 35, 475–479

15  For an excellent, accessible introduction to brain plasticity: Doidge, Norman, *The Brain that Changes Itself* (Penguin, 2007)

16  Carré, Justin M. & Putnam, Susan K. (2010), 'Watching a previous victory produces an increase in testosterone among elite hockey players', *Psychoneuroendocrinology*, 35, 475–479

17  Jecker, John, & Landy, David (1969), 'Liking a person as a function of doing him a favor', *Human Relations*, 22 (4), 371–378; Franklin, Benjamin, *The Autobiography of Benjamin Franklin* (Courier Dover Publications, 1996)

## Chapter 4

18  Pinker, Stephen, *The Blank Slate: The Modern Denial of Human Nature* (Viking, 2002)

19  Smelser, N. J., Wright, James, Baltes, P. B., 'Autonomy at work', *International Encyclopedia of the Social & Behavioral Sciences* (Pergamon, 2001)

20  Marmot, M. G., Davey Smith, G., Stansfield, S., *et al.* (1991), 'Health inequalities among British civil servants: the Whitehall II study', *Lancet*, 337 (8754), 1387–1393

21  Fine, Leslie M., & Bolman Pullins, Ellen (1998) , 'Peer mentoring in the industrial sales force: an exploratory investigation of men and women in developmental relationships', *Journal of Personal Selling and Sales Management*, XVIII (4), 89–103

## Chapter 5

22  Lyubomirsky, Sonja, *The How of Happiness: A Scientific Approach to Getting the Life You Want* (Penguin, 2007)

23  Taleb, Nassim Nicholas, *Fooled by Randomness* (Random House, 2001)

24  Schulman, Peter (Winter 1999), 'Applying learned optimism to increase sales productivity', *Journal of Personal Selling and Sales Management*, XIX (1), 31–37

25  Gottfried, Adele Eskeles, Flemming, James S. Gottfried, Allen (March 2001), 'Continuity of academic intrinsic motivation childhood to late adolescents: a longtitudinal study', *Journal of Educational Psychology*, 91 (3); Karageorghis, Costas (2000), *Research Quarterly for Exercise and Sport*

26  Rowling, J. K. (July/August 2011), 'The fringe benefits of failure and the importance of the imagination', Harvard Commencement, *Harvard Magazine*

27  Pennebaker, James W. (May 1997), 'Writing about emotional experiences as a therapeutic process', *Psychological Science*, 8 (30)

28  Bevin Bavelas, Janet (1973), 'Effects of the temporal context of information', *Psychological Reports*, 32, 695–698

## Chapter 6

29  Shellenberger, Sylvia (1992), 'Review of positive illusions: creative self-deception and the healthy mind', *Family Systems Medicine*, 10 (1)

30  Bartolomé, Fernando, & Weeks, John (April 2007), 'Finding the gold in toxic feedback', *Harvard Business Review*, 85 (4), 24–26

31  Ferguson, Eamonn, James, David, O'Hehir, Fiona, & Sanders, Andrea (February 2003), 'Pilot study of the roles of personality, references, and personal statements in relation to performance over the five years of a medical degree', *BMJ*, 326 (7386), 429–432

32  Mehta, P. H., & Josephs, R. A. (2006), 'Testosterone change after losing predicts the decision to compete again', *Hormones and Behavior*, 50, 684–692

33  Lyttle, Nigel, Dorahy, Martin J., Hanna, Donncha, & Huntjens, Rafaële J. C. (Nov 2010), 'Conceptual and perceptual priming and dissociation in chronic posttraumatic stress disorder', *Journal of Abnormal Psychology*, 119 (4), 777–790

34  Bushman, B. J. (2002), 'Does venting anger feed or extinguish the flame?', *Personality and Social Psychology Bulletin*, 28, 724–731

35  McCullough, Michael E., Root, Lindsey M., & Cohen, Adam D. (2006), 'Writing about the benefits of an interpersonal transgression facilitates forgiveness', *Journal of Consulting and Clinical Psychology*, 74 (5), 887–897

## Chapter 7

36  Dobreva-Martinova, Tzvetanka (October 2002), 'Occupational role stress, its association with individual and organizational well-being', *Dissertation Abstracts International*, Section B: The Sciences and Engineering, 63 (4B)

37  Gilbert, Daniel T., Gill, Michael J. & Wilson, Timothy D. (May 2002), 'The future is now: temporal correction in affective forecasting', *Organizational Behaviour and Human Decision Processes*, 88 (1), 430–444

38  Dobson, Keith S., Dozois, & David J. A. (2001), 'Historical and philosophical bases of the cognitive-behavioral therapies', in Dobson, Keith S., *Handbook of Cognitive-Behavioral Therapies* (2nd ed.) (Guilford Press, New York, 2002)

39  Damasio, Antonio R., *Descartes' Error: Emotion, Reason and the Human Brain* (Penguin Books, New York, 2005), 193–194

40  Jackson, Jamie, *Guardian* (8 August 2009), 'Chelsea put faith in Bruno Demichelis's science to get results'

41  Beauchamp, Pierre, & Beauchamp, Marla K. (2001), 'Winning performance using biofeedback for sport psychology and better athletic training', *Advance for Physical Therapy and Rehab Medicine*, 21 (21), 24

42  Williams, S. L., & Zane, G. (1997), 'Guided mastery treatment of phobias', *Clinical Psychologist*, 50, 13–15

43  Reivich, Karen, & Shatté, Andrew, *The Resilience Factor: 7 Keys to Finding Your Inner Strength and Overcoming Life's Hurdles* (Broadway, 2002)

44  Bandura, A. (1977), 'Self-efficacy: towards a unifying theory of behavioral Change', *Psychological Review*, 84 (2), 191–215

## Chapter 8

45  Fry, D. P. (2000), 'Conflict resolution in cross-cultural perspective', in Aureli, F., & de Waal, F. B. M. (2000), *Natural Conflict Resolution* (Berkeley: University of California Press); Maynard Smith, John, and Szathmary, Eors, *The Major Transition in Evolution* (Oxford University Press, 1997); Wright, Robert, *NonZero: The Logic of Human Destiny* (Pantheon Books, 2000)

46  Willemsen, Martijn C., Böckenholt, Ulf, & Johnson, Eric J. (August 2011), 'Choice by value encoding and value construction: processes of loss aversion', *Journal of Experimental Psychology: General*, 140(3), 303–324; De Dreu, Carsten K. W. & McCusker, Christopher (May 1997), 'Gain–loss frames and cooperation in two-person social dilemmas: a transformational analysis', *Journal of Personality and Social Psychology*, 72 (5), 1093–1106

47  Tajfel, H., *Human Groups and Social Categories* (Cambridge University Press, 1981)

48  Jecker, John, & Landy, David (1969), 'Liking a person as a function of doing him a favor', *Human Relations*, 22 (4), 371–378

49  'Can mess make us racist?', broadcast on *All in the Mind*, BBC Radio 4 (25 May 2011)

50  Peterson, C., & Seligman, M. E. P. (2003), 'Character strengths before and after September 11', *Psychological Science*, 14, 381–384; Peterson, C., Park, N., & Seligman, M. E. P. (2006), 'Greater strengths of character and recovery from Illness', *Journal of Positive Psychology*, 1, 17–26

51  Haidt, J. (2000), 'The positive emotion of elevation', *Prevention and Treatment*, 3; Algoe, S., & Haidt, J. (2009), 'Witnessing excellence in action: the other-praising emotions of elevation, admiration, and gratitude', *Journal of Positive Psychology*, 4, 105–127

## Chapter 9

52  Finkelstein, Stacey R., & Fishbach, Ayelet (June 2012), 'Tell me what I did wrong: experts seek and respond to negative feedback', *Journal of Consumer Research* (published online 26 July 2011)

53  The survey was conducted by YouGov on behalf of Threshold.

54  Gilbert, D. T., & Malone, P. S. (1995), 'The correspondence bias', *Psychological Bulletin*, 117, 21–38

55  Ross, L. (1977), 'The intuitive psychologist and his shortcomings: distortions in the attribution process', in Berkowitz, L. (ed.), *Advances in Experimental Social Psychology*, 10, 173–220

56  Pittenger, David J. (Fall 1993), 'Measuring the MBTI and coming up short', *Journal of Career Planning & Placement*

57  Interview with Dr Tim Rees by Luckwinder Goulsbra, on behalf of Threshold.

## Chapter 10

58  Barefoot, W., *et al.*, *The Health Consequences of Hostility* (1983)

59  Loehr, Jim, *The Power of Full Engagement* (Free Press, 2004)

60  Carney, Dana R., Cuddy, Amy J. C., & Yap, Andy J. (October 2010), 'Power posing: brief nonverbal displays affect neuroendocrine levels and risk tolerance, *Association for Psychological Science*, 21 (10), 1363–1368

61  Nolen-Hoeksema, Susan, and Davis, Christopher (October 1999), *Journal of Personality and Social Psychology*, 77 (4), 801–814

62  Haidt, Jonathan, *The Happiness Hypothesis* (Arrow Books, 2006)

# REFERENCES

Algoe, S., & Haidt, J. (2009), 'Witnessing excellence in action: the other-praising emotions of elevation, admiration, and gratitude', *Journal of Positive Psychology*, 4, 105–127

Apicella, Coren L., Dreber, Anna, Gray, Peter B., Hoffman, Moshe, Little, Anthony C., & Campbell, Benjamin C. (February 2011), 'Androgens and competitiveness in men', *Journal of Neuroscience, Psychology, and Economics*, 4 (1), 54–62

Bandura, A. (1977), 'Self-efficacy: towards a unifying theory of behavioral change', *Psychological Review*, 84 (2), 191–215

Barefoot, W., *et al.*, *The Health Consequences of Hostility* (1983)

Barkow, J., Cosmides, L., & Tooby, J. (Eds.), *The Adapted Mind: Evolutionary Psychology and the Generation of Culture* (Oxford University Press, 1992)

Bartolomé, Fernando, & Weeks, John (April 2007), 'Finding the gold in toxic feedback', *Harvard Business Review*, 85 (4), 24–26

Bavelas, J. (1973), 'Effects of the temporal context of information', *Psychological Reports*, 32, 695–698

Beauchamp, Pierre, & Beauchamp, Marla K. (2001), 'Winning performance using biofeedback for sport psychology and better athletic training', *Advance for Physical Therapy and Rehab Medicine*, 21 (21), 24

Borton, J. L. S., & Casey, E. C. (2006), 'Suppression of self-referential negative thoughts: a field study', *Self and Identity*, 5, 230–246

Britt, Thomas W. (January 2003), 'Black Hawk Down at work', *Harvard Business Review*

Burnham, Terry, and Phelan, Jay, *Mean Genes from Sex to Money to Food* (Perseus Publishing, Cambridge, 2000)

Bushman, B. J. (2002), 'Does venting anger feed or extinguish the flame?', *Personality and Social Psychology Bulletin*, 28, 724–731

Camilleri, Joseph A. (8 November 2002), 'Evolutionary forensic psychology perspectives', Lecture delivered at Westfield State University, Westfield Massachusetts

Carney, Dana R., Cuddy, Amy J. C., & Yap, Andy J. (October 2010), 'Power posing: brief nonverbal displays affect neuroendocrine levels and risk tolerance', *Association for Psychological Science*, 21 (10), 1363–1368

Carré, Justin M. & Putnam, Susan K. (2010), 'Watching a previous victory produces an increase in testosterone among elite hockey players', *Psychoneuroendocrinology*, 35, 475–479

Cherniss, Cary (2000), 'Emotional intelligence: what it is and why it matters', *The Consortium on Emotional Intelligence*, Graduate School of Applied and Professional Psychology, Rutgers University

De Dreu, Carsten K. W., & McCusker, Christopher (May 1997), 'Gain–loss frames and cooperation in two-person social dilemmas: a transformational analysis', *Journal of Personality and Social Psychology*, 72 (5), 1093–1106

Dobreva-Martinova, Tzvetanka (October 2002), 'Occupational role stress, its association with individual and organizational well-being', *Dissertation Abstracts International*, Section B: The Sciences and Engineering, 63 (4B)

Dobson, Keith S., & Dozois, David J. A., (2001), 'Historical and philosophical bases of the cognitive-behavioral therapies', in Dobson, Keith S., *Handbook of Cognitive-Behavioral Therapies* (2nd ed.), (Guilford Press, New York, 2002)

Doidge, Norman, *The Brain that Changes Itself* (Penguin, 2007)

Drabant, E. M., Kuo, J. R., Ramel, W., Blechert, J., Edge, M. D., Cooper, J. R., Goldin, P. R., Hariri, A. R., & Gross, J. J. (1 March 2011), 'Experiential, autonomic, and neural responses during threat anticipation vary as a function of threat intensity and neuroticism', *Neuroimage*, 55 (1), 401–410

Ferguson, Eamonn, James, David, O'Hehir, Fiona, & Sanders, Andrea (February 2003), 'Pilot study of the roles of personality, references, and personal statements in relation to performance over the five years of a medical degree', *BMJ*, 326 (7386), 429–432

Fine, Leslie M., & Bolman Pullins, Ellen (1998), 'Peer mentoring in the industrial sales force: an exploratory investigation of men and women in developmental relationships', *Journal of Personal Selling and Sales Management*, XVIII (4), 89–103

Finkelstein, Stacey R., & Fishbach, Ayelet (June 2012), 'Tell me what I did wrong: experts seek and respond to negative feedback', *Journal of Consumer Research* (published online 26 July 2011)

Franklin, Benjamin, *The Autobiography of Benjamin Franklin*, (Courier Dover Publications, 1996)

Fry, D. P. (2000), 'Conflict resolution in cross-cultural perspective', in Aureli, F., & de Waal, F. B. M. (2000), *Natural Conflict Resolution* (Berkeley: University of California Press)

Gilbert, Daniel T., Gill, Michael J., & Wilson, Timothy D. (May 2002), 'The future is now: temporal correction in affective forecasting', *Organizational Behaviour and Human Decision Processes*, 88 (1), 430–444

Gilbert, D. T., & Malone, P. S. (1995), 'The correspondence bias', *Psychological Bulletin*, 117, 21–38

Gottfried, Adele Eskeles, Flemming, James S., & Gottfried, Allen (March 2001), 'Continuity of academic intrinsic motivation childhood to late adolescents: a longtitudinal study', *Journal of Educational Psychology*, 91 (3)

Haidt, Jonathan, *The Happiness Hypothesis* (Arrow Books, 2006)

Haidt, J. (2000), 'The positive emotion of elevation', *Prevention and Treatment*, 3

Inoff-Germain, Gale, Arnold, Gina Snyder, Nottelmann, Editha D., Susman, Elizabeth J., Cutler, Gordon B., Jr., & Chrousos, George P. (Jan 1988), 'Relations between hormone levels and observational measures of aggressive behavior of young adolescents in family interactions', *Developmental Psychology*, 24 (1), 129–139

Jecker, John, & Landy, David (1969), 'Liking a person as a function of doing him a favor', *Human Relations*, 22 (4), 371–378

Karageorghis, Costas (2000), *Research Quarterly for Exercise and Sport*

Liening, S. H., Josephs, R. A., & Mehta, P. A., 'HBEV: 00100 Competition', University of Texas, USA

Loehr, Jim, *The Power of Full Engagement* (Free Press, 2004)

Lyttle, Nigel, Dorahy, Martin J., Hanna, Donncha, & Huntjens, Rafaële J. C. (November 2010), 'Conceptual and perceptual priming and dissociation in chronic posttraumatic stress disorder', *Journal of Abnormal Psychology*, 119 (4), 777–790

Lyubomirsky, Sonja, *The How of Happiness. A Scientific Approach to Getting the Life You Want* (Penguin, 2007)

Marmot, M. G., Davey Smith, G., Stansfield, S., *et al.* (1991), 'Health inequalities among British civil servants: the Whitehall II study', *Lancet*, 337 (8754), 1387–1393

Maynard Smith, John, and Szathmary, Eors, *The Major Transition in Evolution* (Oxford University Press, 1997)

McCullough, Michael E., Root, Lindsey M., & Cohen, Adam D. (2006), 'Writing about the benefits of an interpersonal transgression facilitates forgiveness', *Journal of Consulting and Clinical Psychology*, 74 (5), 887–897

Nisbett, R. E., & Cohen, D., *Culture of Honor: The Psychology of Violence in the South* (Westview Press, Boulder, CO, 1996)

Nolen-Hoeksema, Susan, and Davis, Christopher (October 1999), *Journal of Personality and Social Psychology*, 77 (4), 801–814

Peterson, C., Park, N., and Seligman, M. E. P. (2006), 'Greater strengths of character and recovery from illness', *Journal of Positive Psychology*, 1, 17–26

Peterson, C., and Seligman, M. E. P. (2003), 'Character strengths before and after September 11', *Psychological Science*, 14, 381–384

Pinker, Stephen, *The Blank Slate: The Modern Denial of Human Nature* (Viking, 2002)

Pittenger, David J. (Fall 1993), 'Measuring the MBTI and coming up short', *Journal of Career Planning & Placement*

Reivich, Karen, & Shatté, Andrew, *The Resilience Factor: 7 Keys to Finding Your Inner Strength and Overcoming Life's Hurdles* (Broadway, 2002)

Ross, L. (1977), 'The intuitive psychologist and his shortcomings: distortions in the attribution process', in Berkowitz, L. (ed.), *Advances in Experimental Social Psychology*, 10, 173–220

Rowling, J. K. (July/August 2011), 'The fringe benefits of failure and the importance of the imagination', Harvard Commencement, *Harvard Magazine*

Savitsky, Kenneth, Gilovich, Thomas, & Husted Medvec, Victoria (2000), 'The spotlight effect: an egocentric bias in estimates of the salience of one's own actions and appearance', *Journal of Personality and Social Psychology*, 78 (2), 211–222

Schulman, Peter (Winter 1999), 'Applying learned optimism to increase sales productivity', *Journal of Personal Selling and Sales Management*, XIX (1), 31–37

Shackleford, Todd K. (2005), 'An evolutionary psychological perspective on cultures of honor,' *Evolutionary Psychology*, 3, 381–391

Shellenberger, Sylvia (1992), 'Review of positive illusions: creative self-deception and the healthy mind', *Family Systems Medicine*, 10 (1)

Smelser, N. J., Wright, James, & Baltes, P. B., 'Autonomy at work', *International Encyclopedia of the Social & Behavioral Sciences* (Pergamon, 2001)

Tajfel, H., *Human Groups and Social Categories* (Cambridge University Press, 1981)

Taleb, Nassim Nicholas, *Fooled by Randomness* (Random House, 2001)

Willemsen, Martijn C., Böckenholt, Ulf, & Johnson, Eric J., (August 2011), 'Choice by value encoding and value construction: processes of loss aversion', *Journal of Experimental Psychology: General*, 140 (3), 303–324

Williams, S. L., & Zane, G., (1997), 'Guided mastery treatment of phobias', *Clinical Psychologist*, 50, 13–15

Wright, Robert, *NonZero: The Logic of Human Destiny* (Pantheon Books, 2000)

Wright, Robert, *The Moral Animal: Evolutionary Psychology and Everyday Life* (Pantheon, New York, 1994)

# INDEX

# ABOUT THE AUTHORS

**James Brooke** is a director and co-founder at Threshold, an international training and consulting firm dedicated to helping companies, teams and individuals to communicate and work together better. James has twenty years' experience in the field of internal communication and change management. He has held senior positions with a number of consultancies and has directed multi-national programmes for a number of high-profile companies. He has led major research programmes for international institutes and business schools, and is a regular contributor and speaker on business courses and seminars.

**Simon Brooke** is a communications strategist and journalist with 25 years' experience in communications training and development. Having started his career in corporate, financial and consumer PR, he moved into political strategy and has held senior communications positions with major political parties on both sides of the Atlantic. Simon now works with senior executives to develop their communications strategies, identify their key messages and to help them to express their ideas in both speech and writing. As a journalist, he currently writes and edits on a freelance basis for most of the national newspapers, on subjects ranging from business and management to marketing, education and the media. He is also the author of two novels.

## More about Threshold

In addition to James Brooke, Peter Nicholas and Dr Amy Silver are also principals of Threshold. Threshold's clients include Aviva, BP, Coca-Cola, Rolls Royce and Pfizer.

www.threshold.co.uk

## The Be Bulletproof Project

The Be Bulletproof Project offers a series live interactive workshops which offer the opportunity to develop and practice the techniques of Be Bulletproof, with expert guides, feedback and practice with live actors. For more information visit: www.bebulletproof.net